Reference and Access
for Archives and Manuscripts

ARCHIVAL FUNDAMENTALS SERIES III
Peter J. Wosh, Editor

1 **Leading and Managing Archives and Manuscripts Programs**
Peter Gottlieb and David W. Carmicheal, Editors

2 **Arranging and Describing Archives and Manuscripts**
Dennis Meissner

3 **Advocacy and Awareness for Archivists**
Kathleen D. Roe

4 **Reference and Access for Archives and Manuscripts**
Cheryl Oestreicher

5 **Advancing Preservation for Archives and Manuscripts**
Elizabeth Joffrion and Michèle V. Cloonan

6 **Selecting and Appraising Archives and Manuscripts**
Michelle Light and Margery Sly

7 **Introducing Archives and Manuscripts**
Peter J. Wosh

Reference *and* Access
for Archives *and* Manuscripts

Cheryl Oestreicher

SOCIETY OF
American Archivists
CHICAGO

The Society of American Archivists
www.archivists.org

© 2020 by the Society of American Archivists

All rights reserved. No part of this publication may be reproduced, stored in a retrieval system, or transmitted in any form or by any means without prior permission from the publisher.

Library of Congress Control Number: 2020941908

Printed in the United States of America.

ISBN: 978-1-945246-38-8 (paperback)
eISBN: 978-1-945246-39-5 (epub)
eISBN: 978-1-945246-40-1 (pdf)

Graphic design by Sweeney Design, kasween@sbcglobal.net.

Table of Contents

FOREWORD: The Evolution of a Book Series ix
    Peter J. Wosh

PREFACE xiii
    Acknowledgments xiv

INTRODUCTION 1
    Reference and Access: Historical Influences and Innovations 2
    Conclusion 10

1 Contextualizing Reference Within an Archives Program 13
    Acquisition and Appraisal 15
    Arrangement and Description 17
    Preservation 18
    Digital Content 18
    Outreach and Advocacy 19
    Conclusion 20

2 Reference Skills and Knowledge 22
    Knowledge 23
    Technical Skills and Knowledge 24
    Interpersonal Skills 25
    Reference Manual 26
    Training 27
    Conclusion 29

3 Users 31
    Information Seeking 31
    Archival Literacy and Intelligence 32
    Levels of User Experience 34
    User Types 34
    Conclusion 38

4 Reference Interaction ... 39
- Behavior and Communication ... 39
- Reference Interview ... 41
- Virtual and Remote Reference ... 45
- Dealing with Difficult Patrons ... 47
- Conclusion ... 50

5 Physical Access ... 52
- Reading Room and Research Area ... 52
- Staffing ... 54
- Registration ... 56
- Use and Handling ... 58
- Security ... 60
- Conclusion ... 62

6 Intellectual Access ... 65
- Arrangement and Description ... 65
- Access Outputs ... 69
- Conclusion ... 73

7 Virtual Access ... 74
- Websites ... 75
- Digital Collections ... 77
- Systems and Formats ... 80
- Metadata ... 81
- Virtual Reading Room ... 82
- Innovations in Digital Research ... 83
- Conclusion ... 85

8 Ethics, Patron Privacy, and Accessibility ... 87
- Ethics ... 87
- Patron Privacy ... 88
- Accessibility ... 90
- Conclusion ... 93

9 Legal Regulations ... 95
- Archivists' Responsibility ... 96
- Freedom of Information Act ... 96
- Family Educational Rights and Privacy Act (FERPA) ... 97
- Health Insurance Portability and Accountability Act (HIPAA) ... 99
- Privacy Act ... 99
- Public Company Accounting Reform and Investor Protection Act ... 99
- Copyright ... 100
- Restrictions ... 109
- Conclusion ... 112

10 Use Policies 115
- Types of Uses 115
- Reproductions 116
- Copyright and Public Domain 122
- Procedures 123
- Loans 124
- Attributions 125
- Conclusion 126

11 Outreach 127
- Development and Strategy 128
- Social Media 130
- Crowdsourcing 131
- Friends Groups 132
- Conclusion 133

12 Assessment of Reference Programs 134
- Public Services Metrics 135
- User Studies 136
- Data Ethics and Privacy 138
- Conclusion 139

13 The Future of Access and Reference 140

POSTSCRIPT 142

APPENDIXES
- A Examples of Reference Manuals 144
- B Examples of Registration Forms 146
- C Examples of Online Reference Request Forms 149
- D Examples of Access Outputs, Alternative Formats 152
- E Examples of Reproduction Request Forms 158
- F Examples of Permission to Publish Forms. 161

BIBLIOGRAPHY 165

ABOUT THE AUTHOR 189

INDEX 190

FOREWORD

The Evolution of a Book Series

The Society of American Archivists (SAA) first conceived the notion of developing and publishing "manuals relating to major and basic archival functions" in the early 1970s. Charles Frederick Williams (popularly known as C. F. W.) Coker (1932–1983), a former US Marine Corps captain and North Carolina state archivist who recently had been appointed to head the Printed Documents Division of the National Archives and Records Services, edited the initial Basic Manual Series. The first five basic manuals, which appeared in 1977, illustrated the ways in which archivists defined and classified their core concepts at that historical moment:

- *Archives & Manuscripts: Appraisal & Accessioning* by Maynard J. Brichford
- *Archives & Manuscripts: Arrangement & Description* by David B. Gracy II
- *Archives & Manuscripts: Reference & Access* by Sue E. Holbert
- *Archives & Manuscripts: Security* by Timothy Walch
- *Archives & Manuscripts: Surveys* by John Fleckner

The entire series accounted for only 163 pages of text, which included numerous illustrations, graphics, sample forms, charts, and bibliographic insertions. Each 8.5" by 11" softbound pamphlet contained three holes, punched down the left side, for easy insertion into a loose-leaf binder that might be handily referenced at an archivist's desk. Individual volumes sold for $4, though SAA members received a $1 discount.

Archivists operated within a far different cultural, legal, and professional framework during the early and middle years of the 1970s. In 1973, the same year that SAA began work on the Basic Manual Series, IBM introduced the Correcting Selectric II typewriter as its major technological breakthrough, thereby eliminating the need for such popular tools as rubber erasers, correction fluid, and cover-up tape. This revolutionary product seemed destined to alter the nature of document creation forever. During this period, a few archivists had begun grappling with the challenges of something known as "machine-readable records," but a bibliographer who surveyed this puzzling development could still confidently conclude in a 1975 *American Archivist* article that "only a few archival establishments" appeared to be "developing programs for accessioning" such materials. Other momentous—and occasionally unsettling—changes appeared on the horizon. A new copyright law, which was enacted by Congress in 1976 and became effective on New Year's Day 1978, contained significant implications for how archivists would manage collections and serve researchers. Richard Nixon's resignation in 1974 prompted the promulgation of new legislation in 1978 that declared for the first time that presidential and vice presidential records are public documents. Professionally, the archival landscape seemed to be shifting as well. The Association of Canadian Archivists launched an exciting new journal, *Archivaria*, in winter 1975/1976, a development destined to deepen the discipline's intellectual discourse. Regional archival associations formed, became fruitful, and multiplied in the United States. In addition, a new era in archival education began as library schools and history departments inaugurated archives-based graduate programs in the late 1970s, ultimately resulting in a highly credentialed and formally trained corps of professional practitioners.

Such transformations, and many others too numerous to mention here, convinced the Society of American Archivists that only an active publications program that regularly refreshed the existing literature could provide its membership with easy access to rapidly changing trends and best practices. SAA accordingly published the Basic Manual Series II—a second set of five volumes—in the early 1980s:

- *Archives & Manuscripts: Exhibits* by Gail Farr Casterline
- *Archives & Manuscripts: Automated Access* by H. Thomas Hickerson
- *Archives & Manuscripts: Maps and Architectural Drawings* by Ralph E. Ehrenberg
- *Archives & Manuscripts: Public Programs* by Ann E. Pederson and Gail Farr Casterline
- *Archives & Manuscripts: Reprography* by Carolyn Hoover Sung

Over the years, SAA published scores of other titles, each illustrating the rich diversity of archival work: administration of photo collections, conservation, machine-readable records, law, management, a basic glossary, collections of readings on archival theory and practice, and books specific to archives in a variety of institutional settings (i.e., colleges and universities, businesses and corporations, religious and scientific institutions, museums, government agencies, historical societies, etc.). Even with the proliferation of publications, the bedrock of archival practice rested on the core knowledge represented in the basic manuals, which were reconceptualized and rechristened between 1990 and 1993 as the Archival Fundamentals Series:

- *Understanding Archives and Manuscripts* by James O'Toole
- *Arranging and Describing Archives and Manuscripts* by Fredric M. Miller
- *Managing Archival and Manuscript Repositories* by Thomas Wilsted and William Nolte
- *Selecting and Appraising Archives and Manuscripts* by F. Gerald Ham
- *Preserving Archives and Manuscripts* by Mary Lynn Ritzenthaler
- *Providing Reference Services for Archives and Manuscripts* by Mary Jo Pugh
- *The Glossary of Archivists, Manuscript Curators, and Records Managers* by Lynn Lady Bellardo and Lewis Bellardo

A second iteration of the seven books in this revamped series appeared roughly fifteen years later as the Archival Fundamentals Series II:

- *Understanding Archives and Manuscripts* by James O'Toole and Richard J. Cox
- *Arranging and Describing Archives and Manuscripts* by Kathleen D. Roe
- *Managing Archival and Manuscript Repositories* by Michael Kurtz
- *Selecting and Appraising Archives and Manuscripts* by Frank Boles
- *Preserving Archives and Manuscripts* by Mary Lynn Ritzenthaler
- *Providing Reference Services for Archives and Manuscripts* by Mary Jo Pugh
- *A Glossary of Archival and Records Terminology* by Richard Pearce-Moses

Mary Jo Pugh and Richard J. Cox edited these multivolume compilations, which almost instantaneously became required texts in archival education courses and necessary additions to archivists' bookshelves. The Archival Fundamentals Series I and II differed in scope and scale from the initial Basic Manual Series. For example, John Fleckner's comprehensive treatment of surveys did not appear in need of revision and dropped out of the series. Security became incorporated into a broader manual on preservation. SAA commissioned an introductory overview of the field, added a new book that focused on managerial issues, and developed a glossary with the goal of defining and historicizing key archival concepts. Beginning in the 1970s, both Archival Fundamentals Series I and II incorporated and delineated the evolving descriptive standards that defined professional practice, dissected the contentious debates surrounding appraisal and deaccessioning that enlivened archival discourse in the 1980s, and reflected the growing emphases on an expanding user base and more complex reference services that revolutionized reading rooms and repositories in the late twentieth century.

This third edition—Archival Fundamentals Series III—contains important continuities and significant departures from its predecessors:

- A new book, *Advocacy and Awareness for Archivists* by Kathleen D. Roe, reflects an increased understanding that these functions undergird all aspects of archival work.
- The management volume, *Leading and Managing Archives and Manuscripts Programs* edited by Peter Gottlieb and David W. Carmicheal, has been reconfigured to focus especially on leadership and to provide readers with opportunities to explore their individual managerial styles.
- *Advancing Preservation for Archives and Manuscripts* by Elizabeth Joffrion and Michèle V. Cloonan addresses digital challenges and focuses on such current issues as risk management, ethical considerations, and sustainability.
- *Arranging and Describing Archives and Manuscripts* by Dennis Meissner, *Reference and Access for Archives and Manuscripts* by Cheryl Oestreicher, and *Selecting and Appraising Archives and Manuscripts* by Michelle Light and Margery Sly may appear familiar topics to readers of the previous two series, but each book illustrates the innovations in thought and practice that have transformed these archival functions over the past fifteen years.
- A general overview volume that I am preparing, *Introducing Archives and Manuscripts*, provides a broad introduction to the historical, philosophical, and theoretical foundations of the profession.

One contribution that constituted a cornerstone of the previous series has been reformatted to maximize its currency and usability. Although not part of the Archival Fundamentals Series III, the *Dictionary of Archives Terminology* (dictionary.archivists.org) will replace *A Glossary of Archival and Records Terminology* and will be maintained and updated as a digital resource by SAA's Dictionary Working Group.

We hope that undergraduate and graduate students, new professionals, seasoned archival veterans, and others in the information science and public history fields will find the seven volumes in the Archival Fundamentals Series III helpful, provocative, and essential to both their intellectual life and their daily work. As Richard J. Cox observed in his preface to an earlier edition of the series, the time has long passed "when individuals entering the archival profession could read a few texts, peruse some journals, attend a workshop and institute or two, and walk away with a sense that they grasped the field's knowledge and discipline." This series provides an entry point and a synthetic distillation of a much broader literature that spans an impressive array of academic disciplines. We encourage you, of course, to do a deeper dive into each of the individual topics covered here. But we also remain confident that this series, like its predecessors, provides an honest and accurate snapshot of archival best practices at the beginning of the third decade of the twenty-first century.

The authors, of course, deserve full credit for their individual contributions. The Archival Fundamentals Series III itself, though, constitutes a collaborative enterprise that benefited from the work of SAA Publications Board members, editors, and interns throughout the past decade. These individuals helped to define the series parameters, reviewed proposals and manuscripts, and shepherded various projects to conclusion. Special shout-outs (in alphabetical order) are owed to: Bethany Anderson, Jessica Ballard, Roland Baumann, Cara Bertram, Mary Caldera, Amy Cooper Cary, Jessica Chapel, Paul Conway, J. Gordon Daines, Todd Daniels-Howell, Sarah Demb, Jody DeRidder, Keara Duggan, Margaret Fraser, Thomas J. Frusciano, Krista Gray, Gregory Hunter, Geoffrey Huth, Petrina Jackson, Joan Krizack, Christopher Lee, Donna McCrea, Jennifer Davis McDaid, Kathryn Michaelis, Nicole Milano, Lisa Mix, Tawny Nelb, Kevin Proffitt, Christopher Prom, Mary Jo Pugh, Aaron Purcell, Colleen Rademaker, Caryn Radick, Dennis Riley, Michael Shallcross, Mark Shelstad, Jennifer Thomas, Ciaran Trace, Anna Trammell, Joseph Turrini, Tywanna Whorley, and Deborah Wythe. Nancy Beaumont has been an inspirational executive director for SAA, as well as a brilliant editor in her own right. Abigail Christian, SAA's editorial and production coordinator, has skillfully shepherded design and layout. Teresa Brinati, keenly insightful and good-humored as always, remains the epitome of competent leadership and has transformed the SAA publications program into a model for professional associations. It has been a privilege and great fun to work with everyone on this project.

PETER J. WOSH
Editor, Archival Fundamentals Series III
Society of American Archivists

Preface

As the nature of archives continues to evolve, so does the need for archivists to keep abreast of who users are, why patrons use archival collections, how to improve access, how to advance reference services, and the skills and knowledge required to be excellent reference professionals. Writing this book about reference and access prompted me to reflect on my nearly twenty years working in libraries and archives. I have worked in a historical society, an art museum, and a public library and have spent most of my career in academic archives. Each institution had different practices, but all were united in the goal of creating access to rare and unique materials. The intellectual stimulation I get from working with patrons and collections increases my desire to aid in the discovery and knowledge found in archives.

Archives manuals tell the story of how reference and access have moved from being a tangential notion for professionals to today's environment in which nearly all archival functions are employed with access as the ultimate goal. Early archives manuals prioritized appraisal, arrangement, and description, with reference mentioned only briefly. Then in 1977, SAA created the Basic Manual Series to advance archival practices and theories as well as to provide fundamentals and standards, including *Archives and Manuscripts: Reference and Access* by Sue E. Holbert. Later, in 1992 and 2005, Mary Jo Pugh authored editions of *Providing Reference Services for Archives and Manuscripts* as part of both Archival Fundamental Series I and II. In the nearly thirty years between Holbert's manual and Pugh's second edition, the value of reference services became clear.

The third edition of this manual continues the established legacy of accentuating the topic's importance, encouraging use and understanding users and their behaviors, and exploring ways in which to provide excellent services. This book outlines the components of reference and access, explores how they fit within other archival functions, and offers strategies and practices that can be modified for any type of institution. The ideas put forth are meant to be part of a comprehensive overview, with the intent that archivists will learn new ideas, adapt methods to their institutions, and be motivated to advance access for their repositories.

There is a constant influx of new articles, books, blog posts, newsletter articles, presentations, and other discourse about reference and access. I had a strong desire to include everything I read, but that journey is never-ending. Archivists continuously share their experiences to benefit others and to create a shared understanding of the similarities and differences that govern practices. And that is one of the greatest pleasures of being an archivist—the opportunity to develop, share, and advance how access to archives affects both other archivists and society. I encourage archivists to be future-oriented and to think about how all of these ideas can advance future access.

A few housekeeping items to keep in mind when reading this book: I use the phrases "reference archivist," "reference professional," "reference staff members," and "archivists" to encompass anyone who performs reference services, whether as a sole responsibility or as one of many job duties. There are occasions when I offer specific repository types as examples, but the ideas proffered are meant for any repository type. I recognize that not all practices directly apply to all institutions but the text is couched this way for easier readability. Although this book often discusses reference and access with the goal of reaching "the public," I also recognize that many archives have only internal constituents who are considered the "public." Last, I use "researcher," "user," and "patron" interchangeably, again, to ease readability. The intended purpose behind these uses is not to narrowly define the practices and theories described or present them as the only options but to show that archivists can take and modify those theories and practices to work with all audiences.

As you read this manual, I encourage you to examine existing theories and practices, both at your institution and within the profession. Use this book and other manuals but also talk with your colleagues, consult other professionals, attend conferences, seek educational opportunities, and read additional literature. There are always new ideas and developments about how to bring people into the archives and bring archives to the people—and I encourage you to add your ideas to the conversations.

Acknowledgments

Through writing this book, I came to appreciate, even more than I already had, the thousands of archivists who have made incredible accomplishments toward access. They established archives, opened up to patrons, advocated for legislation, acquired and processed collections, created standards, and implemented technology, all with the goal of access. Without those archivists, we would not be where we are today.

I must recognize the multitude of people who helped me through the process of writing this book. I thank former SAA Publications Editor Chris Prom and the Publications Board, who invited me to write this book, and series editor Peter Wosh for his unending support and encouragement. Caryn Radick was invaluable for her conversations and feedback. SAA staff members Teresa Brinati and Abigail Christian were always resourceful and helpful, and I am grateful for the work of the copyeditor, reviewers, and all others involved in the book's production.

Learning from professional colleagues is something I highly value, and I appreciate the conversations, input, and resources I gained from many along the way, particularly Anne Ackerson, Krystal Appiah, Terry Baxter, Christina Bryant, Liz Call, David Carmicheal, Wesley Chenault, Lisa

Cruces, Sarah Demb, Elizabeth Dunham, Christian Dupont, Jim Duran, Rachel Frazier, Nancy Godoy, Brenda Gunn, Pam Hackbart-Dean, Michelle Harvey, Alexis Horst, Polina Ilieva, Laura Uglean Jackson, Elizabeth Joffrion, Joshua Kitchens, Nicole Laflamme, Samip Mallick, Alexis Braun Marks, Kathy Marquis, Dennis Meissner, Nicole Milano, Stephanie Milne-Lane, Lisa Mix, Malgosia Myc, Tawny Ryan Nelb, Andrew K. Pace, Lizette Pelletier, Fernanda Perrone, Charlotte Priddle, Colleen McFarland Rademaker, Dennis Riley, Kathleen Roe, Amy Schindler, Deena Schwimmer, Mollie Spillman, Barbara Teague, and Audra Eagle Yun. If I have missed adding anyone to this list, please know that I appreciate all contributions.

I want to thank my colleagues at Boise State University, particularly Mary Aagard, Jodie Brown, Nancy Donahoo, Cheri Folkner, Isabell Greensky, Gwyn Hervochon, Marlena Hooeyboer, Rita Huffstetler, Pam Kindelberger, Allison Look, Alex Meregaglia, and Nancy Rosenheim, who were always interested and supportive. I want to offer a special recognition to those who processed my constant interlibrary loan requests, helped me find the hard-to-find resources, and made sure I had current editions.

Last, I thank all of the current and future archivists who tirelessly strive to collect, create access to, and advocate for the archival record. Keep up the great work!

CHERYL OESTREICHER

Introduction

In the second decade of the twenty-first century, the archival landscape in the United States is vastly different than the concept that emerged during the seventeenth and eighteenth centuries, when colonial governments collected official documents but placed strict limitations on access. Archives now collect materials on virtually every topic, and many archives are open to the general public. Archivists work in historical societies, state and public libraries, museums, historic sites, genealogical societies, religious institutions, medical centers, tribal archives, corporations, nonprofits, governments, community-based organizations, academic departments, and other types of repositories.[1] Further, an archives professional is no longer just a custodian of records but rather, as archival educator Anne J. Gilliland writes, a "highly trained archival expert who advocates for the record and who may also take on roles as a record-keeping systems analyst, metadata architect, digital curator, digital asset manager, videographer, oral historian, ethnographer, or community activist."[2] As the numbers and types of institutions and professionals grow, so do their roles within society. They enable citizens' rights to information in a democratic society, empower people to contribute to the historical record, and promote unlimited possibilities for research and advancing knowledge.

All of this is part of the changing nature of archives themselves. Historically, archives were often viewed as elite places for scholars or others interested in historical research. Today, more people see archives as vital institutions and places for reflection and discovery, not just as sites that preserve the historical record. More and more people encounter the power of archives, from researching their genealogical roots, to extrapolating information for scholarly pursuits, to presenting discoveries through public discourse, to exercising their rights as citizens for access to records. Indeed, there is no end to the possibilities that archives can fulfill.

Access and reference services are central to advancing knowledge and offering people opportunities to engage with historical resources. *Access* is the ability to use resources to find information, and *reference* is how archivists facilitate that ability. Although the ways in which reference and access have been viewed have remained consistent throughout history, the ways in which they are executed continue to evolve. Since Mary Jo Pugh's second edition of this book came out in 2005, many developments—particularly advancements in technology—have transformed both how archivists do their jobs and how researchers locate materials.

The core foundation of services has remained the same since the early days of archives: conducting reference interviews, helping researchers find relevant materials, ensuring proper handling and use of collections, providing reproductions, adhering to copyright and other legal regulations, granting permissions to use and publish, and performing outreach activities to engage audiences. However, the specific functions and activities continually progress. Instead of paper finding aids and inventories, archives offer online portals to finding aids, digital collections, inventories, and other descriptive resources. Instead of calling or writing to an archives to find out information about collections, users search online to find repositories that have materials about their research topics. Instead of waiting for researchers to find collections, archives actively seek opportunities to engage current audiences and bring in new audiences.

All of this culminates in access. Archivists attend to tasks with access as the ultimate goal, from acquisition through processing. Whether prioritizing internal or external audiences, archivists strive to organize collections, create metadata, implement digitization programs, conduct outreach, and promote archives with the intent to bring collections to users.

Reference and Access: Historical Influences and Innovations

Archivists continually reenvision how to bring users to the archives and materials to the users. Centuries of practice in the United States have seldom altered the overarching concepts of access and reference, yet they are constantly transformed as new technologies, privacy considerations, user-centered approaches, systematic description, and other innovations influence the growth and development of access policies and reference procedures. This brief overview offers a historical framework that illuminates the changing nature of access policies, reference practices, description trends, and repository clientele.

Users

The user is central to access, and archival repositories have always grappled with the circumstances of who might use their holdings. Until the twentieth century, the majority of U.S. archival institutions were historical societies, along with a few academic archives. Most historical societies limited access to fee-paying members, though some advocated opening to the general public. Academic archives primarily retained records for internal use, granting public requests or permitting access to outside researchers only occasionally. The overall approach of access to archives was to privilege limited and selective audiences.[3]

Movements to purposely allow public access to archives grew slowly. In the nineteenth century, internal constituents, historians, and patrician hobbyists were the dominant user types in historical societies and academic archives. Not until the early twentieth century, when government archives were founded intentionally to allow public access to their holdings, did this climate shift significantly. Early state archives, such as that of Alabama in 1901, often combined the functions of public repositories and historical societies, but they augured a new commitment toward serving a broader public. The long movement to open federal records to scholarly and popular use finally culminated in the creation of the National Archives in 1934, but access policies remained somewhat idiosyncratic. That same year, the Society of American Archivists (SAA) was founded, which propelled further discussion about access and users. In his 1938 presidential address at the SAA Annual Meeting, Albert Ray Newsome articulated the necessity of establishing state and local laws to preserve and make available public archives. At that time, thirty-three states had archival agencies.[4]

Opening archives to the public proved to be a slow process, as was expanding the user base. In 1939, pioneering Illinois state archivist Margaret Cross Norton succinctly categorized archival users into three types: government departments (using their own records), historical, and legal. She described research purposes as the desire to obtain internal information, legal documentation, historical background, or genealogical data. Thirteen years later, the National Archives' handbook similarly prioritized requestors as follows: government and congressional employees, people investigating legal rights, those whose work made significant contributions, and others whose needs could only be met by National Archives records.[5] Both of these documents assumed a relatively narrow and consistent category of archival patrons who exhibited limited purposes for reviewing records during the first half of the twentieth century.

Nearly thirty years after Albert Ray Newsome's call for legislation to make records available to the public, the federal government finally responded. In 1967, Congress passed the federal Freedom of Information Act (FOIA), which codifies the principle that citizens have the right to inspect federal documents.[6] Perhaps more than any other legislative enactment, FOIA set a national precedent that all citizens have the right to access information, and the implications transcended government archives by affecting access policies at other repositories. All public institutions, which include public colleges and universities as well as publicly funded historical societies and museums, necessarily adhere to local, state, or federal laws regarding access. Many other repositories, however, do not fall under that umbrella. Private universities, corporations, museums, Native American communities, religious institutions, and nonprofits typically establish access policies based on their institutional missions, which may or may not include public access.

As a direct result of FOIA, libraries and archives, already brokers of knowledge, did more to develop practices and services that focused on users and their right to information. Simultaneously, academic scholarship shifted from documenting the stories of "dead white men" to chronicling the events and lives of ordinary people. Archives quickly adapted to the changing landscape of users and uses in this new climate of citizens' rights and social history. In the 1960s and 1970s, archivists noted that their patrons included high school students, television newscasters, radio broadcasters, undergraduates, "advertising people," avocational historians, publishers, genealogists, novelists, scholars, journalists, and graduate students. Into the 1980s and 1990s, archivists further noted that there were more "nontraditional" user types whose interests were cross-disciplinary, such as the "administrator, ecologist, urban planner or journalist," as well as international students, archaeologists, and documentary filmmakers.[7]

The broadening of audiences changed how archivists viewed users and, subsequently, how they modified reference practices to address this shift. As the philosophy moved toward access, the user became more central to all archival functions. To further incorporate this attitude, archivists called for more proactive methods to investigate who users were, explore the nature of research, and evaluate the effectiveness of reference services.[8]

In 1989, an influential study and publication by Page Putnam Miller et al apprised the National Archives of strategies that could transform this administrative agency into a premier research institution. The authors of this report, which was a synthesis of data from interviews with more than 200 archivists and users, prioritized users and their needs, a revolutionary concept at the time. In addition to recognizing the existence of different audience types, the report's authors noted the necessity to serve inexperienced users, scrutinize the usefulness of reference tools, investigate how to conduct successful reference entrance and exit interviews, and examine archivist-user dialogues for efficacy. Overall, the recommendations focused on the importance of the user perspective and the influence of patrons in archival functions, strategies, and priorities.[9]

Particularly since the 1990s, archives have focused more on user experiences. User studies and surveys analyze the similarities and differences in users' needs to create resources that better facilitate access. Archivists proactively engage their internal and external constituents to broaden their audiences, host events, and promote their collections and services through various outreach activities. As these initiatives have progressed, early practices of limiting access to select users (outside of those who serve internal constituents only) have almost completely dissolved, and many repositories have welcomed the varied publics into their domains.

Technological advancements also transformed access, and the digital age has required archivists to modify access policies in efforts to meet patrons' expectations. By the early 2000s, massive digitization projects and the increasing need for archivists to accession born-digital materials altered the relationship between users and physical repositories. Many researchers believe in the myth that "everything is online," even though archivists understand that only a small percentage of their holdings can be, or ever will be, accessed remotely. Electronic access has introduced new audiences to archival materials, simultaneously creating unprecedented challenges for user education. One special undertaking is increasing the number of opportunities to reach users who perhaps know little about or have never visited an archives. Online research enables archival descriptions or content to appear in search results, leading both new and seasoned users to find and access collections.

Today, the user remains central to archival functions. Collections are processed, metadata created, and digitization projects prioritized with careful attention to the user experience through physical and virtual access. No longer narrowly defined, the population of users is expected to be broad and varied, new and experienced, and continually changing.

Reference

Archives owe the concept of reference services to early library history. The phrase "reference work" evolved from the term "reference book" (any noncirculating book). The groundwork for the concept began as early as 1876, when librarians started to create indexes, catalogs, and subject headings to use as aids in finding books. Within a short time, articles, presentations, and reports appeared that described the importance of reference books, allowing "free access" to reference books, and implementing cross-referencing for efficient research. Further, several authors emphasized the importance of the librarian-patron relationship and encouraged librarians to be accessible and provide personal assistance to satisfy their clientele and create self-sufficient users. By the turn of the century, library reference was viewed as a core responsibility that required dedicated and trained personnel.[10]

The movement to formalize reference work in archival contexts emerged in the 1930s. Early discussions about archival reference appear in English archivist V. H. Galbraith's 1934 manual; the inaugural issue, in 1938, of *American Archivist*'s description of the National Archives; and Margaret Cross Norton's 1939 article in *Illinois Libraries*. These writings describe practices that set standards that are still followed today. Galbraith described the process of patrons filling out forms, gathering in a reading room, requesting items by identifying record group and box/folder numbers, using proper citations, remaining mindful of restrictions, and paying fees. At the National Archives, most requests were handled within the agency that created the records, with nongovernment requests funneled to a separate Division of Reference. Norton specifically contextualized the difference between libraries and archives, describing how the knowledge required of staff differed; while librarians often had broad knowledge of many subjects, archives reference staff benefited from deep knowledge of specific subjects, including local, regional, and national history.[11]

Over the next two decades, reference gained slightly more attention. Both British archivist Sir Hilary Jenkinson and American archivist Theodore R. Schellenberg, two of the most influential archival theorists of the twentieth century, devoted some attention to reference in their pathbreaking works. Jenkinson framed use as the *raison d'être* for archival work. He described creating indexes and descriptive lists to aid patrons and noted that a "Search Room" staffer acts as an adviser and guide, remains current on research trends, maintains an encyclopedic grasp of reference books, and exhibits traits of "intelligence and good nature."[12]

Schellenberg's manual outlined policies related to reference, including taking public interest into account and preventing access to confidential personal information; advocating for equal and free access; basing services on the nature of the request and not the requestor; formalizing procedures for reproductions and loans; presenting proper identification to use collections; and respecting proper handling techniques. He also advocated for a user-oriented approach to reference, urging staff to proactively ask questions and do everything possible to meet researcher needs.[13]

The National Archives was a leader in advancing reference services as central to the archival mission. In the 1950s, its procedural handbook and code of ethics set standards for the profession. The handbook directed staff to assist patrons in locating and using materials, provided that they completed the required user application and paid reasonable fees for extensive research. Prepared for use in the National Archives Inservice Training Program, "The Archivist's Code" specified the need for archivists to predict future research needs, promote public access, and provide courteous service.[14]

These seminal works were largely procedural. In the 1970s and 1980s, archival literature elevated the importance of the user experience and perspective. Manuals encouraged archivists to share their knowledge and develop relationships with researchers but emphasized the user's responsibility to find relevant materials and conduct research. Further, archivists proposed the importance of studying reference interactions to provide high-quality service, motivating and training staff, and helping users be well prepared for research. There was also recognition that most manuals were written by or catered to government and academic archives. Acknowledging that the core concepts of reference were applicable to most repositories, professionals compiled a 1986 volume with essays from museum, academic, government, business, religious, and other repository types to demonstrate how the execution of services varied across institutions.[15]

As archivists elevated the importance and quality of reference services, the 1990s proved an equally transformative decade. Technological changes advanced the ways in which archives described and produced finding aids, email and virtual reference altered the archivist-patron relationship, and websites revolutionized how users found information about collections. Notably, because so much research occurs in an online environment, archivists lost some of their knowledge about and control over who accessed their holdings. This drastically changed the scope of reference services. Although the user increasingly became more central to archival functions, technology provided ways to more openly and broadly share information about collections. Reference archivists no longer waited for users to seek out archives but actively pursued ways to bring in new audiences and more researchers.

Well into the twenty-first century, reference practices and procedures have become a frequent topic in archival literature. Based on decades of practice, the foundational concepts remain the same: helping users find relevant materials and setting policies for access. Yet the components of those practices and the ways in which they are carried out have changed tremendously and will continue to evolve. Technology will continue to transform how to make information available, how users find materials, what skills are required of reference staff, and, especially, what expectations users have about accessing and using content. Particularly, the exponential increase in born-digital and digitized collections has greatly increased access as well as patrons' expectations of remote retrieval of information. Going forward, technology will be the crux of expanding reference and access.

Arrangement and Description

Collection information is the key component of reference and access. Since the first archives were established, archivists have recognized that patrons cannot find or use collections without inventories, finding aids, catalog records, or other descriptive information. For nearly two centuries, archives commonly published pamphlets, newsletters, circulars, bibliographies, or printed guides that summarized specific institutions' holdings.[16] Influenced by library practices, archivists believed that more detailed cataloging was the best assistance for patrons searching for relevant materials.[17] As libraries adopted the Library of Congress classification scheme and adhered to the *Anglo-American Cataloging Rules*, archivists desired similar standardization but experienced difficulties fitting their unique, and often voluminous, collection descriptions within the strict rules meant for published materials. Advancements came when the Library of Congress published *Archives, Personal Papers, and Manuscripts* in 1983, the same year that MARC-AMC (Machine-Readable Cataloging for Archival and Manuscripts Control) became the first American archival cataloging standard.[18] These standards provided ways to give brief descriptions about collections but did little to address the deeper description required for archival materials.

Knowing how researchers benefited from detailed inventories, archivists also meticulously arranged collections at the item level and created extensive bibliographic details about individual or small groups of items, now known as "traditional" processing. Though no formal definition exists, this method is generally understood to be highly detailed arrangement, description, and preservation at the item level. Some components of traditional processing include evaluation of each item in a collection, removal of metal fasteners, specific arrangement of items in folders (such as chronological or alphabetical), creation of extensively detailed item- or folder-level descriptions, encasement of all photographs in protective sleeves, preservation photocopying of newspaper articles or other fragile papers, refoldering and reboxing of all contents into acid-free cases, and other aspects that require item-level handling. The purpose of thorough arrangement and description was to precisely inform the researcher of available items and, often, to read materials in the order of creation, topic, or format. The approach facilitated a purposeful reading of most or all documents to determine exact arrangement and description and was believed to be the most effective method for both staff and researchers to find and use materials.

These processes remained standard in some repositories for many decades. In the 1980s, however, at a moment nearly simultaneous with the emerging professional emphasis on users and access, processing methods became a more frequent discussion topic. Arrangement and description practices were called into question as acquisitions increased at a rate faster than processing output and as backlogs grew voluminously, budgets diminished, and the number of users increased. These reasons motivated many archivists to review and implement adaptive methods, though some perpetuated traditional practices. Archivists assessed time and costs spent on processing, promoted the notion that not all collections (or series) need to be processed to the same level, determined priorities based on research potential, implemented strategic work plans, and coordinated team processing.[19]

Some repositories implemented these practices in efforts to facilitate access to more collections, but the challenges of keeping up with acquisitions and reducing backlogs remained. Defining access as a "means to discovery," a 2003 white paper by the Association of College and Research Libraries noted institutions' responsibilities to review existing arrangement and description procedures to meet the expanding user base and increased demand for access. It provides an overview of considerations to document hidden and unprocessed collections: exploring various levels of processing and description, dealing with security risks, collecting data to make decisions, examining the effect on public services staff, and establishing workflows to accommodate various approaches.[20]

In 2005, Mark Greene and Dennis Meissner wrote a seminal article that directly addressed these challenges: "More Product, Less Process: Revamping Traditional Archival Processing" (MPLP). The authors offered practical solutions scalable to any institution's size and type to address seemingly unmanageable backlogs and to gain physical and intellectual control over holdings. They favored creating intellectual order over physically rearranging materials, describing at the box level instead of the folder or item level, and skipping any minuscule preservation tasks, such as removing metal fasteners and preservation photocopying. In short, Greene and Meissner encouraged taking a flexible approach to processing that focused on employing a minimal amount of arrangement and description to make more collections available while maintaining scalable techniques to modify processing techniques as necessary or based on demand.[21]

Yale University had already approached reducing their extensive backlog through principles that were similar to those promoted by Greene and Meissner. Primarily, Yale's archivists implemented an "accessioning as processing" technique. To reduce the amount of time between acquisition and access, they arranged at the series level, wrote box-level inventories, and created collection-level catalog records so that collections did not enter the backlog. Influenced by discussions with, and expectations of, donors, the Yale system made folder-level arrangement and description an exception rather than a rule.[22]

More recently, in his book *Extensible Processing for Archives and Special Collections: Reducing Processing Backlogs*, archivist Daniel A. Santamaria has combined many of these practices into an effective strategy in which the concepts are adaptable to any repository type and size. The goal is to have a "baseline level of access," meaning minimal descriptions of all holdings. From there, user demand drives processing priorities, hence creating access to collections based on the knowledge that they are of high research value. Santamaria further extends these practices to digitization, whether scanning is conducted during processing or done on-demand, and allows for repurposing existing metadata. He intends that this approach be scalable from small- to large-scale projects. Like Greene and Meissner, Santamaria emphasizes flexibility to ensure that all collections are accessible to users.[23]

These principles and practices are again in flux as they are applied to born-digital records. Traditional arrangement and description focused on extensive or item-level details, often appropriate for collections of electronic records. However, some archivists are developing MPLP and flexible processing methods for digital content, whether digitized or born digital. Following the continuing focus to make as much material as possible available for research, arrangement and description practices are being evaluated and new standards are emerging. Whether these standards mirror or deviate from long-standing practices remains to be seen.

All of these developments are geared toward facilitating access to collections. Archivists now routinely assess workflows, revise practices, and analyze methods in ways that demonstrate how the user, and therefore access, is the focal point of arrangement and description.

Technology

There is no question that technology has transformed all aspects of archival functions and practices. Early on, some skeptical archivists thought computers were a fad, while others predicted the benefits of collecting and disseminating information via computer-generated and machine-readable records.[24] Today, it is nearly impossible to imagine reference interactions or accessibility of collections without using some form of technology. Software to produce description and finding aids, online platforms and websites to share information and content, options for virtual interactions, and the explosion of digitized and born-digital content have affected, and will continue to advance, reference services.

The computer's capabilities toward reference and research were documented as early as the 1940s, when the archives profession discussed the effect of technology on historical research. In that era, an advancement in technology was the punch card system, which coded information for quicker retrieval. Soon after, in the 1950s, archivists started to examine the effect of computers on recordkeeping. Many archivists contemplated how to handle collecting machine-generated records and experimented with automating description. Proponents emphasized systemization and continuity and also encouraged archivists to rethink "old" practices and embrace the potential for new and more efficient ways to move forward.[25]

By the 1960s, archivists lauded the capacity for computers to automate, enhance, and accelerate information retrieval. Over the next two decades, archivists endeavored to automate finding aids and cataloging through applications. Indeed, while acquisition, preservation, and arrangement of electronic records were crucial, archivists knew the key component was description. Records could not be found and used for research without adequate description.[26]

The revolutionary breakthroughs for description came in the 1990s. As automated access became increasingly central to archival functions and services, archivists searched for ways to better promote and share collection information and incorporate the researcher perspective. Two 1993 developments forever transformed the user experience: the advent of the World Wide Web and the creation of Encoded Archival Description (EAD).

Early on, archivists recognized the web's potential to disseminate collection information and publicize holdings.[27] Creating websites that offered information about the repository, hours, and lists of collections paved the way for today's robust sites that are portals to digital collections, finding aids, audiovisual materials, and remote reference interactions. Perhaps the most significant development was the ability to share finding aids online, thereby making collection information more broadly available and searchable.

EAD allowed institutions to move beyond the constrictive structure of basic MARC and catalog records and toward a configuration that permitted the inclusion of detailed inventories. Further, searches take place across collections, among multiple institutions, and in networked environments.[28] Although EAD was purposely created to facilitate sharing and searching via the web, presenting finding aids was not, and still is not, limited to this output. Repositories use Word documents, PDF files, websites, searchable databases, and other means to provide access to collection inventories.

To ease implementation of EAD and enhance consistency among finding aids, archivists then created collection management systems tailored to archives. The first open source systems were the Archivists' Toolkit (AT) and Archon, which in 2015 merged to become ArchivesSpace, although AT and Archon remain in use by some repositories. The premier benefit of these applications is that they produce EAD-encoded finding aids without the need for knowledge of coding. Both Archon and ArchivesSpace also have an online public interface, enabling repositories to immediately publish collection information, whether accessions, collection-level records, or full finding aids. While a focal point of these systems is to create more consistent description, the option of using the public interface was transformative for smaller repositories because they no longer required extensive staffing and resources to build a technical infrastructure to produce and share collection information online.

Since the early twentieth century, archives have endeavored to broadly share not just information about collections but their contents as well. Early reproductions were provided in the formats of microfiche or microfilm, which were usually available for loan or purchase. This type of reproduction remained in practice for decades until scanning equipment and technology made possible searchable electronic facsimiles of items on disks or hard drives.[29] By the mid-1990s, archivists were rapidly implementing tools and software to share materials through various electronic means. These early initiatives quickly evolved into the robust systems available today that support sharing of reproductions online with searching capabilities.

Also during this time, discussions about electronic records proliferated. Although extensive efforts started in the 1980s and 1990s, common practices and standards in preservation, collection, processing, and accessibility of born-digital content are still in development.[30] Archivists are continually challenged to corral obsolete media, software releases, file types, systems, and voluminous production of records. Confronted with constantly changing electronic forms of communication that have replaced written forms, such as texting, voicemail, email, and social media, archivists strive to keep abreast of all the different modes of electronic records. How to address collection-, folder-, and item-level metadata and description; whether to allow for any user to download and manipulate files; continual migration to adapt to technological changes; and the creation of systems for access are only a few of the issues still in development. While access is always the eventual goal, archivists wrestle with the conundrum of how to properly preserve born-digital material in a way that will enable future research.

Conclusion

This overview describes how access has grown in importance to become the crux around which archival functions are centered. Archival developments in the past few decades are indicative of how access—and reference in particular—are paramount to a repository's success.

NOTES

[1] Victoria Irons Walch, "Part 3. A*CENSUS: A Closer Look (Expanded Version)" (Chicago: Society of American Archivists, 2006), 17–20.

[2] Anne J. Gilliland, *Conceptualizing 21st-Century Archives* (Chicago: Society of American Archivists, 2014), 46.

[3] Leslie W. Dunlap, *American Historical Societies, 1790–1860* (Philadelphia: Porcupine Press, 1974), 40; Louis Leonard Tucker, *The Massachusetts Historical Society: A Bicentennial History, 1791–1991* (Boston: Massachusetts Historical Society, 1995), 235–237, 310; Walter Muir Whitehill, *Independent Historical Societies: An Enquiry into Their Research and Publication Functions and Their Financial Future* (Boston: Boston Athenaeum, 1962), 225; Clifford K. Shipton, "The Reference Use of Archives," in *University Archives: Papers Presented at an Institute Conducted by the University of Illinois Graduate School of Library Science*, ed. Rolland E. Stevens (Champaign, IL: The Board of Trustees of the University of Illinois, 1965), 74–75.

[4] Albert Ray Newsome, "Uniform State Archival Legislation," *American Archivist* 2, no. 1 (1939): 1–16, https://doi.org/10.17723/aarc.2.1.32tk6267g256l5n8.

[5] Margaret Cross Norton, "The Comparison of Archival and Library Techniques," in *Norton on Archives: The Writings of Margaret Cross Norton on Archival and Records Management*, ed. Thornton W. Mitchell (Chicago: Society of American Archivists, 2003), 102–105; *Handbook of Procedures* (Washington, DC: National Archives and Records Service, 1952), V-101.00.

[6] U.S. Department of State, "The Freedom of Information Act," https://foia.state.gov/Learn/FOIA.aspx.

[7] Whitehill, *Independent Historical Societies*, 213; Kenneth W. Duckett, *Modern Manuscripts: A Practical Manual for Their Management, Care, and Use* (Nashville: American Association for State and Local History, 1975), 6–7; Lucille Whalen, "The Reference Process in Archives: An Introduction," in Whalen, ed., *Reference Services in Archives* (New York: Haworth Press, 1986), 5.

[8] Elsie T. Freeman, "In the Eye of the Beholder: Archives Administration from the User's Point of View," *American Archivist* 47, no. 2 (1984): 111–123, https://doi.org/10.17723/aarc.47.2.a373340078502136; William Saffady, "Reference Service to Researchers in Archives," *RQ* 14, no. 2 (Winter 1974): 139–144.

[9] Page Putnam Miller, "Developing a Premier National Institution: A Report from the User Community to the National Archives," National Coordinating Committee for the Promotion of History, 1989, 16–22.

[10] David A. Tyckoson, "History and Functions of Reference Service," in *Reference and Information Services: An Introduction*, 4th ed., ed. Richard E. Bopp and Linda C. Smith (Santa Barbara, CA: Libraries Unlimited, 2011), 8–9; Lisa Janicke Hinchliffe, "Instruction," in Bopp and Smith, *Reference and Information Services*, 222; Louis Kaplan, *The Growth of Reference Service in the United States from 1876 to 1893* (Chicago: Publications Committee of the Association of College and Reference Libraries, 1952), 2–5.

[11] V. H. Galbraith, *Introduction to the Use of the Public Records* (Oxford: Clarendon Press, 1934), 101–105; "News Notes," *American Archivist* 1, no. 1 (1938): 149–150, https://doi.org/10.17723/aarc.1.3.633w7541151113h8; Norton, "Comparison of Archival and Library Techniques," 102.

[12] Sir Hilary Jenkinson, "The English Archivist: A New Profession," in *Selected Writings of Sir Hilary Jenkinson*, ed. Roger H. Ellis and Peter Walne (Chicago: Society of American Archivists, 2003), 255–256.

[13] T. R. Schellenberg, *Modern Archives: Principles and Techniques* (Chicago: The University of Chicago Press, 1956), 224–236.

[14] National Archives and Records Service, *Handbook of Procedures*, V-101.00; National Archives and Records Service, "The Archivist's Code," *American Archivist* 18, no. 4 (1955): 307, https://doi.org/10.17723/aarc.18.4.g027u80688293012.

[15] George Chalou, "Reference," in *A Manual of Archival Techniques*, ed. Roland M. Baumann (Harrisburg, PA: Pennsylvania Historical and Museum Commission, 1979), 48; Duckett, *Modern Manuscripts*, 236, 239–240; Whalen, *Reference Services in Archives*.

[16] Dunlap, *American Historical Societies*, 86–89, 95–108; Tucker, *Massachusetts Historical Society*, 29; Philip M. Hamer, ed., *A Guide to Archives and Manuscripts in the United States, Compiled for the National Historical Publications Commission* (New Haven: Yale University Press, 1961), vii.

[17] Jane Aikin Rosenberg, *The Nation's Great Library: Herbert Putnam and the Library of Congress, 1899–1939* (Urbana, IL: University of Illinois Press, 1993), 45.

[18] Rosenberg, *Nation's Great Library*, 45; Kris Kiesling, "EAD as an Archival Descriptive Standard," *American Archivist* 60, no. 3 (1997): 345, https://doi.org/10.17723/aarc.60.3.r7v8555610121244; Gilliland, *Conceptualizing 21st-Century Archives*, 93.

[19] Helen W. Slotkin and Karen T. Lynch, "An Analysis of Processing Procedures: The Adaptable Approach," *American Archivist* 45, no. 2 (1982): 155–156, https://doi.org/10.17723/aarc.45.2.63q172t634g386l4; Terry Abraham, Stephen E. Balzarini, and Anne Frantilla, "What Is Backlog Is Prologue: A Measurement of Archival Processing," *American Archivist* 48, no. 1 (1985): 35–36, https://doi.org/10.17723/aarc.48.1.m677m48014427332; Megan Floyd Desnoyers, "When Is a Collection Processed?," *Midwestern Archivist* 7, no. 1 (1982): 7–8, https://minds.wisconsin.edu/handle/1793/44721.

[20] Association of Research Libraries, "Hidden Collections, Scholarly Barriers: Creating Access to Unprocessed Special Collections Materials in North America's Research Libraries," White Paper, June 6, 2003, 11–13, https://www.arl.org/wp-content/uploads/2003/06/hidden-colls-white-paper-jun03.pdf, captured at https://perma.cc/ZZ3R-4W2A.

[21] Mark A. Greene and Dennis Meissner, "More Product, Less Process: Revamping Traditional Archival Processing," *American Archivist* 68, no. 2 (2005): 208–263, https://doi.org/10.17723/aarc.68.2.c741823776k65863.

[22] Christine Weideman, "Accessioning as Processing," *American Archivist* 69, no. 2 (2006): 274–283, https://doi.org/10.17723/aarc.69.2.g270566u745j3815.

[23] Daniel A. Santamaria, *Extensible Processing for Archives and Special Collections: Reducing Processing Backlogs* (Chicago: ALA Neal-Schuman, 2015), ix, 89–93, 122.

[24] Thornton Mitchell, "The State of Records Management," *American Archivist* 24, no. 3 (1961): 261, https://doi.org/10.17723/aarc.24.3.f4285k8x40516158; "Writings on Records Management: A Select List," *American Archivist* 36, no. 3 (1973): 379–380, 394–395, 476, https://doi.org/10.17723/aarc.36.3.m737p5531801l656.

[25] Murray G. Lawson, "The Machine Age in Historical Research," *American Archivist* 11, no. 2 (1948): 143, https://doi.org/10.17723/aarc.11.2.k10wv0736708370q; Barbara Fisher, "Byproducts of Computer Processing," *American Archivist* 32, no. 3 (1969): 216–217, https://doi.org/10.17723/aarc.32.3.y7x58648782q6720.

[26] Frank G. Burke, "The Application of Automated Techniques in the Management and Control of Source Materials," *American Archivist* 30, no. 2 (1967): 255, https://doi.org/10.17723/aarc.30.2.a427563789262223; Maynard Brichford et al., "Intellectual Control of Historical Records," *American Archivist* 40, no. 3 (1977): 167–177, https://doi.org/10.17723/aarc.40.3.30436v4722504547; Trudy Huskamp Peterson, "Archival Principles and Records of the New Technology," *American Archivist* 47, no. 4 (1984): 391–392, https://doi.org/10.17723/aarc.47.4.30u45640617n2184.

[27] David Bearman, "Archival Strategies," *American Archivist* 58, no. 4 (1995): 409, https://doi.org/10.17723/aarc.58.4.pq71240520j31798; James M. O'Toole, "The Future of Archival History," *Provenance* 13, no. 1 (1995): 17, https://digitalcommons.kennesaw.edu/provenance/vol13/iss1/2/.

[28] Gilliland, *Conceptualizing 21st-Century Archives*, 99.

[29] John H. Whaley, Jr., "Digitizing History," *American Archivist* 57, no. 4 (1994): 660, 667–668, https://doi.org/10.17723/aarc.57.4.6w4443523781g154.

[30] The following journal issues were dedicated to electronic records: *American Archivist* 53 no. 1 (1990); *Archival Issues* 20, no. 1 (1995); *Archivaria* 36 (Fall 1993).

1

Contextualizing Reference Within an Archives Program

From appraisal through advocacy, archives programs function in complex ways. Access is the outcome of all functions and activities: selection, acquisition, appraisal, arrangement, description, preservation, reference, outreach, and advocacy. Whether an archival staff consists of one person or a large department, all archivists must comprehend how access, and reference in particular, intellectually and practically intersects with and informs all other functions.

To set the direction of an archival program and all its functions, institutions develop mission statements and strategic plans. These are established most often at the highest organizational level and are sometimes written for departmental or perhaps individual functions, such as reference. When determining access and reference policies and procedures, aligning them to the larger organizational structures and goals ensures an effective program.

As archivist Peter Gottlieb writes, a mission statement reflects "the values and philosophy of an archives."[1] The examples in Figure 1 highlight public access, promotion, programming, research, and user communities, all of which are aspects that shape reference and access programs. By creating a user-oriented mission, repository leaders can guide archivists on how to provide effective reference services. A well-crafted mission statement also serves to communicate realistic expectations to public audiences and patrons.

To execute the mission, a strategic plan guides programs and activities for a specific period of time, identifies accomplishable goals and initiatives, and defines successful outcomes.[2] A strategic plan can be at the unit, department, and/or institutional level. Creating a shared mission and goals is good groundwork for unifying services and developing specific objectives, policies, and core practices. If the parent institution's strategic plan does not include components related to archives, or to reference and access, there is an opportunity to identify and advocate for those needs.[3] Though

Academic (department)**:** The OSU [Oregon State University] Libraries Special Collections and Archives Research Center (SCARC) stimulates and enriches the research and teaching endeavors of Oregon State University through primary sources. As part of the University's land grant mission, SCARC makes these resources available to the OSU community, Oregonians, and the larger community of scholars and independent researchers. As the repository for and steward of the Libraries' rare and unique materials, we build distinctive and unique collections in our signature areas: natural resources, the history of science, university history, and Oregon's multicultural communities. These collections encompass manuscripts, archives, rare books, oral histories, photographs, ephemera, audio/visual materials, electronic and born digital records.

Academic (unit)**:** The mission of the [University of Arkansas] Manuscripts Unit is to collect, organize, preserve, and provide access to research materials documenting the state of Arkansas and its larger role in regional, national, and international communities.

Community: The ONE Archives Foundation, Inc. collects, preserves, and protects LGBTQ history, art, and culture in collaboration with ONE Archives at the [University of Southern California] Libraries. To provide access to the ONE collection, the Foundation presents and supports projects, programs, exhibitions, and education to share the LGBTQ experience with diverse communities worldwide.

Corporate: The Hershey Community Archives' mission is to collect, preserve, and facilitate access to the records documenting the lives of Milton and Catherine Hershey and to promote the study and understanding of their vision and legacy as embodied in the businesses and communities they established.

Government: [The National Archives and Records Administration's] mission is to provide public access to Federal Government records in our custody and control. Public access to government records strengthens democracy by allowing Americans to claim their rights of citizenship, hold their government accountable, and understand their history so they can participate more effectively in their government.

Historical Society: [The Massachusetts Historical Society's mission is] to promote understanding of the history of Massachusetts and the nation by collecting and communicating materials and resources that foster historical knowledge.

Museum: The mission of the Library and Archives at the San Diego Air and Space Museum is to collect, preserve, and make available for research published, documentary, and visual materials that chronicle the development of Air and Space technology and experience.

Religious: The Mennonite Church USA Archives seeks to inspire people worldwide to follow Jesus Christ by engaging them with the historical record of Mennonite Christian discipleship.

FIGURE 1. Statements of Mission and Strategic Planning

Sources: Oregon State University Libraries, Special Collections and Archives, 2020, http://scarc.library.oregonstate.edu/about-us.html; Timothy G. Nutt and Diane F. Worrell, "Planning for Archival Repositories: A Common Sense Approach," *American Archivist* 78, no. 2 (2015): 325, https://doi.org/10.17723/0360-9081.78.2.317; ONE Archives Foundation, "History," 2018, www.onearchives.org/about/history/; Hershey Community Archives, "About Us," https://hersheyarchives.org/about-us/; National Archives and Records Administration, "Mission, Vision and Values," www.archives.gov/about/info/mission; Massachusetts Historical Society, "Mission, Vision, and Values," 2020, www.masshist.org/mission; San Diego Air and Space Museum, "Library and Archives Overview," http://sandiegoairandspace.org/research/; Mennonite Church USA, "Mennonite Church USA Archives," http://mennoniteusa.org/what-we-do/archives/.

strategic plans often are considered internal documents, some repositories share them with broader audiences to increase public transparency.

The National Archives and Records Administration (NARA) is an example of a repository with a publicly accessible strategic plan. Two of the goals in its 2018–2022 strategic plan are "Make Access Happen" and "Connect with Customers." Within the first goal, initiatives focus on digitization, description, and processing; the second comprises customer service, public participation, and outreach.[4] Together, the goals merge both the technical and public aspects of access and offer an example of how reference and access operate within a broader archival context.

Strategic plans of professional archival organizations also inform the ways in which individual repositories might carry out reference and access activities. For example, SAA's Strategic Plan contains a vision, mission, core values, and goals statements. Specific to reference, Goal 1: Advocating for Archives and Archivists includes, "Provide leadership in ensuring the completeness, diversity, and accessibility of the historical record."[5] This goal offers broad guidance to the profession while allowing flexibility for individual repositories to interpret and apply that guidance based on their unique institutional missions and goals.

Mission statements and strategic plans are foundational frameworks that guide the execution and advancement of all archival functions, including reference and access. Keeping these frameworks in mind helps to understand the connections among all aspects of an archives program.

Acquisition and Appraisal

Acquisition and appraisal lead directly to access. Through the appraisal process, archivists focus on identifying collections deemed valuable for acquisition and subsequent research.[6] Determining value begins with record creation, often before an archivist is involved. Societal factors influence how organizations and persons document their activities, including legal, economic, political, and individual perspectives on what is important to save and what to discard. Creators first determine why records are produced and why they are kept, which helps archivists to assess their long-term value (see Figure 2). More recently, archivists have expanded the concepts of value to address diversity, underrepresented groups and subjects, and community relations.[7]

A collection development policy is what communicates these values to donors and patrons. This policy outlines what the repository collects, including subject areas, physical formats, electronic records, preservation needs, institutional capacity, or other factors. Directly connected to access, a good policy considers users, stakeholders, and other communities while addressing current and future research. While it is impossible to predict all potential research topics, curating collections with the anticipation of future use promotes growth with patrons in mind.

Such strategies work for both analog and digital collections. However, appraising born-digital records also requires technical evaluation of file formats, physical media, software, technical characteristics, system functionality, and the institution's technical infrastructure for preservation, storage, and access.[8] Archivists are becoming more proactive in educating creators on how to adhere to standards before and during the creation of electronic records.[9] This includes advising on what records are valuable, establishing file name structures, recognizing the software and systems used for creation, and, subsequently, determining ways to provide access.

Value: 1. APPRAISAL (RECORDS MANAGEMENT): the usefulness, significance, or worth that determines a record's retention; 2. APPRAISAL: the amount of money something might bring if offered for sale; 3. COMPUTING: the information found within a record, field, or variable; 4. DIGITAL RECORDS PHOTOGRAPHY: the level of brightness or color in an image

Notes

"Value" is a heavy-laden word in archivy. Besides meaning the importance of the record in cultural and societal terms, it means the worth of a record in cash, not to mention its specialized uses in digital archives and photography. Beyond these basic, single-word senses, our field uses dozens of additional multi-word terms for different kinds of value, which include gradations of meaning so fine as to rarely be observed in the archivist's actual practice of communicating with words. Permanent and enduring value may have no difference in meaning. Legal and evidentiary value may cover essentially the same concept. Some of these "values" we share with the rest of the world, and some we have made only for ourselves. This plethora of terms underlines the deep need in archivists to identify records that are truly worth keeping. Value is a difficult concept to corral and tame; thus, we use many terms so we might have many additional lenses through which to appraise and select records for a period of time we designate as "permanent."

Archival value: The ongoing usefulness or significance of records, based on the administrative, legal, fiscal, evidential, or historical information they contain, justifying their continued preservation

Artifactual value: The usefulness or significance of an object based on its physical or aesthetic characteristics, rather than its intellectual content

Associational value: The usefulness or significance of materials based on their relationship to an individual, family, organization, place, or event

Continuing value: The usefulness or significance of records based on the information they contain that justifies their ongoing preservation

Enduring value: The usefulness or significance of records based on the information they contain that justifies their permanent or ongoing preservation

Ephemeral value: Useful or significant for a limited period of time

Genealogical value: The continuing usefulness of records to support research into a person's or family's ancestry

Historical value: 1. The importance or usefulness of records that justifies their continued preservation because of the enduring administrative, legal, fiscal, or evidential information they contain; 2. The usefulness or significance of records for understanding the recorded human past

Indefinite value: The ongoing usefulness or significance of records, based on the administrative, legal, fiscal, evidential, or historical information they contain, justifying their continued preservation

Research value: The usefulness or significance of materials based on their content, independent of any intrinsic or evidential value

Secondary value: The usefulness or significance of records based on purposes other than that for which they were originally created

Symbolic value: The importance that accrues to records because of their cultural, social, and psychological significance to a society

FIGURE 2. Definitions of Value

Source: *Dictionary of Archives Terminology*, Society of American Archivists, https://dictionary.archivists.org.

Record creation, collecting scope, and archival value are important to the reference process. These aspects are communicated to patrons to provide context. In turn, reference archivists' interactions with researchers provide solid data to use in cycling back and informing appraisal and collecting decisions. Tracking collection use, recognizing research trends, and knowing about patrons' subject interests informs future collection development.

Arrangement and Description

Of all archival functions, processing most informs reference services. To provide effective service, reference archivists must have knowledge of professional standards and their institutional arrangement and description practices. Staff turnover and changes in approaches over decades lead to vastly different procedures. This leaves archivists and patrons to navigate and interpret a wide variety of finding aids, inventories, metadata, catalog records, and other descriptive outputs.

Approaches to arrangement and description vary greatly. Traditional processing is executing folder- or item-level arrangement and description to provide extensive collection details. Since the 1980s, several archivists have proposed implementing more flexible procedures that range from item- through collection-level arrangement and description. Megan Desnoyers, Mark Greene, Dennis Meissner, Christine Weideman, and Daniel A. Santamaria provide strategies, guidelines, and recommendations for quicker processing while maintaining physical protection and control.[10] MPLP, extensible processing, accessioning as processing, and similar approaches focus on increasing access by providing collection-level records, describing all holdings, and implementing patron-driven processing strategies. All of these authors propose focusing on improving collection management as a way to give the user access to more materials.

Developments in technology and professional standards have helped small and large institutions implement and improve processing workflows. In particular, advances in archives-specific cataloging and collection management software have led to standardized finding aids, more robust online information, better inventories, and other discovery tools. Such software creates consistent descriptive output structure and, at times, better adherence to such standards as Machine Readable Cataloging (MARC), Resource Description and Access (RDA), and *Describing Archives, a Content Standard* (DACS). Combined with the ability to post seemingly unlimited information online, access to collection descriptions and contents has greatly increased and will continue to do so. This improved access aims to reach more users but can also increase demands on reference staff to field questions and facilitate use.

Reference cannot occur without at least nominal description of collections. Whether working on a basic record with a creator and minimal subject headings or an extensive inventory, an archivist's solid processing procedures enable patrons to find and use collections. Further, reference interaction helps inform processing strategies and effectiveness of arrangement and description. By monitoring requests and interactions, reference archivists learn about research demands and trends and thereby have the opportunity to offer input on processing priorities.

Preservation

At first glance, reference and preservation appear to be at odds. Preservation tasks are conducted with the goal of minimizing deterioration of materials, while reference encourages the handling and use that can cause deterioration. However, both focus on long-term availability of materials: preservation tasks protect items, and reference ensures proper handling and use that safeguard those actions.

Though wear and tear naturally occur over time, protective measures mitigate excessive deterioration of materials. Creating a physical setup conducive to handling various formats, implementing reading room procedures, communicating the proper procedures to patrons, and monitoring use and handling are basic steps to minimizing damage to materials.

The bulk of preservation measures are discovered and completed during processing. However, some preservation needs may be overlooked or extensive handling can cause the need for protection at a later time. By communicating the purpose of and enforcing proper handling procedures to users, reference staff members play a key role in supporting long-term preservation. Both patrons and reference archivists can point out problems discovered during use. Whether a torn photograph needs to be encased in protective sleeves or a box of letters seems too brittle to unfold, raising these matters proactively safeguards materials for future handling.

One particular function in which preservation and access intersect is digitization. A general objective of creating digital reproductions is to facilitate online access, as well as an alternate method that alleviates physical handling. To be clear, digitization does not equal or supercede preservation, but, particularly with high-use and high-demand materials, providing access to digital reproductions prevents harm to the original items.

Ultimately, preservation activities are conducted with access in mind. However, there are ongoing challenges in trying to balance protecting materials with the desire to make them accessible and usable. For physical materials, ongoing use can cause damage. For digital materials, more is required to fix the content and formats to forestall damage or manipulation. Regardless of the format, preservation remains a crucial component of access to materials.

Digital Content

Since the advent of the World Wide Web in the early 1990s, archives have strived to place reproductions from collections, as well as born-digital items, online. While this has greatly increased access and broadened audiences, it has also escalated users' expectations for electronic access to archival materials. The discrepancy between those expectations and repositories' abilities to deliver extensive online content will only increase over time. Further, this necessitates constant and continuous communication to patrons about how the process works and the multitude of challenges to online access. Although archives struggle to meet (often unrealistic) user demands, they have exponentially increased access to collections through digital means.

Many archives have strategies—whether formal or *ad hoc*—for digitization of collection contents. Larger programs have entire departments devoted to digitization, while small ones may operate on an as-needed basis. One strategy that has increased in popularity is the patron-driven approach, in which the driving factor behind creating digital surrogates is based on user demand. With any type of digitization strategy, reference interactions are instrumental in guiding digitization activities. Much like patron-driven processing, reference archivists monitor research trends and collection use statistics to make informed decisions about digitization. In addition, being on the front lines enables reference archivists to monitor cases in which preservation concerns, whether individual items or groups of items, merit digitizing.

Born-digital records necessitate different strategies. Archives are responsible for maintaining the authenticity, completeness, and reliability of electronic records. This entails maintaining storage platforms with multiple copies in different locations, monitoring storage, and specifying who has access to the content, but it also entails detail-oriented tasks such as using write blockers, conducting virus checks for incoming content, establishing fixity of content, evaluating formats for accessibility, repairing files, migrating data periodically to prevent obsolescence, and standardizing metadata.[11] These details are the back-end tasks for electronic records management, which affect the front end of access. Without fixing formats and content, creating metadata, and establishing systems for presentation, there can be no access to these records.

The availability of digital content has also removed the reference archivist from some interactions. Some users may find what they need through search engines without consulting an archivist. Metadata and descriptions are optimized through search engines and often harvested through multiple portals, providing numerous avenues for results. On the one hand, when users find materials through online searches, they may contact a repository with a query for more details or more information. On the other hand, they may find what they need and have no need for further support.

As the world becomes more and more digitally focused, archives will continue to strive to meet patrons' expectations of providing digital content. The amount of digital resources will only increase, as will the ways of making them accessible. Reference archivists' roles are to monitor and assess what patrons are looking for, gauge their capabilities of navigating systems and software, and use this information to suggest strategies and priorities for making digitized and born-digital records accessible.

Outreach and Advocacy

Collections will not be used if people do not know they exist. In the past few decades, archival practice has changed from passively waiting for patrons' calls or visits to actively engaging existing audiences and seeking new ones through outreach activities. While outreach is important for individual institutions, this trend also affects the profession as a whole. The more people who are aware of archives and their purposes, the more respect the profession gains within society.

In one respect, an archivist can approach all archival functions as though they are outreach activities. Typically, outreach activities involve publicity, websites, social media, tours, publications, and events. On a deeper level, research guides, finding aids, and digital collections also encompass outreach. Even further, donor relations, pleasant reference interactions, and any engagement with people about archives also leaves an impression. Some institutions establish specific outreach programs, but another approach is to incorporate outreach as a framework for all activities. Doing so enables archivists to recognize the importance of tailoring services to reach appropriate constituencies.

Outreach is action that is a crucial component of advocacy. Archivist Kathleen Roe defines advocacy as "giving a focused purposeful message to a targeted audience in order to effect a positive change."[12] While outreach focuses on promoting collections and services, advocacy goes further to justify the importance of archives and their existence. This is accomplished through establishing partnerships with stakeholders, engaging in activism and politics on behalf of archives, and developing financial support, whether within the parent institution or local, state, or regional communities, or on national or international levels.

Reference both directly and indirectly intersects with both outreach and advocacy. As the most public-facing archives personnel, reference professionals are responsible for patrons' or other stakeholders' impressions of the archives. Directly, reference staff members often perform outreach activities, such as tours, presentations, or instruction, as well as research assistance. Indirectly, these interactions have potential for greater reach than the initial point of contact in emphasizing the significance of archives. For example, a tour for a community group may lead to an acquisition, a presentation to an internal group may accentuate the archives' relevance to the parent institution, or fulfilling a reference inquiry may lead to acknowledgment in a publication. Because any direct or indirect interaction can reap benefits, using outreach as a framework helps archivists approach all activities with that goal in mind.

Conclusion

This book contains many illustrations of and details about how reference and access are central to all archival functions. Reference archivists have a responsibility to communicate patron activities and use to their colleagues to inform other functions, strategies, and priorities. Documenting oft-requested collections, trending research topics, and preservation issues helps further appropriate institution-wide planning, which in turn emphasizes the priority of patrons and use.

Archivists have taken reference work beyond informational interactions to include a greater focus on outreach and advocacy. In other words, archivists no longer wait for users to appear on their doorsteps but instead actively connect to new audiences on local and global levels, engage a wide variety of patrons, and educate communities on the value of archival records.

As the number and type of institutions and professionals proliferate, their social role continues to expand. Archival institutions enable citizens' rights to access information within a democratic society, empower people to contribute to the historical record, and offer unlimited possibilities for conducting research and advancing knowledge. The following chapters explore the ways in which a solid reference program and a focus on access will allow archivists to fulfill these goals, now and in the future.

NOTES

[1] Peter Gottlieb, "Strategic Leadership," in *Leading and Managing Archives and Manuscripts Programs*, ed. Peter Gottlieb and David Carmicheal (Chicago: Society of American Archivists, 2019), 26.

[2] Carol E. B. Chosky, "Leading a Successful Records Management Program," in *Leading and Managing Archives and Records Programs: Strategies for Success*, ed. Bruce W. Dearstyne (New York: Neal-Schuman Publishers, 2008), 80.

[3] Larry J. Hackman, "Advocacy for Archives and Archivists," in ed. Larry J. Hackman, *Many Happy Returns: Advocacy and the Development of Archives* (Chicago: Society of American Archivists, 2011), 12–13.

[4] U.S. National Archives and Records Administration, "Strategic Plan 2018–2022," February 2018, https://www.archives.gov/files/about/plans-reports/strategic-plan/2018/strategic-plan-2018-2022.pdf, captured at https://perma.cc/98NA-TMJ6.

[5] Society of American Archivists, "Strategic Plan 2020–2022," May 2019, www2.archivists.org/governance/strategic-plan/2020-2022, captured at https://perma.cc/DU9J-7DVN.

[6] *Dictionary of Archives Terminology*, s.v. "appraisal," Society of American Archivists, https://dictionary.archivists.org/entry/appraisal.html, captured at https://perma.cc/B2QL-53UT.

[7] Tom Nesmith, "Documenting Appraisal as a Societal-Archival Process: Theory, Practice, and Ethics in the Wake of Helen Willa Samuels," in *Controlling the Past: Documenting Society and Institutions, Essays in Honor of Helen Willa Samuels*, ed. Terry Cook (Chicago: Society of American Archivists, 2011), 32; Randall C. Jimerson, *Archives Power: Memory, Accountability, and Social Justice* (Chicago: Society of American Archivists, 2009), 13, 300–301.

[8] Geof Huth, "Appraising Digital Records," in *Appraisal and Acquisition Strategies*, ed. Michael Shallcross and Christopher J. Prom (Chicago: Society of American Archivists, 2016), 29, 33–34.

[9] Gabriela Redwine et al., *Born Digital: Guidance for Donors, Dealers, and Archival Repositories* (Washington, DC: Council on Library and Information Resources, 2013).

[10] Desnoyers, "When Is a Collection Processed?"; Greene and Meissner, "More Product, Less Process"; Weideman, "Accessioning as Processing"; Santamaria, *Extensible Processing for Archives and Special Collections*.

[11] Erin O'Meara and Kate Stratton, "Preserving Digital Objects," in *Digital Preservation Essentials*, ed. Christopher J. Prom (Chicago: Society of American Archivists, 2016), 13.

[12] Kathleen D. Roe, *Advocacy and Awareness for Archivists* (Chicago: Society of American Archivists, 2019), 6.

2

Reference Skills and Knowledge

Reference services are only as good as the people who provide them. In the past, archivists seemed like "dragons at the gate," meaning patrons relied almost solely on archivists' guidance and extensive knowledge of collections. Over time, this approach shifted as archives became more public-facing institutions with an increasing variety of audiences. Today, while knowledge and expertise are still essential, many archives also prioritize a service-oriented approach.

The pertinent reference skills and knowledge are codified primarily in statements made by three organizations: the Society of American Archivists, the Academy of Certified Archivists, and the Association of College and Research Libraries. Offering standards that archivists need to perform all archival functions, the portions of these statements that pertain to reference focus on research strategies, technical abilities, interpersonal relations, understanding user behaviors, collection knowledge, subject expertise, and awareness of internal and external laws and regulations.[1]

Recent job advertisements (see Figure 3) present a snapshot that aligns with these standards. The job descriptions have common threads, including communication and interpersonal skills, computer and research skills, and knowledge of best practices for reference and archival standards. These examples illustrate that knowledge of collections and subjects is expected to be learned on the job, but understanding of cataloging and metadata, research strategies, communication skills, and the ability to work with the public are the competencies desired. It is the combination of knowledge, technical skills, and good interpersonal relations that make a well-rounded reference archivist.

Patrons rely on archivists for their expertise and ability to find relevant resources, but good customer service and communication facilitates a pleasant interaction for both user and archivist. This chapter examines the skills, knowledge, and competencies that reference archivists at all repository types and staffing levels require to be successful.

> Recent postings for archival positions list the following requirements:
>
> **Head of Public Services:** Commitment to implementing, planning, and assessing customer service; written and verbal interpersonal and communication skills; knowledge of trends and technologies; strong foundation in intellectual property
>
> **Library Subject Specialist and Reference Librarian:** Strong background in library science and subject/discipline history; familiarity with automated library cataloging systems; excellent computer and communications skills; and a demonstrated ability to work with the public
>
> **Reading Room and Front Desk Coordinator:** Detail-oriented and organization skills; understanding of best practices for handling fragile materials; oral and written communication skills
>
> **Reference Archivist:** Familiarity with professionally accepted library and/or archival standards of classification, indexing and cataloging, and knowledge of automated records storage and retrieval systems; excellent interpersonal, oral and written, analytical, and organization skills; and be able to communicate and collaborate effectively
>
> **Reference Internship:** Strong research, writing, organizational, and communication skills; attention to detail and professionalism
>
> **Research Librarian:** Experience in a special collections or archives with significant responsibilities for instruction and education; knowledge of best practices and current methods in special collections pedagogy and reference services; experience in the effective use of research tools (scholarly resources, citation management tools, etc.)

FIGURE 3. Sample Job Postings

Note: These job postings summarize requirements to demonstrate similarities and differences across institution types. For analysis purposes, the postings selected represent a variety of repositories and aspects of reference but excluded jobs in which reference was not the primary duty. These postings, which were anonymized, are a sampling from the *Archives Gig* blog in February 2017.
Source: Meredith Lowe, *Archives Gig* (blog), https://archivesgig.wordpress.com/tag/reference-services/.

Knowledge

Patrons rely on archivists for their knowledge. Overarching knowledge encompasses the process of records creation, context of archives within society, and ways in which reference fits within other archival functions. On a more detailed level, knowledge is familiarity with the institution's history, biographies and histories of records creators, and specifics about the contents of collections. To help define these areas of knowledge, a 2013 survey of archivists and patrons examined what both groups identified as knowledge that is expected of archivists. The results described three main categories of knowledge that archivists need: interaction, collection, and research. Each category encompasses specific components, which directly relate to the standards delineated by the aforementioned professional organizations. The study's descriptions outline the varied aspects that make up core knowledge required to provide effective reference service.[2]

Interaction knowledge includes understanding users, institutional practices and policies, and access systems. Identifying user types and their information-seeking behaviors helps reference professionals understand the user's perspective and cater services appropriately. Interaction knowledge also includes knowing the procedures to share with researchers, from the basics of using materials in the reading room through how to gain permission to publish. Further, this skill includes identifying the appropriate systems and tools needed to construct research strategies, effectively navigating databases, and interpreting finding aids and other collection information.[3] Essentially, interaction knowledge means recognizing the institution's user base, research trends, procedures and policies, and legal and ethical issues.

Collection knowledge and research knowledge are interrelated yet distinct, and both serve to connect patrons with information. As noted in the 2013 survey, collection knowledge involves gaining comprehension of the institution's holdings and the contextual information about those holdings to point patrons toward relevant materials. Researchers are also interested in collection gaps or learning what relevant materials might be located in other repositories.[4] Archivists build collection knowledge over time and through interactions with patrons and collections, but it is acceptable that archivists not expect to know all the details about every collection. Instead, focusing on building broad knowledge about all holdings is beneficial long-term.

Research knowledge expands on collection knowledge to include subjects, artifactual literacy, and research methodologies. This includes identifying thematic research potential across collections, developing the ability to read and interpret texts and other materials as objects, and working with various methods to assist patrons in creating search and interpretative strategies.[5] Some archivists may have formal research methods training through undergraduate or graduate programs, but broadening knowledge to a variety of disciplines aids in effective research service.

In addition to knowledge of collection contents and research methods, archivists must be conversant with legal and copyright issues, donor and/or use restrictions, institutional policies, and any other stipulations that regulate access. Archivists need not have the proficiency of a lawyer, but they must be aware of institutional practices and policies, how and where to check for mandates, and who to consult when the need arises. Examples of situations in which such legal issues come into play include determining appropriate access to entire collections or portions of them, responding to publishing requests, and creating reproductions for use.

Essentially, knowledge encompasses all aspects about collections, subject areas, research methods, access regulations, and patrons. These components of knowledge are relevant to all repository types, but the detailed components vary by institution.

Technical Skills and Knowledge

A reference question is rarely addressed without the use of some form of technology. There is no formal definition of technical skills, but essentially they are practices and procedures in which some form of hardware or software is used. As archives continue to implement more technical ways to facilitate access to collections, reference archivists are required to maintain and advance their skills and knowledge in this area.

Once again, job postings offer guidance on requisite skills and job knowledge. Some of the skills that employers desired or preferred in the job postings in Figure 3 include the effective use of research tools (such as scholarly resources and citation management tools), knowledge of automated records storage and retrieval systems, familiarity with library cataloging systems, and website design. Employers specify these skills when required for job duties, but skills are also learned on the job.

The primary skill required is the ability to use systems to locate relevant materials. These can be external tools, such as websites, finding aids databases, online catalogs, or digital collections portals, or internal resources, such as Access databases, Excel worksheets, Word documents, or collection management systems. Typically, skills in searching systems involve understanding the components of the interface, how to enter search terms to find the best results, and how to interpret the results. Most repositories have multiple sources that contain collection information, and reference archivists must know how and where to find what is needed. In addition, patrons may ask for assistance in finding related materials using other institutions' platforms.

Though systems vary across repositories, the commonality is metadata, which requires a combination of skill and knowledge. The skill is recognizing the structure, and the knowledge is understanding the content. To deftly utilize any platform, archivists must recognize the description and metadata standards used. Reference professionals do not need to be experts in the nuts and bolts of all schema, but they should have the ability to identify fields and to effectively search for specific information. This knowledge is frequently communicated to patrons, and archivists often teach users how to search for and identify the necessary metadata to find what they need.

As well as being familiar with metadata structure, reference professionals must have the ability to think critically about terms and subjects. Often, a collection described decades earlier has different terminology than is used today. For example, *foreign* was once a common descriptor, while today cataloguers might refer to the same concept as *international* or *global*.

Archivists are proactively examining options to adapt more inclusive and representative metadata.[6] Time and resources seldom allow archivists to comprehensively evaluate and redescribe all materials; therefore, reference staff members are required to consider both current and previous terminology. At times, past language is considered offensive but it is also necessary in order to understand historical context. Think of *negro* instead of *African American* or *Black*, or *crippled* instead of *disabled* or *differently abled*. These are educational moments, and explaining historical contexts of language use to patrons better informs them on how to execute successful searches.

Beyond searching systems, archivists need capabilities to use general computer software, scanning equipment, audiovisual equipment, and other tools that directly relate to access of materials. Knowing how to convert a Word document to a PDF, download photos from a phone or camera, or digitize a folder's contents are examples of tasks that can arise as part of a reference interaction.

To attempt to identify all of the technical skills reference archivists need is challenging due to the constant changes in technology, growing types of formats and equipment, and job expectations. It can also greatly vary by institution, and tools change over time. As archives advance in implementing technology for access, the necessity for technical skills also grows.

Interpersonal Skills

There are probably a number of archivists who enter the profession with the expectation of working with collections and do not always expect nor desire a public service role. Yet all archivists will interact with patrons, donors, stakeholders, or others as part of working in an archives.

Interpersonal skills are the "soft skills" that enable effective and professional interactions. These qualities include communication, active listening, sympathy and empathy, service orientation, patience, the ability to build rapport, sensitivity, self-control, flexibility, a sense of humor, good judgment, and confidence.[7] Adopting professional, interpersonal, and communication-oriented conduct elicits the same in-kind behavior from patrons.

In a 2003 survey, employers ranked "skills such as interpersonal and communications" as the highest desirable skills for entry-level personnel and second after experience for mid- or senior-level archivists.[8] This is supported by requirements in the job advertisements in Figure 3, which also indicate the importance of communication, interpersonal skills, customer service, and ability to work with the public. Overall, reference professionals must be proficient in communicating and working with people.

These soft skills extend beyond general communication and into providing good customer service. Indeed, as library and information services manager Sheila Corrall writes, customer service "is at the heart of what we do and why we exist."[9] Archives typically use the terms *patron*, *user*, and *researcher services*, though *customer* is emphasized in some library manuals, and the National Archives uses *customer* in its strategic plan.[10] Infusing reference services with a customer service ideal elevates the expectations of the archivist-user interaction.

Interpersonal skills and customer service are vital aspects of reference services. Archivists must develop the ability to clearly communicate at the point of interaction without overloading the patron with information.[11] It is a balance between quickly assessing needs with providing information usefully and efficiently, which includes figuring out how to utilize resources, estimating length of time required for research, or providing external resources. Archivists truly are what archivist George Chalou describes as the "most valuable finding aid."[12] Archivists who provide excellent customer service through effective interpersonal interactions cause patrons to view those archives and archivists as assets in their searches for information. Creating a customer service–focused culture requires establishing standards, expectations, benchmarks, and training for all staff members.

Reference Manual

A reference manual is a resource that establishes expectations, standards, and procedures for providing consistent services. A manual focuses on how staff members conduct all aspects of both the public and technical sides of reference and access, which encompasses the aforementioned knowledge and skills. The manual also serves as a tool that ensures reference archivists' compliance with policies and procedures (see Appendix A for examples of reference manuals).

The larger the staff, the more important a manual is to ensure consistency of reference service. A solo archivist or small staff may not need an extensive manual, but documenting services is beneficial for backup staff members or future employees. Creating a comprehensive manual takes time and commitment from all reference archivists. For a large staff, assigning sections helps spread out the work. For a lone arranger, taking time to document activities as they occur will eventually result in a comprehensive manual. Building a reference manual is a worthwhile investment that benefits both archivists and users.

A reference manual ought to be flexible and easily revisable. Scheduling regular review of the manual (e.g., annually, quarterly) affirms that it is up to date, but revisions can occur whenever new systems or procedures are implemented. Components of a reference manual may include:

- Patrons: greeting, registration, forms, explaining policies, guidelines for in-person and remote research
- Retrieval/circulation: handling materials, security, stacks maintenance
- Policies: copying/reproduction, fees, permission to publish, copyright, restrictions
- Assessment: tracking use, collecting statistics
- Staffing: hours of operation, schedule, reading room monitoring
- Systems and tools: finding aids, digital collections, website, collection management

A manual and policies can also offer behavioral standards for customer service and reference interiews.

The format of a manual varies, but an online or electronic document is easiest for maintenance and access. Wiki software, Google Sites, Word documents, PowerPoint slides, or similar platforms are good tools because they are accessible from any computer, allow multiple people to edit, and can be updated immediately. Because staff members may have different learning preferences, a manual can include written procedures, instructional photographs and videos, and links to internal and external resources. For example, written instructions paired with walk-through videos or screen captures of tasks such as scanning photographs or proper use of audiovisual equipment helps staff members to follow procedures. These options are particularly helpful for those who only occasionally conduct these tasks and for training personnel.

Reference manuals are primarily internal documents, but institutions can opt to open all or portions of them to their audiences. Reasons for broadening a manual's access include increasing patron understanding of services, creating a resource for non-archives staff members who are backup personnel, or streamlining information for both reference professionals and patrons. Opening a manual to the public allows them to see what is involved in conducting services, which could result in a better understanding and respect for an archives' policies and procedures.

Overall, a reference manual is an important foundational resource for any repository. It assists with training, implementing consistent and cohesive services, and change management. Although writing a manual is a time commitment, it brings a high return on investment. Once written, it is a living document that guides reference staff members in performing technical and public services. Involving all reference archivists in contributing to and maintaining a manual keeps archives personnel up to date on any changes and gives them the opportunity to identify any new skills or resources needed.

Training

Implementing a standard approach to training staff members facilitates consistent reference services, provides professional development, and encourages job satisfaction. Training is not limited to a new hire; it also is an opportunity for ongoing growth and development for all archivists with reference duties. While some tasks, such as registering patrons and sharing reading room procedures, are often accomplished through a quick orientation, developing knowledge of collections and users requires time and effort. Collections, access tools, technology, and patron types change and evolve, and archivists must strive to advance their knowledge and skills.

One option is to create a checklist of goals and outcomes for both the trainer and trainee. This can include defining the skills, knowledge, and competencies required to perform reference services; devising step-by-step instruction of the components of reference services; setting a training schedule; and incorporating recent reference interactions as practice examples (see Figure 4). This checklist may also include a training schedule to document how tasks progress and build on each other. When training, it is important to consider how much information a staff person can retain and process. Walking through a few steps at a time allows the person to better master and use the information. Further, spreading tasks over days, weeks, or even months facilitates a better understanding of how all processes and procedures connect and build on each other. Combined with a checklist, a schedule gives everyone an expected outline for successful training.

Even if an archivist's primary job duty is reference, hands-on training in the basics of other archival functions enhances contextual knowledge. An archivist may not fully process collections, but going through the exercises of sorting a box, writing front matter, typing an inventory, or other tasks enhances understanding of arrangement and description practices. Observing or completing preservation tasks helps ensure better handling procedures for archivists and patrons. Further,

---

Suggested components of training include:

General
- Training goals and outcomes
- How long training lasts
- Outlines of tests/tasks to be completed
- Expectations of both trainer and trainee

Knowledge
- How reference intersects with other archival functions
- Collections overview; collecting policy; reading in subject areas collected
- Customer service standards
- Policies (reading room use, copyright, reproduction, etc.)
- Procedures (registration, paging, reproduction, etc.)
- Archival standards and best practices

Skills
- Conducting entrance and exit interviews
- Shadowing/practicing in-person and remote reference
- Developing basic customer service skills and interpersonal behaviors
- Reading and interpreting finding aids
- Developing search strategies
- Using systems, software, and equipment

FIGURE 4. Training Checklist

archivists whose responsibilities are not primarily reference services will benefit from cross-training on assisting patrons and developing search strategies to augment how to perform processing or preservation. Cross-training and continually keeping all repository staff informed of procedures not only facilitates good reference services but also promotes an understanding of others' job responsibilities and how all positions and functions are connected.

Feedback is crucial to developing skills, abilities, and competencies. Trainers should coach, evaluate outcomes, and offer constructive feedback, which may include explaining what the trainee overlooked but also commending what was done well. The trainee ought to also have the opportunity to comment on how the training works, what could be improved, and what was most helpful. Most important, an open communication loop benefits developing skills and knowledge while also improving training tools and procedures.

Working directly with patrons and answering reference questions is where most collection and research knowledge is developed. Conducting or shadowing reference interactions provides better insight than just reading through a collection's front matter or inventory. Along these same lines, talking with coworkers is a vital way to learn. Because each archivist has different knowledge of collection contents, patron interactions, and research strategies, sharing that information improves wisdom of all staff. This can be done one-on-one or in group meetings where staff members share reference interactions, questions that patrons ask, collections used, recent uses and publications, or any other relevant information. In addition, reviewing past inquiries assists in skill development.

New professionals, students, interns, or volunteers require different training strategies. These personnel may not be as familiar with archives as a workplace or have extensive knowledge of archival functions. Providing readings or other resources that offer a foundation of the importance of archives and why they exist helps contextualize why reference is important and how it intersects with other functions. Further, books, articles, or other publications about the history of the institution or specific collections bestow much information and insight.

Another option for new or seasoned professionals is incorporating training outside the department. Library schools, archives programs, and professional organizations offer classes on theories, concepts, and practices for reference. The parent institution may also offer classes or resources on how to develop skills. For example, the Arizona State Library has a continuing education program for any library staff members, and Simmons College School of Library and Information Science created the Massachusetts Municipal Clerks Archival Education Program.[13] Although it takes time to find and create such instruction, participating in educational opportunities is important for professional development.

Ongoing training for all archivists enhances their abilities to provide excellent and consistent services. For seasoned reference archivists, refreshers on customer service standards, observations and feedback on interactions, and self-evaluations are helpful tools to keep skills honed. As the numbers of user types, access tools, research methods, and collections grow and as those aspects of the profession evolve, training refreshers ensure that services continually meet users' needs.

Conclusion

There are many skills and much knowledge and training required to provide effective reference services. A successful reference archivist needs a mix of skills and competencies that encompass knowledge, technology, and interpersonal relations. Seemingly a tall order, these areas coalesce into the simple concept of connecting patrons and information.

NOTES

[1] Academy of Certified Archivists, "Role Delineation Statement," www.certifiedarchivists.org/get-certified/role-delineation-statement/#domain3, captured at https://perma.cc/SB33-JQDW; Society of American Archivists, "GPAS Curriculum," www2.archivists.org/prof-education/graduate/gpas/curriculum, captured at https://perma.cc/L7LQ-6GWJ; Association of College and Research Libraries, "Guidelines: Competencies for Special Collections Professionals," revised March 6, 2017, www.ala.org/acrl/standards/comp4specollect, captured at https://perma.cc/3T6K-DEDE; Society of American Archivists, "Real-World Reference: Moving Beyond Theory," www2.archivists.org/prof-education/course-catalog/real-world-reference-moving-beyond-theory, captured at https://perma.cc/2KQP-ZLN8.

[2] Wendy M. Duff, Elizabeth Yakel, and Helen R. Tibbo, "Archival Reference Knowledge," *American Archivist* 76, no. 1 (2013): 85, https://doi.org/10.17723/aarc.76.1.x9792xp27140285g.

[3] Duff, Yakel, and Tibbo, "Archival Reference Knowledge," 87.

[4] Duff, Yakel, and Tibbo, "Archival Reference Knowledge," 79–80, 87.

[5] Duff, Yakel, and Tibbo, "Archival Reference Knowledge," 86.

[6] Archives for Black Lives in Philadelphia, Anti-Racist Description Working Group, *Anti-Racist Description Resources* (Philadelphia, 2019), https://archivesforblacklives.files.wordpress.com/2019/10/ardr_final.pdf, captured at https://perma.cc/5HWG-64D9; Erin Baucom, "An Exploration into Archival Descriptions of LGBTQ Materials," *American Archivist* 81, no. 1 (2018): 65–83, https://doi.org/10.17723/0360-9081-81.1.65; Irene Lule et al., "Transforming the Archive: Increasing Inclusivity Through Language" (Society of American Archivists Annual Meeting, Austin, TX, August 4, 2019); Karen Smith-Yoshimura, "Strategies for Alternate Subject Headings and Maintaining Subject Headings," *Hanging Together* (blog), October 29, 2019, http://hangingtogether.org/?p=7591, captured at https://perma.cc/A94X-8NTP.

[7] M. Kathleen Kern and Beth S. Woodard, "The Reference Interview," in Bopp and Smith, *Reference and Information Services: An Introduction*, 75–78.

[8] Walch, "Part 3. A*CENSUS," 56–57.

[9] Sheila Corrall, "Planning and Policy Making," in *Building a Successful Customer-Service Culture: A Guide for Library and Information Managers*, ed. Maxine Melling and Joyce Little (London: Facet Publishing, 2002), 27.

[10] Maxine Melling and Joyce Little, eds., *Building a Successful Customer-Service Culture: A Guide for Library and Information Managers* (London: Facet Publishing, 2002); Darlene E. Weingand, *Customer Service Excellence: A Concise Guide for Librarians* (Chicago: American Library Association, 1997); Guy St. Clair, *Total Quality Management in Information Services* (London: Bowker-Sauer, 1997); U.S. National Archives and Records Administration, "Strategic Plan."

[11] Weingand, *Customer Service Excellence*, 80–81.

[12] Chalou, "Reference" in Baumann, *A Manual of Archival Techniques*, 50.

[13] Arizona State Library, Archives, and Public Records, "Continuing Education," https://azlibrary.gov/libdev/continuing-education; Gregor Trinkaus-Randall and Kaari Mai Tari, "The Massachusetts Municipal Clerks Archival Education Project: A Study in Collaboration" (CoSA Member Webinar, May 26, 2016), www.statearchivists.org/files/8714/6774/5531/CoSAMemberWebinar_May_2016_05_26.pdf, captured at https://perma.cc/96BM-ACF7.

3

Users

Users are central to how reference services are implemented and executed. In SAA's *Dictionary of Archives Terminology*, the definition of a user is "an individual who uses the collections and services of a repository; a patron; a reader; a researcher; a searcher."[1] Through archivists' increasing focus on outreach and advocacy, more audiences are exposed to the accessibility and reliability of archives and historical records. As a result, the types of users, their purposes for accessing records, and their information-seeking behaviors continually change. While users' intentions are individual and varied, all repositories can identify certain traits and patterns to guide services, practices, and procedures.

Users may be scholarly, vocational, avocational, or institutional. Although user types are found across different repositories, each repository recognizes its most common users. For example, corporate and museum archives prioritize internal constituents; academic archives cater to scholarly and educational pursuits; and government archives and historical societies see many genealogists, local historians, and K–12 groups. Although most services are applicable to any user type, some require specific approaches tailored to their ways of inquiry, expectations, and desired outcomes. This chapter broadly categorizes patrons and their information-seeking behaviors to provide context for understanding and recognizing common user types.

Information Seeking

People seek information on a daily basis. Whether they realize it or not, they exhibit specific behaviors, motivations, and patterns in why and how they look for information. Broadly defined, information seeking incorporates what information behavior experts Donald O. Case and Lisa M.

Given call "active and intentional behavior" to find and use relevant resources.[2] Over the past half century, librarians and archivists have spent considerable time attempting to understand how users search for information, how those behaviors change and evolve, and how that knowledge helps institutions create effective services.

An early library study about information-seeking behavior found that people moved through the reference process in one of two ways: consulting a professional or searching for information in their own way, without support.[3] Users approach archival research similarly, and the increasing availability of information online today has shifted both types of information-seeking behaviors. While some users may find answers online without interacting directly with an archivist, others may not find answers, may need assistance to interpret the information, or may desire more information than they find online and therefore seek reference help.

Archival literature includes many illustrations and investigations of researchers' behaviors. Often, this literature incorporates case studies of surveys and/or interviews with users to understand their needs and behaviors. Approaches to studying patrons and their information-seeking patterns have primarily focused on the following points:

- Individual types of researchers
- Types of materials used
- How users find materials
- Tailoring resources to specific user types
- The effectiveness of outreach activities
- Other aspects that analyze how users find, use, and interpret content

Seldom are these points assessed individually; instead, they are usually investigated with multiple goals in mind. For example, the types of users are better understood when considered with the types of materials used, how users access collections, users' levels of research abilities, and how users develop search strategies.

By developing an understanding of users' information-seeking behaviors, archivists can foster constructive relationships with their patrons and strengthen reference interactions. Archivists prepare their resources and practices with an eye toward accommodating both those users who want to "go it alone" and those who want or need personal attention. Observing researchers' information-seeking behaviors, engaging in conversations, and conducting user studies provide insights that contribute to excellent reference services.

Archival Literacy and Intelligence

Archival literacy, which has only recently gained traction, traces its roots to the library field's concept of information literacy. Librarians teach skills in bibliographic instruction, now often referred to as library or user instruction. In the 1970s, these sessions included such tasks as how to use a card catalog, understand call number classifications, and make sense of subject headings. By the 1980s and into the 1990s, information literacy became a trendy professional concept as librarians focused more on their roles and what information science educator Shirley J. Behrens describes as their "connection between user education, information literacy, and lifelong learning."[4] Librarians, particularly those in academic and public institutions, continue to utilize and advance these concepts for all learning environments, disciplines, and education.[5]

In the past two decades, archivists have taken library literacy concepts and applied them specifically to archival contexts. Proponents state that "archival literacy" helps communicate the unique components of archival research to a diverse clientele. Although the concept is similar in libraries and archives, the content and strategies diverge because of the difference in the structure of information. Whereas libraries have catalogs and databases with item-level detail, archives present information about items or groups of items through finding aids, inventories, or other descriptive formats that may be unfamiliar to users. Further, developing search terms and strategies requires more effort and yields different results than a typical database search does. The vast and complex information world continues its growth, making it necessary for archivists to consider how to incorporate archival literacy into their reference programs.

The concept of "archival literacy" first appeared in *American Archivist* in 1998, when information studies educator Anne Gilliland-Swetland noted that developing archival literacy and bibliographic instruction was an area for future research to help K–12 teachers learn about archival research methods.[6] By 2014, archivists had expanded archival literacy competencies and skills to include developing research strategies, critically interpreting and evaluating content, placing primary sources within their historical context, and using sources effectively.[7]

Archival educators Elizabeth Yakel and Deborah Torres have augmented archival literacy with their concept of "archival intelligence." They recommend going further than the basics of archival literacy by promoting that a researcher should also understand archival principles, practices, and procedures; ways to develop meaningful search strategies; and connections between primary sources and their surrogates. They assert that knowledge of the framework behind archival management and practices strengthens archival literacy competencies, meaning that understanding how archivists manage, appraise, arrange, and describe collections helps researchers better find and use materials.[8] In this respect, archival literacy is a component of the more expansive concept of archival intelligence.

Related to both archival literacy and archival intelligence, archivists have dedicated time to creating curriculum, case studies, unconferences, presentations, and other resources promoting primary source literacy. Recognizing the growing need for formal guidelines on primary source literacy, the Association of College and Research Libraries (ACRL), the Rare Books and Manuscripts Section of the American Library Association (RBMS), and the Society of American Archivists (SAA) created the Joint Task Force on the Development of Guidelines for Primary Source Literacy. The group identified specific learning objectives as the ability to conceptualize; find; read, understand, and summarize; interpret, analyze, and evaluate; and use and incorporate primary sources.[9] These resources are generally geared toward teachers, archivists, and librarians who regularly work with K–12 or higher education students but also apply to any type of user or repository.

Reference and outreach archivists are key to developing strategies for promoting archival literacy and intelligence. Archivists already spend a portion of their time explaining some archives principles and search strategies in their reference interactions. Although archival literacy is central to most services, the nuance is deciding when, and to what extent, to integrate archival intelligence into reference interactions; archivists must assess when those skills and competencies are applicable and relevant. For example, working with the local media to quickly find photographs for a news story does not require understanding of all archival concepts, whereas undergraduate history students will benefit from those skills to enhance their educational pursuits.

Using archival literacy, archival intelligence, and primary source literacy is a good foundation for developing users into skilled researchers. The more adept users are at finding, interpreting, and using archival materials, the more valuable archives become. Teaching such skills and competencies gives users what they need to apply that knowledge and contributes to lifelong learning.

Levels of User Experience

Archivists work with users who have various levels of experience with archival research. New users need extensive guidance, while seasoned researchers are often well prepared for visits. Figure 5 shows some of the basic traits of users at different levels and strategies for working with them. These are only general outlines, and there is crossover between the groupings. For example, an expert researcher may still require a reminder of reading room rules, or a beginner may be adept at research strategies. One must not assume the levels of knowledge and skills a user has but use the reference interview to assess how much assistance a patron requires.

User Types

In the early twentieth century, users primarily were scholars, government employees, or institutional staff. Today, patron types include donors, genealogists, hobbyists, journalists, filmmakers, television and radio producers, K–12 students and teachers, undergraduate and graduate students,

---

Beginner Users
- Have seldom or never done archival research
- Need a longer reference interview to establish the scope of their inquiry
- Expect more from the archivist because they lack knowledge and experience
- Need information and instructions repeated to ensure comprehension
- Need more in-depth explanations on how to use resources, develop search strategies, and use materials
- Need more supervision to ensure that they appropriately handle materials

Intermediate Users
- Have used archives or done archival research but sporadically or not extensively
- Have some familiarity with the rules but may need a refresher
- Have some knowledge about using resources and developing search strategies but may require additional instruction

Expert Users
- Use archives regularly and/or have visited multiple repositories
- Are familiar with reading room rules and use guidelines
- Expect little interaction with the archivist beyond retrieving materials, or
- Take up a lot of time because they seek out the archivist's knowledge to ensure they are accessing as much as possible

FIGURE 5. User Traits

authors, photographers, artists, urban planners, lawyers, legislators, and many others. A major factor of this expansion is the availability of descriptions of and information about collections through online sources, making them more discoverable by the general public. Following is a broad overview of user categories. Recognizing their primary user groups will assist repositories in building programs and tools that best meet the various needs of their constituents.

Internal and Institutional Users

Internal and institutional users are found in most, if not all, repositories. This group comprises the archives' or parent institution's staff members and related stakeholders. With these patrons, archivists usually provide research assistance using, primarily and sometimes solely, institutional records. Working with internal and institutional users often goes beyond answering questions and helping them find information. It also encompasses building relationships and partnerships, advocating for the value and necessity of archives, and integrating the archives into organizational functions.[10]

Who: Examples of these groups include departments of public relations, legal counsel, communications, marketing, facilities, research, and product development, as well as exhibit designers, executive offices, boards, and trustees. For some archives, such as corporate or religious, the primary or only type of user is internal, while for others, internal users are only a subset.

Institution Types: All

Research Outputs: Select types of use include advertising, obituaries, exhibits, events, anniversaries, retirements, honors/awards, and publications.

Reference Assistance: Internal users often expect archivists to provide the answers and resources they need because they may not have the time or inclination to conduct archival research. Archivists can determine what works best for their constituents. Small requests are often easiest for reference archivists to handle with efficiency, but if users from a certain department are frequent requestors or have projects that require deeper inquiries, it might be worth training them to do archival research.

Scholarly Users

In recent years, more scholars have come to view repositories as more than physical storage spaces for historical materials; they see archives as "knowledge producers" that help shape narratives and produce data for analysis and synthesis. Scholars still seek specific collections and information but take that further by contextualizing archives as a place that selects, acquires, and processes materials—therefore, the archive is both a resource and a subject. Some scholars now view archives as powerful cultural and political institutions integral to the documentation and existence of society and democracy.[11]

Because of this, some scholars view archivists less as service providers and more as research partners, strategic consultants, and/or collaborators for projects. This attitude elevates the role of archivists and has encouraged archivists to take a more proactive approach to engage with and promote archives to the scholarly community. When appropriate, archivists assume a responsibility to be more transparent about the administrative framework that guides decisions about appraisal, selection, processing, and other archival functions. These conversations contribute to advocacy for archives and also break down the behind-the-scenes barriers between archives and the public.

Who: Scholarly users come from a wide variety of disciplines that include the humanities, sciences, education, social sciences, and business.

Institution Types: Any, with a focus on historical societies and government and academic institutions

Research Outputs: Traditionally, scholars have focused on writing books and articles geared toward their peers within their disciplines. Today, while some scholarship remains sequestered in academic communities, many scholars purposely encourage participation with and engagement from the public through television interviews, documentaries, podcasts, social media, magazines, ebooks, and other popular outputs.[12]

Reference Assistance: Scholars range from beginner to expert researchers. What is most helpful is asking the scholar to describe the project—thesis, dissertation, book, journal article, digital humanities project, or other outputs—to determine the appropriate level of assistance and/or collaboration.

Public Users

In general terms, public audiences include anyone who is not affiliated with the repository. The more the public becomes aware of archives, the more expansive the user base becomes. Identifying public audiences varies greatly by repository type and size, geographical area, and collecting scope.

Who: Select examples of public users include genealogists, hobbyists, journalists, filmmakers, television and radio producers, authors and novelists, photographers, artists, urban planners, lawyers, and legislators. This list is not exhaustive, and individual repositories likely have other identifiable groups.

Institution Types: Any that are open to the public, but, most often, historical societies and government and academic institutions

Research Outputs: As with their research purposes, their potential outputs are vast and varying. In addition, some outputs may be solely for personal use with no formal intent.

Reference Assistance: Public users range from beginner to expert. While some are seasoned researchers, it is just as likely that someone who has never heard of archives, much less set foot in one, may request resources.

Educational Users

Working with student and teacher groups is a long-standing practice of archivists. K–12 initiatives, such as National History Day and Common Core standards, require and encourage students to evaluate and present evidence, including from primary sources.[13] Although most often associated with history, integrating primary sources is applicable to many disciplines, including English, art, computer science, mathematics, astronomy, psychology, music, science, and visual arts. To provide adequate assistance, archivists need to understand teacher expectations, familiarize themselves with specific assignments, and understand disciplinary norms.[14]

In addition to K–12 groups, many archives receive visits from undergraduate and graduate students. Faculty may bring classes in for a "show-and-tell" to introduce students to primary sources, require assignments that utilize collections, or encourage graduate students to use collections for their thesis or dissertation projects.

Who: These users include students, teachers, professors, and other educators.

Institution Types: Primarily government and academic institutions and historical societies

Research Outputs: Students generally write papers, produce simple projects, or look for examples of primary sources. Apart from bringing in student groups to the archives, teachers are poised to conduct somewhat deeper research to develop lesson plans and assignments.

Reference Assistance: K–12 students are less apt to delve deeply into topics, so it is sufficient to guide them to a minimal amount of materials. These users primarily need an introduction to select materials to contextualize how primary sources help document and shape historical narratives. In higher education, undergraduate and graduate students may go more in depth in their research and require more assistance.

Archivists

There are three primary purposes for archivists to conduct research beyond answering reference inquiries: to complete projects directly related to job duties, to produce content for organizational use, or to write and publish historical or professional works.

Some of the job duties that require archivists to conduct research include writing front matter for finding aids, creating subject and research guides, developing class instruction and/or assignments, and curating exhibits. As part of processing collections, archivists note relevant information found during arrangement and description, as well as additional research when necessary, to write biographical and historical notes.

Preparing for instruction sessions and curating exhibits requires more extensive research on a common theme or purpose. Instruction sessions are designed around a particular course and the instructor may have specific requests. This is most often related to educational users but can be geared toward institutional staff, community or public groups, or any other user type that expresses interest in learning more about a repository's collections. Similarly, exhibit curators conduct research on a certain theme or historical topic to select materials for public display.

Archivists may also serve as institutional historians, whether formally or informally. Some archivists regularly write about institutional history, people, or events for institutional newsletters, magazines, blogs, or social media. Institutional staff members may request histories or facts and therefore view archivists as the keepers of history. Also, archivists often take initiative to engage constituents in their institutional history.

Conclusion

To provide services effectively, reference archivists must develop an understanding of the variety of user types. Cultivating an awareness of one's user base occurs primarily through working directly with users, as well as by conducting formal investigations of users and their research behaviors. Chapter 12 describes the importance of user studies that can further facilitate archivists' understanding of these researchers and their methods.

NOTES

[1] *Dictionary of Archives Terminology*, s.v. "user," Society of American Archivists, https://dictionary.archivists.org/entry/user.html, captured at https://perma.cc/RN59-MP8C.

[2] Donald O. Case and Lisa M. Given, *Looking for Information: A Survey of Research on Information Seeking, Needs, and Behavior*, 4th ed. (Bingley, UK: Emerald Group Publishing Limited, 2016), 93.

[3] Robert S. Taylor, "Question-Negotiation and Information Seeking in Libraries," *College & Research Libraries* 29, no. 3 (1968): 179, https://doi.org/10.5860/crl_29_03_178.

[4] Shirley J. Behrens, "A Conceptual Analysis and Historical Overview of Information Literacy," *College and Research Libraries* 55, no. 4 (1994): 313, https://doi.org/10.5860/crl_55_04_309; ACRL has several information literacy frameworks: "ACRL Standards, Guidelines, and Frameworks," www.ala.org/acrl/standards/alphabetical.

[5] Elizabeth Yakel and Deborah Torres, "AI: Archival Intelligence and User Expertise," *American Archivist* 66, no. 1 (2003): 57, https://doi.org/10.17723/aarc.66.1.q022h85pn51n5800.

[6] Anne J. Gilliland-Swetland, "An Exploration of K–12 User Needs for Digital Primary Source Materials," *American Archivist* 61, no. 1 (1998): 156, https://doi.org/10.17723/aarc.61.1.w851770151576l03.

[7] Elizabeth Yakel and Doris Malkmus, "Contextualizing Archival Literacy," in *Teaching with Primary Sources*, ed. Christopher J. Prom and Lisa Janicke Hinchliffe (Chicago: Society of American Archivists, 2016), 9; Magia Krause, "Undergraduates in the Archives: Using an Assessment Rubric to Measure Learning," *American Archivist* 73, no. 2 (2010): 519, https://doi.org/10.17723/aarc.73.2.72176h742v20l115.

[8] Yakel and Torres, "AI," 51, 78.

[9] Society of American Archivists, "Guidelines for Primary Source Literacy: Final Draft," www2.archivists.org/groups/saa-acrlrbms-joint-task-force-on-primary-source-literacy/guidelines-for-primary-source-lite-0, captured at https://perma.cc/NC3P-JXVW.

[10] Emilie G. Leumas, Audrey P. Newcomer, and John J. Treanor, *Managing Diocesan Archives and Records: A Guide for Bishops, Chancellors, and Archivists* (Chicago: Association of Catholic Diocesan Archivists, 2012), 7; Christina Zamon, *The Lone Arranger: Succeeding in a Small Repository* (Chicago: Society of American Archivists, 2012), 104.

[11] Peter J. Wosh, "Research and Reality Checks: Change and Continuity in NYU's Archival Management Program," *American Archivist* 63, no. 2 (2000): 271, https://doi.org/10.17723/aarc.63.2.n00l0588g6157373; Lynée Lewis Gaillet, "(Per)Forming Archival Research Methodologies," *College Composition and Communication* 64, no. 1 (September 2012): 39; Robert Leopold, "The Second Life of Ethnographic Fieldnotes," *Ateliers d'anthropologie* 32 (2008): para. 9, https://doi.org/10.4000/ateliers.3132; Antoinette Burton, ed., *Archive Stories: Facts, Fictions, and the Writing of History* (Durham, NC: Duke University Press, 2005), 6, 9; Kate Eichhorn, *The Archival Turn in Feminism: Outrage in Order* (Philadelphia: Temple University Press, 2013), 3; Lisa Stead, "Introduction," in *The Boundaries of the Literary Archive: Reclamation and Representation*, ed. Carrie Smith and Lisa Stead (London: Routledge, 2013), 4; Lucille M. Schultz, "Foreword," in *Beyond the Archives: Research as a Lived Process*, ed. Gesa E. Kirsch and Liz Rohan (Carbondale, IL: Southern Illinois University Press, 2008), vii.

[12] Jessie Daniels and Polly Thistlethwaite, *Being a Scholar in the Digital Era: Transforming Scholarly Practice for the Public Good* (Bristol, UK: Policy Press, 2016), 95–100; Eric T. Meyer and Ralph Schroeder, *Knowledge Machines: Digital Transformations of the Sciences and Humanities* (Cambridge, MA: MIT Press, 2015), 218–221.

[13] Library of Congress, "Primary Sources and the Common Core State Standards," *TPS Journal* 5, no. 2 (Fall 2012), www.loc.gov/teachers/tps/journal/common_core/index.html.

[14] For detailed assignments and advice, see Anne Bahde, Heather Smedberg, and Mattie Taormina, eds., *Using Primary Sources: Hands-On Instructional Exercises* (Santa Barbara, CA: Libraries Unlimited, 2014); Eleanor Mitchell, Peggy Seiden, and Suzy Taraba, eds., *Past or Portal? Enhancing Undergraduate Learning Through Special Collections and Archives* (Chicago: Association of College and Research Libraries, 2012); Christopher J. Prom and Lisa Janicke Hinchliffe, eds., *Teaching with Primary Sources* (Chicago: Society of American Archivists, 2016). Many journals also have published articles and case studies offering advice.

4

Reference Interaction

Reference connects people to resources and information. Although a simple concept, a reference interaction requires knowledge of the researcher and their information-seeking behaviors, skills in research and interpersonal relations, and technical abilities. As discussed in the previous chapter, users represent a variety of experience levels, knowledge of archives, and abilities to find information. Archivists have a responsibility to treat all patrons equally and with respect, properly guide them through the research process, and maintain high standards of service.

Fundamental to reference interactions is building a relationship with the researcher. That relationship may be a brief or long-term association and is what George Chalou calls a "dynamic, constantly changing relationship." While reference is a service, archivists who approach it more as a collegial partnership create effective interactions while often learning along with the researcher.[1] Reference is not about demonstrating intellectual superiority, but it is instead an opportunity to work together toward discovery.

Overall, assistance to researchers encompasses having collections described and arranged for ease of use, providing appropriate levels of guidance based on user needs and expectations, and offering excellent customer service. This chapter explores the facets of the archivist-researcher interaction that lead to positive and fulfilling experiences.

Behavior and Communication

Often, the user may consider the archivist's manner more important than the interaction's results. A positive attitude, pleasant demeanor, and something as simple as a smile go a long way toward establishing a welcoming environment. It is up to the archivist to set the stage and to create an atmosphere where the researcher will know that archivists are approachable to answer questions and provide assistance. Listening carefully and interpreting nonverbal cues, maintaining a pleasant demeanor, and communicating clearly constitute the core of effective reference interactions. Much of what is described in this chapter might seem to be common sense, but these tips hopefully will stimulate archivists to think about their behaviors.

In 1996, the American Library Association approved guidelines created by the Reference and Adult Services Division's Ad Hoc Committee on Behavioral Guidelines for Reference and Information Services. The "Guidelines for Behavioral Performance of Reference and Information Service Providers," which were revised in 2004 and 2011, are organized into five categories. Each guideline includes specific attributes for creating a positive and productive interaction. Some of the points include:

- Visibility/Approachability: remain visible to patrons, greet and acknowledge patrons, make eye contact, offer initial and ongoing assistance
- Interest: focus attention on the patron, use verbal and nonverbal communication to acknowledge understanding of patron's needs, maintain ongoing contact
- Listening/Inquiring: be cordial and receptive, use welcoming tone and language, ask open-ended questions, restate/rephrase patron's inquiries to verify accurate understanding, be objective
- Searching: work with the patron to construct a search strategy, explain how to access/use sources, be considerate of the patron's timeframe, help evaluate results
- Follow-up: ask if question is answered/information found, encourage patron to return, make appropriate referrals[2]

The common theme throughout these points is communication, which is the crux of reference. Active listening means paying attention to what a person communicates throughout the entire interaction. Being interested, making eye contact, offering open nonverbal cues, and giving encouraging responses shows that the archivist is attentive to the researcher.[3]

Although most interactions are productive conversations, archivists also need to accurately assess the flow of the interaction. Archivists must be good listeners but also adept at redirecting conversations that get off-track. Excited patrons share long stories or background about their research.[4] At times, this additional context helps an archivist better field an inquiry, but if the researcher gets too far off-track, it is appropriate for the archivist to curb that excessive talking—with a professional manner, of course. Responses such as "That is an interesting project, and I should let you get back to your research" or "Thank you for sharing the information about your project, and I hope to hear about what you find, but right now I must attend to other tasks" demonstrate interest but diplomatically remind researchers that the archivist's time is valuable.

Conversely, not all patrons are open to conversation. Although the archivist ought to make it clear that researchers' questions remain confidential, the researcher is under no obligation to share details about their research purposes. This is rare, as most patrons are willing to expound on their topics so that the archivist can help them find all relevant resources. If an archivist helps a user who is uninterested in sharing, it is preferable that the archivist not pursue further conversation and instead do their best to serve the patron based on the information provided, however minimal. For example, some scholars prefer to maintain confidentiality because they are concerned that others will "scoop" their topic; other users need information for confidential legal reasons. And some researchers may just not like conversation. This is a conundrum for reference archivists, because the more they know about the topic, the more input they are able to offer on the research. When the patron does not share details, the archivist must be respectful and, instead, focus on providing more tactical information about searching finding aids, digital collections, or other available resources that can further the research process.

Recognizing both verbal and nonverbal cues allows the archivist to assess how to tailor the interaction. Verbal cues are easy to identify: patrons who ask a lot of questions, express excitement about their research, and prolong a conversation merit more engagement. Those who give short answers or do not ask a lot of questions likely desire little interaction. Nonverbal cues are parallel: patrons who make a lot of eye contact or lean closer demonstrate signs of interest, while less eye contact or standing farther away indicate the desire for less interaction. Facial expressions are also indicative of how to proceed: smiling or excited expressions signal openness to continuing contact; confused expressions indicate that the archivist needs to slow down or review information; and a poker face can indicate that the patron prefers to be left alone.

Archivists ought to balance communication by avoiding excessive jargon or, if jargon is necessary, integrating explanations to effectively connect users to archival processes. For example, using and explaining terms such as *finding aids* and *provenance* will educate users about archival functions, but users need not know details about EAD encoding or Dublin Core schema. Conversely, users may not need to know about processes and tools, such as MPLP or ArchivesSpace, to use collections. Patrons need to know how to find materials, which may or may not require knowing the title of the platform that delivers the information. When integrating jargon into an interaction, explain what it means and why it is relevant to the inquiry.

Communication takes effort, and archivists have varying comfort levels when interacting with patrons. Many archivists thrive on their time working with researchers, but for others, constant contact can cause psychological stress.[5] Both managers and staff must maintain awareness of the amount of time each individual spends on reference and recognize when a break is needed. Alleviating that stress can be accomplished through spending time away from the reference desk, assigning tasks that do not require interacting with people, and providing a safe space to discuss interactions. At times, it is not possible to completely disconnect from interacting with people, but archivists are responsible for knowing their own capacities for engaging with patrons. Stepping away for even a few moments (provided there is adequate coverage) while the patron is immersed in using materials allows a brief breather and time to regroup.

Reference Interview

In SAA's *Dictionary of Archives Terminology,* a reference interview is defined as a "conversation between an archivist and a researcher designed to give the researcher an orientation to the use of the materials, to help the researcher identify relevant holdings, and to ensure that research needs are met."[6] This initial interaction, whether in person or remote, sets the stage for the patron's perception of staff, the institution, and services. Reference interactions can be as short as a patron asking to look at a single book or as long as an extended discussion exploring a research topic. Using communication, technical skills, collection knowledge, and search strategies, the reference interview helps the archivist determine how to interpret and meet the patron's needs.

Reference interviews have multiple components, which vary depending on the depth of the inquiry. Library science educators Catherine Sheldrick Ross, Kirsti Nilsen, and Marie L. Radford usefully delineate the five steps of a reference interview:

1. greeting the interviewee and establishing rapport;
2. general information-gathering or getting the big picture;
3. specific information-gathering;
4. intervention, such as giving information, advice, or instructions; and
5. ending, including feedback or summary.[7]

This concise outline is a good structure for yielding consistent and thorough interviews, whether in person, on the telephone, or via email.

With an in-person interaction, the archivist should start with a smile and a greeting, as well as open-ended questions such as "How may I help you?," "What can I help you with today?," or "What are you looking for today?," instead of a yes-or-no question, such as "Do you need help?" Once the archivist initiates the conversation, patrons typically respond with a question or statement of what they need. The manner in which patrons form their inquiries directly correlates to their level of experience. Patrons with extensive practice in archival research often have well-articulated questions or even a prepared list of resources to consult. First-time or less-experienced patrons may not know what they need, may fear appearing inept or uninformed, may become intimidated by the situation, may remain shy about asking for assistance, may appear hesitant to "bother" staff, or may be reluctant to admit their inexperience.[8] Regardless of experience, a hospitable atmosphere encourages all patrons to be comfortable.

As noted in the second step of Ross, Nilson, and Radford's list, learning the broad scope of the research inquiry allows archivists to achieve the third step, focusing on the details. Listening carefully helps the reference professional discern the context and depth of the patron's purpose and recognize clues that point to appropriate resources. For example, a patron may ask a question that does not quite indicate the true purpose behind the inquiry. An archivist who responds with probing questions will elicit additional information and pinpoint the purpose of the inquiry. In another example, an archivist could ask a genealogist whether they are looking only for evidence about a particular person or would like contextual information about the time period or geographical location. In addition, determining the steps that the patron already attempted or reviewing the resources that they used helps the archivist to assess what not to repeat or to direct the patron to alternate options. These objectives help both the patron and archivist expedite the process and bring about a mutual understanding on necessary next steps. How this is accomplished largely depends on the patron's experience with archives. A seasoned patron may require only cursory directions, while a first-time patron will need more in-depth coaching and assistance.

Developing strategies and conducting searches is best done with involvement from the patron. Some users are unfamiliar with how the systems work and depend on professionals to both find information and explain how to navigate resources. To start, an archivist can ask probing questions to determine a patron's familiarity and comfort level with using resources. It is important to ask user-centered questions as opposed to systems-based questions. For example, instead of asking "Have you searched our finding aids database?," an archivist might ask, "Have you had a chance to get started yet?"[9] The latter question avoids placing pressure on or intimidating the patron and instead frames the interaction more as an investigation that archivist and patron embark on together.

Part of the reference interaction involves teaching researchers how to use tools and develop search strategy skills, particularly through explaining processes. To sit with researchers and patiently show them how to search a database, explain why and how to use related terms, indicate where they can find different types of information, and explore other strategies informs them on how to conduct further or future research and engages them in the process. Empowering the researcher is important, but it is also imperative to recognize that some users prefer, and perhaps require, that the archivist conduct research tasks. For users who are new to archival research or those without advanced skills, performing such tasks is an appropriate service. This helps researchers learn and lets them see whether the search will answer their question.[10]

Once the question is clarified, the fourth step is giving instructions and directing the patron toward appropriate collections. The archivist can advise about the length of time it may take to review relevant materials and realistically assess how and what resources the patron may use to maximize effective research. It is helpful to keep in mind how to match the quantity and type of resources with the depth of the inquiry. A genealogist may desire all possible resources and be willing to spend a lot of time with materials, while a high school student may need only a few items and exhibit limited patience. The goal is to ensure that the patron's time is spent efficiently and productively, and conversations about the inquiry, available time, and resources of interest determine the scope. Once the archivist delivers the initial instructions and the researcher consults resources, the archivist can check in with the researcher to determine whether the information is sufficient to fulfill the inquiry or further investigation is required.

Besides determining the potential length of time for a patron to do research, an archivist must also assess how much time they have available to spend assisting that patron. Some institutions specify the amount of time to spend on research, an amount that depends on the inquiry, patron, ease of research, and staff availability. Other archives focus on working extensively with patrons because reference is the highest priority. At times, archivists may not know, nor have time to investigate, the exact scope or context of a collection, and they need to let patrons figure out what is in a collection without extensive assistance. Although users often rely on archivists for this knowledge, it is likely, and acceptable, that archivists do not have familiarity with all their collections. Archivists can help patrons understand this fact.

Because demands on an archivist's time may not allow them to fully assist a patron in an inquiry, one option is to direct patrons to hire a research assistant. Implementing this strategy serves both the patron's and staff's needs and is particularly common in the case of remote patrons, but anyone can hire a research assistant. A reference archivist may do a cursory estimate of the time expected to conduct thorough research and then connect the patron with a local researcher. Most often, the institution is not directly involved in payment or other arrangements, which are up to the patron and research assistant.

An inquiry may not be completely fulfilled by one institution, and referring to other repositories both demonstrates an archivist's knowledge and helps researchers understand connections between archives. Such referrals may be based on an archivist's knowledge or additional searches. Using Google, ArchiveGrid, catalogs, or databases can expand the list of potential resources available. Again, assessing the depth of information that the patron needs dictates whether referring to outside resources is appropriate.

The last step of the interview is the conclusion. Closing out the interaction is just as important as establishing a welcoming environment at initial contact. At minimum, the archivist should ask whether there are more questions, whether additional resources are required, and whether the patron found the needed information. Further, the archivist can conduct a formal or informal exit interview to find what the researcher found most helpful about their experience. The responses will inform how the archivist works with future researchers. The archivist should maintain excellent standards of respect and communication until the patron departs.

An archivist may make particular mistakes during an interview: not acknowledging the patron, not listening, not asking "sense-making" or open-ended questions, making assumptions, or not following through or following up. There are also signals an archivist may give that will discourage a patron: indicating more should have been done before asking a question, providing only easily found information, discouraging further investigation, claiming information does not exist, or exhibiting a defeatist attitude.[11] Because reference is largely about building relationships and having ongoing conversations, whether short- or long-term, making an effort to be thoughtful and a good listener and taking steps to fulfill patrons' needs demonstrates that the archivist views patrons as a priority.

Another sensitive aspect to a reference interview is the emotional motivation for seeking certain materials or the emotional reaction to a collection's contents. Drawing on investigations of faculty and student users, archivist Helen Willa Samuels identified the fact that users experienced pleasure, excitement, and satisfaction when utilizing intellectual skills from discovering and using resources. In addition to the positive emotions resulting from the process of research, patrons also experience reactions to the materials themselves. A study on users and digital photographs described how looking at images frequently elicited the desire to tell the historical story, partially based on varied emotional responses to the photographer, subject, or creation process.[12] This emotional connection is important, as it emphasizes how users connect with and value archival materials. Further, archivists may find it satisfying to know that an object in a collection has evoked that connection.

Not all research leads to positive emotions. Including notes or descriptions about difficult topics in the finding aids are helpful steps, but archivists are also responsible for informing researchers of potential difficulties when reading or viewing certain materials. For example, viewing photographs of Holocaust concentration camps, reading about acts of discrimination or hate crimes, listening to oral histories of members of the LGBTQA+ community and their challenges within society, or reading letters about death and tragedies may cause emotional reactions. Although these may not be everyday occurrences, recognizing these components helps archivists understand users' personal motivations and be sensitive and supportive to emotional reactions.[13]

The reference interview does not always end with the initial interaction. It is ongoing until the patron departs and sometimes continues after that. When appropriate, periodically checking in on patrons while they are utilizing materials demonstrates interest in ensuring that patrons are finding what they need. As patrons prepare to leave, saying thank you and encouraging them to come back continues the rapport that began on their arrival. Institutions may choose to document a reference interview to assess opportunities for improvements or enhancements.

Virtual and Remote Reference

Remote reference has always been a common practice, and the concepts outlined above also apply to virtual and remote reference interactions. Before archives had the capacity to share information online, users relied on published bibliographies and inventories, footnotes from books and articles, or personal referrals to find relevant collections. Then, they contacted a repository via telephone or mail, or visited in person, to access materials. Today, anyone with an internet connection can more easily find and access archival content, whether purposely or accidentally.

The increased use of digital platforms for contact influences both users' expectations and archivists' employment of research assistance. With email and telephone, as well as chat or social media, users have quick and easy ways to contact archives with questions. These users may or may not be familiar with archives, and therefore they may be unsure of how to clearly define questions or use materials. Further, users often have increased hopes for quick responses and immediate answers, as well as access to digital resources. Archivists know this is not always possible, and good communication is key to facilitating a successful interaction.

Still applicable today, a 1999 study of remote reference inquiries identified the differences between in-person and email questions. Resulting from increased collection descriptions and information online, this study found a change in the type of researcher, increased requests for research of personal interest (as opposed to academic or vocational research), and inquiries that more often included specific collection information instead of general questions. An analysis of the results concluded that into the future, remote researchers would use online information to refine their searches before contact, fewer of the initial remote inquirers would visit in person, remote users might not provide thorough questions, and more queries would involve personal interest.[14] Now, twenty years later, it is clear that the study accurately identified and predicted trends that are central to remote inquiries today.

Limited online information about a collection or topic often increases reference inquiries. A patron may find a reference to a collection and request further details, and the archivist is responsible for providing finding aids or detailed explanations of collections and/or contents. However, with the increasing availability of online finding aids, digital repositories, and websites, it is quicker and easier for users to find information on their own. Often, a user employs a search engine and stumbles on a collection, reviews the finding aid, then contacts the institution to inquire about access or reproductions. This has changed how archivists work, as they may need to educate researchers about how to find the context and other details of the collection. In addition, some users become more adept at finding the specific resources that are most applicable to their research.

Users frequently utilize email for inquiries or fill out online forms when available. Much of what is conveyed during an in-person reference interview can be communicated via email, including establishing rapport, gathering information, and offering research strategies and resources. A greater challenge involves determining the accurate research question. Face-to-face interviews allow for quicker conversations, whereas email discussions can take a short time or span several days or weeks.

Approachability is still important when archivists and users do not meet face-to-face and is harder to convey via email. Much like in-person interactions, archivists have different communication styles for remote inquiries. For some, taking the time to incorporate friendliness and openness is the ideal, while others focus on communicating only the necessary information. Some tips for email interactions are to use a personalized greeting, avoid putting words in all caps, and use friendly and professional language. Archivists who are unfriendly or terse can deter users from continuing the interaction or reaching out again in the future.

The virtual environment has increased the expectation that an answer comes quickly; therefore, users also judge the interaction by how long they wait for a response. Some answers are quick, such as a referral to policies or a link to a finding aid. However, many questions require lengthy explanations that take time to formulate and write out thoroughly. When archivists know the answer will take time, they can acknowledge the receipt of the inquiry, ask the user's timeframe, and provide an estimated amount of time that it will take to reply with the information. Or, they can respond with a website link or a quick answer while offering the possibility of providing additional information. It helps to have sample scripts that can save time and provide consistent communication.[15] Setting institutional standards for appropriate response times helps to facilitate timely interactions. When an archivist at least maintains regular contact indicating that a response is forthcoming, users' trust and appreciation increases.

If it is difficult to ascertain a researcher's real need, it is appropriate to ask the person to schedule a follow-up phone call to discuss details and gain a mutual understanding of the inquiry. Near the end of the interaction, a final response can include a phrase such as "Please let me know whether you have additional questions" or "Please email if this does not answer your question," thereby indicating that the dialogue remains open. To help in all these stages, creating boilerplate language to use for a variety of situations helps with efficient and consistent responses.

An email allows patrons to craft their own inquiries, but online forms guide them in providing structured and detailed requests. Forms can be as simple as asking for a name and email address and providing a text box for the question, or forms can gather more details, such as personal demographics, full contact information, research purpose information, and guided questions. Part of the form can include potential response time, suggested sources to start research, or other pertinent information. This helps a patron formulate a more focused inquiry and can alleviate some back-and-forth communication. The form's purpose can be for remote-only reference or for requesting an appointment and access to specific collections (see Appendix C for examples of online reference forms). Archivists can then enter this data into a spreadsheet or other system that allows for appropriate distribution of inquiries and tracking statistics. This works for any size and type of institution.

The same principles for email interactions apply to telephone inquiries. Because physical, nonverbal cues are not available when speaking on the telephone, there is an increased need for attentive listening and good interview skills. To establish rapport, archivists should use a clear and pleasant voice, acknowledge and restate the inquiry, pose questions to clarify needs, take notes, and explain what they are doing so that users know that they are attending to the questions.[16] Comfort with silences and patience is also required. Communicating resources and information should be done at a pace that gives users time to take notes or type into an internet browser. This requires speaking slowly, waiting while users write or type, and possibly repeating information. If archivists cannot answer a question quickly, they can ask for contact information and offer an approximate timeframe for a response. Even when an archivist is able to answer a question, it is good practice to offer to email resources or a summary of the discussion.

Unlike email inquiries, a telephone interaction has potential to be disruptive to others. Telephones are located at individual staff desks or at a reference desk located inside or outside of the reading room. Although public services archivists are used to the hustle and bustle of daily activities, a telephone within earshot of patrons has a different effect. Often, this is unavoidable due to the physical setup. For example, a small archives may be required to host researchers in staff areas, or a large archives may have one or more telephones in researcher areas for patron calls or for staff-to-staff interactions. Though patron comfort is important, informing patrons that there may be noise and activity in the research area sets the expectation for their experience.

Staff responses to remote inquiries depends on how virtual services are established. Having a general email and/or phone number designated for reference provides continuous service, even with staff turnover, but another option is to provide specific contact information for individual staff members. Establishing a monitoring schedule and response timeframe allows easy incorporation into archivists' daily duties. Creating email templates, documenting repeated questions, and encouraging staff members to review questions facilitates standards and consistency in responses.

Online chat reference is more common in libraries than in archives but is an option. Inquiries about archival research or resources often require more communication and attention than can be provided in this format. Effective chat reference includes utilizing continuous contact, providing appropriate textual abbreviations and shortcuts, clearly stating available hours and maintaining customer service standards.[17] If a question requires deeper attention, the archivist may ask whether the users can call or offer to follow up via email. Some libraries also offer texting as an option, though, again, this is less common in archives.

There is a direct correlation between providing more online content and increasing remote inquiries. Some will lead to in-person visits, while others remain remote interactions. Maintaining effective communication with remote users requires establishing guidelines that are similar to those for in-person interviews. Monitoring and evaluating the frequency, content, and results of remote inquiries will allow for efficient responses and planning. The future is likely to bring new communication platforms, and archivists should assess whether new techniques are applicable and practical to implement.

Dealing with Difficult Patrons

No matter how friendly, accommodating, and helpful archivists are, there are occasions when patrons have demands and expectations that cannot be met. Dealing with difficult patrons is an important customer service skill. There are instances when a patron will leave dissatisfied or unhappy, but there are techniques to make those interactions less antagonistic, thereby leaving the impression that the archivist has been pleasant and helpful, regardless of the outcome.

Everyone can recall an incident (not necessarily in archives) when, as a customer, they were upset or angry with a customer service representative. In archives, sometimes the user is not the sole problem and the issue stems from the interaction between reference professionals and the user.[18] Negative interactions may happen because of the archivist's or patron's behavior, but sometimes it is because the customer is unhappy with an answer or frustrated with the situation.

Frustration is often a result of inflated expectations, whether from the user or the archivist. In our fast-paced world where many answers can be found with a quick Google search, patrons do not always understand that archives operate differently. Users with little or no background in archival literacy may not understand why questions cannot be answered immediately. Archivists are continually challenged to manage these expectations without alienating users and effectively educating them on appropriate methods for archival research. Conversely, archivists may have expectations that their resources, tools, and instructions are clear to any type of user. The crux of managing expectations on both sides is patience and clear communication.

There are other reasons that researchers may be difficult: they are in a bad mood, fear visiting an archives for the first time, think they know more than archivists, or even resent hours of operation or parking options. Some researchers are just difficult people who will not be satisfied, no matter how much staff members attempt to assist and appease. At times, a researcher may become difficult after the interaction starts due to frustration with reading room rules, not comprehending staff instructions or explanations, not understanding procedures, not being able to remove materials from the repository, or not finding answers. Generally, people respond based on their feelings about the situation.[19] Archivists must recognize that such frustrations are seldom personal attacks, although at times they may seem that way. Offering sympathy and support can go a long way toward alleviating a researcher's emotional reactions. Phrases such as "I know that's frustrating" or "I agree, but let's work together to find a solution" indicate the desire to help and make the interaction productive. Regardless of the reason for difficulties, it remains important to conduct such interactions gracefully.

It takes skill and practice to properly handle difficult patrons and situations. Every reference archivist should listen to and be sympathetic about complaints, and everyone working in public services will eventually have to deal with an unhappy patron. It can be hard to keep from reacting defensively, especially if it feels like a personal attack. But complaints are not always detrimental; they can be opportunities for improving services. Having an outside perspective helps to ensure that archivists provide good service and assistance. Complaining may be just what some patrons do and be part of their personality. However, many times the people who choose to raise concerns are demonstrating that they care and want to help both themselves and future patrons.[20]

Librarian Rhea Joyce Rubin's manual *Defusing the Angry Patron: A How-To-Do-It Manual for Librarians* offers detailed information about psychology, verbal and nonverbal communication, staff attitudes and training, policies, incident reports, and strategies. The manual also includes numerous exercises to help reference professionals learn skills for good customer service, understand behaviors and attitudes, and handle difficult interactions. Rubin provides several steps on handling complaints:

- Ask questions
- Restate the problem
- Offer options (if possible)
- Let the patron select the most agreeable solution
- Explain what will happen next
- Ask for a verbal confirmation
- Follow up
- Call in a colleague or supervisor[21]

Many of these steps are part of general good customer service and are regular skills employed by public service archivists.

Dealing with difficult patrons is not limited to in-person confrontations and may occur on the telephone or online. Much of what has already been discussed also applies to these interactions, but there are additional tips. When on the telephone, archivists should speak a bit more slowly, put a smile in their voices, and listen carefully. In virtual interactions, they should use polite (not terse) language, provide a timeframe for a response, and remain courteous.[22]

There is a fine balance between acknowledging a complaint and becoming defensive. It is important to remember that many patrons are not familiar with the inner workings of archives' budgets, staffing levels, and institutional policies. As American society frequently adheres to the tenet that "The customer is always right," some people have difficulty accepting when things do not go exactly as expected. Instead of just saying "no, we can't do that," offering an explanation as to "why" goes a long way to appease a researcher. Frustration often comes with lack of knowledge or understanding, and if a researcher has a fuller context, they can be defused or placated. Also, archivists who show appreciation for patrons' cooperation elicit goodwill.

It is imperative that archivists not create a patron vs. archivist situation but instead show a desire to work together to achieve results. Think of a sign that says "We apologize for any inconvenience," which puts the institution into a subservient role. A better approach is to say "Thank you for your cooperation," which signifies appreciation and teamwork. When a problem arises, the archivist may consider it as an opportunity to educate. If it is appropriate and the patron is willing to listen, taking the time to explain why a certain policy is in place and who is responsible (institutional parking policies, for example) and to identify any efforts that are underway to improve service issues helps with pacification. However, it is not appropriate for an archivist to use a situation as a vehicle for complaining about the institution. Keeping the explanations short, simple, and relatable eases comprehension and understanding.

It is important to not react emotionally or escalate the situation if the patron expresses anger. The archivist must keep their voice even and calm, which will affect the patron's demeanor. Inevitably, incidents will arise that staff members are unable or unsure how to handle. When that happens, the archivist can call a supervisor, especially if the patron asks to speak with a manager. Consulting a supervisor is an appropriate solution, and some patrons prefer to deal with a manager. While the archivist may offer the same solutions or answers, hearing them from a manager may provide the best results and defuse the situation.

Most difficult interactions are one-time incidents. However, if there are ongoing issues, it is important to thoroughly document them. In extreme cases, users can either be removed or banned from the institution, especially if a user has exhibited verbally or physically abusive behavior. Hopefully, an institution has policies and procedures in place to deal with this type of situation. This is primarily applicable to external users, and there may be different policies when the primary audience is internal. If procedures do not exist, working with a legal department, security, and/or other public service departments assists in establishing appropriate guidelines.

Difficult situations cause stress for archivists, which should not be ignored. There are many techniques to alleviate this stress, such as performing muscle relaxation exercises, focusing more on the situation instead of the emotion, reframing the perception by identifying external reasons that caused the patron to act out, discussing the situation with colleagues, not taking things personally, or keeping a journal.[23] Working with colleagues on ways to privately express frustrations offers both stress relief and an opportunity to revisit the situation. Discussing what occurred, what was successful, and what could have been done differently is important, not as a judgment on behavior but as an opportunity for growth and development.

Dealing with difficult patrons is, hopefully, a rare rather than a daily occurrence. Such training techniques as role-playing, sharing stories with colleagues, and establishing guidelines for potential situations helps archivists to be prepared. Reviewing incidents after they happen helps reference archivists to put individual confrontations behind them and learn for future situations.

Conclusion

The purpose of the reference interview is to engage a patron in conversation, facilitate understanding of the nature of the inquiry, perform tasks to meet user needs, and build relationships. Archives benefit greatly from opening conversations and collaborating with patrons. In general, this creates goodwill. It also contributes greatly to archival advocacy as it helps patrons see the value in archives, encourages them to visit again, and potentially cultivates future donors.

NOTES

[1] Chalou, "Reference" in Baumann, *Manual of Archival Techniques*, 50.
[2] American Library Association, Reference and User Services Association, "Guidelines for Behavioral Performance of Reference and Information Service Providers," www.ala.org/rusa/resources/guidelines/guidelinesbehavioral, captured at https://perma.cc/VR5R-FR9T; Rhea Joyce Rubin, *Defusing the Angry Patron: A How-To-Do-It Manual for Librarians* (New York: Neal-Schuman Publishers, Inc., 2011), 10–11.
[3] Weingand, *Customer Service Excellence*, 86–87; Rubin, *Defusing the Angry Patron*, 60.
[4] John H. Slate and Kaye Lanning Minchew, *Managing Local Government Archives* (Lanham, MD: Rowman & Littlefield, 2016), 113.
[5] David R. Kepley, "Reference Service and Access," in *Managing Archives and Archival Institutions*, ed. James Gregory Bradsher (Chicago: The University of Chicago Press, 1989), 161.
[6] *Dictionary of Archives Terminology*, s.v. "reference interview," Society of American Archivists, https://dictionary.archivists.org/entry/reference-interview.html, captured at https://perma.cc/D8XS-MW8V.
[7] Catherine Sheldrick Ross, Kirsti Nilsen, and Marie L. Radford, *Conducting the Reference Interview: A How-To-Do-It Manual for Librarians*, 3rd ed. (Chicago: ALA Neal-Schuman, 2019), 3.
[8] David Isaacson, "Pleasures and Pitfalls That Can Make or Break a Reference Encounter," in *Philosophies of Reference Service*, ed. Celia Hales Mabry (New York: Haworth Press, 1997), 61.
[9] Ross, Nilsen, and Radford, *Conducting the Reference Interview*, 68.
[10] Ross, Nilsen, and Radford, *Conducting the Reference Interview*, 67–68, 109.
[11] Ross, Nilsen, and Radford, *Conducting the Reference Interview*, 51–54, 72–92.
[12] Helen Willa Samuels, *Varsity Letters: Documenting Modern Colleges and Universities* (Metuchen, NJ: Scarecrow Press, 1992), 115; Paul Conway, "Modes of Seeing: Digitized Photographic Archives and the Experienced User," *American Archivist* 73, no. 2 (2010): 442, https://doi.org/10.17723/aarc.73.2.mp275470663n5907.
[13] Bethany Fair et al., "Lumos Maxima! Illuminating Controversial or Restricted Records through Outreach" (Society of American Archivists Annual Meeting, Washington, DC, August 18, 2019); Stephanie Bennett et al., "I Second That Emotion: Working with Emotionally Challenging Collections" (Society of American Archivists Annual Meeting, Atlanta, GA, August 4, 2016).
[14] Kristin E. Martin, "Analysis of Remote Reference Correspondence at a Large Academic Manuscripts Collection," *American Archivist* 64, no. 1 (2001): 38–40, https://doi.org/10.17723/aarc.64.1.g224234uv117734p.
[15] Ross, Nilsen, and Radford, *Conducting the Reference Interview*, 215.
[16] Ross, Nilsen, and Radford, *Conducting the Reference Interview*, 122–125.
[17] Ross, Nilsen, and Radford, *Conducting the Reference Interview*, 194–195.

[18] Rubin, *Defusing the Angry Patron*, ix.
[19] Rubin, *Defusing the Angry Patron*, 5.
[20] Rubin, *Defusing the Angry Patron*, 65.
[21] Rubin, *Defusing the Angry Patron*, 66.
[22] Rubin, *Defusing the Angry Patron*, 84–85.
[23] Rubin, *Defusing the Angry Patron*, 90–96.

5

Physical Access

Patrons who visit in person are common in most archives. It is important to create a comfortable place for research that is conducive to proper handling and use of materials. Setting up a physical space is dependent on the size and type of archives, security options, staffing capability, formats of materials, and equipment and technology required to access materials. Further, the layout of the physical space and resources within are contingent on policies and procedures that specify hours of availability, how to use collections, and appropriate security measures. Because there is no single standard, the following sections outline an array of options for designing the physical space of archives that are adaptable to any repository.

Reading Room and Research Area

A goal of reference is to provide researchers with a designated space that is conducive to accessing materials. SAA's *Dictionary of Archives Terminology* defines a reading room or research area as a "secure space area designed for patrons to work with a repository's holdings."[1] The distinguishing characteristic between a reading room and a research area is that the former is physically separate, while the latter is a designated area located within or combined with staff or other areas.

Before beginning their research, users interact with archivists at a specified service point. Often, one desk serves as the single point of contact for registration, the reference interview, reproduction requests, and any other needs. Locating an area outside or separate from the reading room allows for conversations that do not disturb others.[2] At times, particularly for small repositories or those not open to the public, the physical setup may require locating a reference desk within the reading room or, if there is not a formal reading room, a research area with a designated desk or table.[3]

Having a quiet, well-lit, and functional space with comfortable seating demonstrates the value of the researcher experience. Tables with smooth surfaces alleviate the potential for damage to materials and should be placed far enough apart for ADA compliance, easy maneuverability, and clear sightlines for staff monitoring.[4] Chairs should be comfortable and lighting bright enough to avoid eye strain.

Formats of materials influence the setup of the reading room. Larger institutions may have multiple research areas specific to the material type or format, such as audiovisual, microform, or oversize.[5] Offering a separate area for noisier research, such as viewing a video or using microform machines, prevents disturbing other researchers. Many repositories do not have the option for separate spaces for these situations but can communicate with researchers when the reading room may be noisy or find alternatives for maintaining a quiet atmosphere.

Technology is of increasing necessity to the research experience. Many patrons bring their own laptops, tablets, cameras, or smartphones to utilize during the research process. Most repositories permit the use of those devices, knowing how helpful they are, but may set parameters for how they are used. One option is to make these devices available for those who do not bring their own or to secure access to in-house-only digital materials.[6] For example, a camera is useful when there is a need to control how many photos are taken or to watermark images before release. Some repositories also provide computers that prevent downloading for in-house digital collections.

Connectivity is also important when using laptops or mobile devices. Offering a password-free or guest login to a wireless network, with clear instructions in the reading room, enables patrons to look at online finding aids and resources. Although wireless networks are increasingly common, another alternative is to offer Ethernet or wired connections. For cybersecurity reasons, some institutions may be unable to provide this service. Connectivity options and instructions must be communicated on the institution's website and in the facility so patrons are prepared in advance of their visit.

In addition to connectivity, users need electrical outlets where they can plug in or charge their devices. Many facilities were built before the advent of personal devices—or the sheer proliferation of such devices—and therefore have limited numbers or inconvenient locations of outlets. Extension cords or power strips are an economical and flexible solution, as long as care is taken to keep aisles and walkways clear to avoid tripping hazards.

Many reading rooms or nearby areas offer print or other physical research resources. Many institutions offer printing on demand or other options for making physical copies of finding aids. Oft-used books or other resources are also good to have readily available. For example, historical societies may have reference books about families or local history, academic archives may provide yearbooks or secondary sources about collection creators, and corporate archives may have institutional histories or employee biographies. A designated area for frequently accessed resources alleviates extensive retrieval and enables some self-service research.

Staffing

Staffing is required to monitor the reading room, conduct reference interactions, and retrieve materials. From smaller institutions with a single person or small staff offering limited hours to larger institutions with a large staff offering multiple access points, determining how to staff in-person reference services depends on the size of the staff, expected amount of in-person traffic, and physical setup. There is no single standard for staffing, and individual repositories can determine their optimal operations. Following are typical scenarios for reference staffing.

Single Staff

In some institutions, a sole staff person, or "lone arranger," manages all aspects of an archives, and lone arrangers are found across all types of repositories. A single person who is responsible for acquisitions, processing, preservation, reference, outreach, and more is challenged to extensively focus on any of these functions. Each individual determines the priority of reference based on institutional goals and priorities; some may emphasize reference, while others may consider it less important than other archival functions.

There are several ways for a single staff person to accommodate reference:
- Address inquiries as they occur
- Address inquiries by appointment only
- Offer limited but specific open hours
- Set limits on the amount of time spent on a reference interaction
- Use students, interns, or other institutional staff members to assist

Often, a sole staff person uses a combination of these options.[7] For example, setting a few open hours as well as accepting appointments outside those hours offers flexibility. There are numerous possibilities for this option: for example, one afternoon a week, an afternoon and morning each week, a full day, or every midday. The specific schedule typically is based on how much time staff members determine is necessary for their research community. Whether a small archives is open to the public or serves only internal constituents, archivists can also determine how much of their time is dedicated to reference.

Another option that is occasionally practiced is allowing a researcher to use collections without supervision. This is rare because it is a security risk. However, for small institutions, such as community or corporate archives, placing trust in patrons can build good relations. This does not necessarily mean that a researcher has free reign of the stacks but rather that collections are provided in a specific area and for a predetermined time.[8] This will not work for all repositories but is a consideration that may be appropriate for the community served.

Curatorial Staff

Like sole staff persons, curators often are responsible for multiple archival functions. Large institutions, in particular, have one or more curators who are in charge of cultivating donors and collections around a specific subject area or areas. Depending on the staffing model, some curators are also responsible for processing, reference, instruction, and/or other activities related to their subject expertise.

The benefit of the curatorial model is that a researcher consults a subject expert. Curators can inform researchers about the institution's collections, scholarship produced using theirs or other repositories' collections, connections to archivists at other repositories, and other information directly related to the research.

A challenge to this model is having one person responsible for reference on a particular topic. If that archivist is out of the office, a researcher may lose out on that expertise or not be granted access at all. To address this situation, some repositories are moving away from the curator model. Instead, repositories are implementing models in which multiple people provide reference to all collections. By moving to this model, researchers benefit by not having to rely on one person, thereby allowing greater flexibility in scheduling research. This means that archivists may not have the deep knowledge about a single subject area and its related collections but will have, rather, broad knowledge across all holdings.

Rotating Services

A common approach is to rotate reference duties. Many archivists have job responsibilities in other areas with reference as a small part of their duties. For consistent planning, it is essential to assign a schedule coordinator to ensure that all shifts are filled. Schedules can be set up weekly, monthly, by quarter or semester, or on a permanent basis. Each repository can determine the length of shifts that are manageable for their reference professionals, ranging from one hour to a full day. For some, having one- to two-hour shifts accommodates handling other duties, while repositories with smaller staffs may find that half- or full-day shifts work best. In addition, there should be procedures for covering any scheduled breaks, as well as switching or covering shifts when staff members are out of the office or attending to other duties.

Communication is a crucial aspect of the rotation model, as patrons may have contact with multiple people during the course of their research. Clear communication about which collections researchers are using, their research purposes, or any other pertinent information helps both archivists and users. Patrons may become frustrated if they have to repeat the same information to multiple people, so implementing effective procedures for communication between shifts means that archivists are kept abreast of researcher activities.

Communication can be both verbal and written. Verbal works best for the immediate needs when shifts change. Archivists who are rotating off of reference should communicate each patron's stage of research, whether more material requests are pending, the potential for reproduction requests, or anything else relevant to those currently in the reading room. Written communication also works, such as a log with patron and collections information, a calendar with scheduled appointments, emails describing inquiries and collections requested, and notes about special accommodations.

Functional Services

The functional model is to have one or more archivists who spend all or most of their time on reference activities. This primarily consists of handling in-person and virtual reference inquiries but often includes outreach, instruction, creation of research guides, and other aspects of public services.

Archivists with reference as their sole or main responsibility are a blend of the above models. A small repository may have one reference archivist who serves as the primary person to staff a reference desk, whereas a large repository with multiple reference archivists may use the rotation model. Particularly with larger repositories, a reference department may include archivists, support staff, and/or student employees.

How the duties are shared varies depending on the number of employees. For example, students may be responsible for registering users, retrieving and shelving materials, making reproductions, or monitoring the reading room or reference desk. Archivists and support staff members can handle reference interviews, help patrons develop search strategies, maintain schedules, coordinate security measures, and perform other administrative duties.

Multiple Service Points

Large institutions, such as historical societies and government or academic archives, frequently employ multiple service points. Examples include separate areas for security, information, reception, registration, reference, circulation, and reproductions, as well as one or more reading rooms. Some service points, such as security or information, may be for the entire building and not managed solely by the archives.

Having several service points streamlines services conducted by staff members and provides users with places offering specific types of assistance. This option can ease a patron's burden of figuring out where to go with specific questions but also means that staff members must be capable of fulfilling all of a patron's needs, including reference, circulation, and reproduction. Service point shifts can be assigned for certain lengths of time and, if a high traffic volume is expected, may include multiple staff members. For example, the Minnesota Historical Society has a general information desk for the building; a reception/registration desk outside the reading rooms staffed by employees and volunteers; two reference desks staffed by professionals, one in the main reading room and one in the microform room; a point to submit call slips to request materials; and one to submit reproduction requests.

Registration

Patron registration is a common procedure in most institutions. The ultimate purposes of registration are informing patrons about rules and regulations, documenting collection use, capturing relevant user data for assessment, and security. A registration form, sometimes called a researcher application, is essentially a contract for the user to acknowledge and agree to established terms and conditions to access collections. Along with the standard reading room stipulations, these forms may include notices of copyright, digital photography use, reproductions, or other aspects, as outlined in Figure 6.

Registration forms can be available as a hard copy, online, or through software systems such as Aeon. There are also different options for how often to require registration. For visits that span

- No food or drink
- Pencils only; no ink
- Using one box/folder at a time
- Keeping materials in existing item and folder order
- No leaning on, writing on, tracing, or manipulating materials
- No bags, coats, or umbrellas
- Laptops and mobile devices allowed
- Personal scanners allowed
- Personal cameras allowed
- Cell phone use (excluding camera) discouraged or not allowed
- Use of gloves for certain materials
- Paper provided for notetaking

FIGURE 6. Suggested Reading Room Rules to Include on a Registration Form

Note: See Appendix B for examples of registration forms.

more than one day, there can be a daily sign-in register or note about multiple visits on the original form. If needed, there can also be separate forms for collections that have extra stipulations, restrictions, copyright issues, or specific formats that require special handling, as well as limits on photography and duplication. These forms might stand alone or constitute additions to the standard registration form. Some institutions require registration annually or in some other designated period of time to maintain current patron information.

Generally, the minimum requirements on a registration form are name, address, phone number, and email address. Optional components might include type of user (student, faculty, community, etc.), photo ID information, purpose of research, method for locating the repository or collections, and whether the archives has permission to share the user's research purpose and collection use. A repository need not require all of this information but select the components deemed appropriate. For example, some repositories ask for contact information but not for a photo ID. Some institutions photograph patrons as part of the registration process to create temporary identification cards required to enter the facility or for inclusion in a system such as Aeon.[9]

Often, registration details are collected for statistics about patron demographics and collection use. Developing a profile of a repository's audiences provides great information for developing services. For example, a high occurrence of genealogist visits and inquiries may inspire the creation of specific research tools geared toward that audience. In addition, registration is also a security measure. If materials disappear, archivists can return to this documentation to assess whether theft occurred or the item was misfiled or shelved incorrectly. Collecting this information informs patrons that the repository emphasizes security and, hopefully, helps alleviate potential theft because the information is recorded.

The registration form serves as a way to document the collections accessed. While patrons are responsible for keeping their own notes about materials accessed for their research purposes, recording notes on the registration form about collections is a backup to verify citations or alleviate duplication of efforts. Simultaneously, these notes are beneficial for a repository's statistical information. Depending on the level of analysis desired, this documentation can be at the collection, series, box, folder, or item level or some combination thereof. Collection use statistics assist in reporting, planning, and assessment needs.

Recently, repositories have been reexamining registration within the context of inclusivity and patron privacy. Some elect to not require any documentation at all.[10] Eliminating registration protects patron privacy and removes barriers for those without the required identification or who prefer not to divulge personal information. This does not preclude patrons from following research rules, but it eliminates a step to access and use. With this option, the institution considers whether to ask for certain patron information to collect data for assessment and statistics. Options are to ask verbally or have a form that does not require personal data but instead gathers general information, such as user type or research purpose, thereby allowing the archives to amass anonymized data.

One final aspect of registration involves determining whether or how long to retain registration forms. The statistics collected are used to create digitization and processing plans, support grant applications, identify staffing needs, determine future acquisitions and collection development, justify budget and functional needs to administration or management, and compile data about patron profiles and collection use. When pertinent statistics are compiled in a separate format, forms need not be retained. However, it is not unusual for users to inquire, months or years later, about the collections or items they used. By retaining the documentation, the repository can cultivate long-term patron relations. There is no standard procedure regarding registration form retention; the institution decides whether to save the data for a specified amount of time or in perpetuity.

A concern about the retention of forms is patron privacy. The American Library Association notes that the 2001 USA PATRIOT Act permits law enforcement agencies to request access to patron records, which contradicts protecting user privacy (see Chapter 8).[11] To alleviate this potential request, the repository has the option to collect relevant statistics without keeping personal data. While it is unlikely that most institutions will have to deal with such a scenario, privacy is an aspect to consider.

Use and Handling

Archival collections consist of a wide variety of formats, including textual records, photographs and negatives, audio, video, artifacts, books, maps, oversize materials, and electronic records. Repeated use creates mild wear and tear, but informing patrons on proper handling prevents extensive deterioration or damage. Access policies based on formats and preservation include care and handling and equipment use. Policies are written to encompass handling procedures, but it is important to note when materials have special requirements.[12]

Historically, paper collections provided the basis for access policies as that was the primary format for archival records. Standard preservation policies for paper-based materials include no writing, leaning on, or bending/folding materials. Fragile or torn documents are placed or encapsulated in protective sleeves or provided through preservation photocopies or digital reproductions. A frequent perception of archives is that users are required to wear gloves while handling any format type. However, cotton gloves are more likely to cause damage than preserve papers, as the seams (and often inadequate fit) catch on and tear the paper. Instructing how to gently handle paper by its corners or edges is a better approach, as is providing book cradles for scrapbooks or volumes with tight or fragile bindings to prevent damage to spines.[13]

Photographs, negatives, and microforms require special handling. Unlike with papers, cotton or other types of gloves are appropriate when handling photographic items to counteract fingerprints and residue. Light tables, slide viewers, and magnifiers aid in viewing.[14] If feasible, encasing negatives and slides in protective sleeves offers easier and protected handling, which then reduces or eliminates the necessity of gloves. Even with gloves, a good practice is to handle these items gently by the edges. Microfiche and microfilm also require careful handling to avoid leaving fingerprints and residue, and they require specific equipment for viewing. It is necessary to note that not all patrons are familiar with how to handle microforms or use microform machines, and many require hands-on instruction.

Maps, architectural records, posters, and other oversize items require special procedures. At minimum, archivists must make sure that folders and items are fully supported on the research table and do not droop over the edges. Other recommendations include using cradles or large flat carts for transport, limiting the quantity of materials provided at one time to prevent unnecessary handling, and sliding or shifting items instead of flipping them.[15] What is also helpful is to have enough surface or a separate surface for the user to place a laptop or notepaper so these are not set directly on the items.

One option to minimize handling is to create digital reproductions. Most institutions are not equipped with scanners capable of making high-resolution files of oversize items. A lower-budget option is to use a camera with a stand or a safe hanger to photograph all or parts of oversize items. If items are frequently requested or possess high research value, it is wise to invest in outsourcing high-quality reproductions funded by the institution or patron.

Audiovisual items pose further access challenges. Patrons often assume that the repository has the appropriate equipment to access videocassettes, film, audiocassettes, record albums, or other analog audiovisual materials, yet few archives are equipped to provide access to every format in their holdings. To address this issue, institutions can acquire appropriate equipment, partner with nearby institutions for reformatting or use, or charge the patron to outsource reformatting. If the proper equipment to play or reformat is unavailable or the materials are fragile, indicating this in finding aids or on the website informs patrons ahead of time so that they can plan accordingly.[16]

Users are seldom privy to the internal discussions and strategies about how archives deal with obsolete formats. By openly communicating the challenges, such as the cost of equipment or reformatting, archivists have the opportunity to educate researchers on these challenges. Many users understand such explanations, and archives can use research demands to strategize how to move forward to facilitate access to outdated formats.

Some patrons view use and handling rules as intimidating or discouraging, and it is best to address this outright. Communicating in a positive tone fosters a more welcoming environment that encourages access. Forms and statements include what to do and what not to do, but adding explanatory contexts for why the rules exist educates patrons. For example, the University of Georgia Libraries' Special Collections Libraries state that materials are noncirculating "to protect rare and valuable items." The Oklahoma Historical Society's statement, "To help protect library materials, we ask that researchers write in pencil only (provided)," clearly puts forth a reason and is phrased as participatory rather than prohibitive. The National Archives phrases their policies in a question format, which creates a conversational tone between institution and patron.[17] Policies usually include at least a few "do not" statements, but taking time to reword some in a more positive tone provides balance and solicits willing compliance.

Reference archivists are responsible for educating researchers on proper procedures and to intercede if a researcher does not obey the rules. Such an interaction can be tricky and requires a tactful yet authoritative approach. For example, researchers may lean on materials, mix up the order, bend items, lick their fingers to flip through papers, ignore the no-pen rule, or engage in a host of other mishandling behaviors. Because the ultimate goal is to protect materials, reference staff members must approach the patron without being accusatory. Instead of adopting a "you're doing it wrong" attitude, using a quiet tone and phrases such as, "I neglected to inform you that proper handling is . . ." or "Just a reminder, to help us protect our materials, we ask that you. . . ." In general, patrons are willing to adhere to the rules if they are informed the rules exist for long-term use and preservation. If a user ignores a request, it becomes more challenging and further measures may be necessary.

Security

Security measures play an especially critical role in safeguarding collections, and reference archivists participate in both the front and back end of procedures. Security measures consist of collection access within and outside the reading room, policies to deter theft and damage, and stacks maintenance.

A standard procedure is to not allow bags, coats, umbrellas, or other personal items in the reading room. Primarily, this is to prevent patrons from stealing items. Designating a space with cubbyholes, lockers, and coat racks offer a safe place for personal belongings. A small archives may not have the option to create a physically separate area for personal items and instead can keep them under a table, behind a staff desk, or another designated place. Some repositories also inspect personal items when the patron enters or departs the reading room.[18] A bag-check procedure is fraught with issues, such as creating an impression that patrons are not trustworthy and placing additional demands on reference professionals. However, if thefts have occurred or if high-value items are often accessed, this is a viable option.

Another standard procedure is to limit the amount of materials used at one time. A common archival policy is to allow only one box and/or folder on a table at a time, which aids in monitoring use. When a researcher requests multiple boxes, options are to place a cart of boxes inside the reading room or require asking for each box individually. When placing carts near tables, it is important to keep the sightlines clear for monitoring. For valuable collections or fragile items, repository staff members can use their discretion about imposing stricter procedures, such as viewing one or a few items at a time or seating researchers where the archivist can monitor them.

Monitoring the reading room is an important aspect of security. Preferably, having a service point or designated spot either in the room or just outside, with clear sightlines, permits staff members to observe researchers and how they handle materials.[19] Archivists should walk through the room periodically to maintain visual contact and create a visible presence, which simultaneously serves as an opportunity to check in with researchers and determine whether they need further assistance.

In-person monitoring is preferable, but an alternative is to install security cameras. If cameras are in place, patrons should be informed of this during the registration process and with clear statements on the website. The challenge with monitoring the reading room is balancing the respect for the patron's privacy with the protection of materials. Ultimately, the end goal is to preserve materials and deter theft, but it is important that patrons do not feel under suspicion to the extent that it leaves a bad impression or dissuades them from returning.

Staff members of smaller repositories, particularly those with a single staff person, are often challenged to monitor a reading room while performing other duties. At times, it is possible that the archivist must leave the patron unattended in the research area, perhaps to assist another patron or retrieve materials. Archivists can use their discretion as to how to best handle the situation, which may involve asking researchers to exit for a period of time, even though it disrupts their research; leaving them unattended; asking a colleague to monitor; or trusting them by telling them they will be alone. Regardless of how often this transpires, it is helpful to have a plan in place.

When archives have items or collections that have a high-theft potential, such as extremely rare documents, artifacts, maps, or other materials, an option is to restrict circulation by requiring special permission to view them. In some cases, archives might remove them permanently from circulation and provide researchers with preservation copies or digital reproductions. When researchers have a demonstrated need to access the original, the archives might allow viewing only on an individual basis and only under direct supervision.[20]

Security procedures are also intended to prevent users from tampering with documents. In 2011, the National Archives discovered that an amateur historian had altered an Abraham Lincoln letter in 1998 by changing its date to support his research, which later influenced scholarly works about the Civil War. The letter became notorious, and people began requesting access not because of the letter's contents but because of the incident itself. As a preventative measure, NARA chose to keep the letter in a locked vault.[21]

Institutions need policies and plans to handle suspected or observed theft. Preferably, such policies are written in conjunction with the institution's administration and/or legal counsel. Patrons must be informed—through signage, the registration form, and verbal instructions—of any policy that states that thefts will be prosecuted. Two common reasons for theft are that the person wants to keep valuable materials for themselves or sell them for a profit. In the past, thefts from archives were seldom publicized. Today, incidents are reported in the news more often, but there are no readily available statistics on how often they occur. Publicly announcing thefts elicits assistance from dealers, collectors, researchers, or others to identify materials if they materialize on the market.[22] Further, publicity might deter future thefts once potential felons know that an archives tracks and monitors access.

Security also takes place outside of the reading room. It is typical to have closed stacks because archives utilize unique identification and wayfinding systems. Permitting only archives staff members to access stacks maintains better control, lessens the chances that materials will be misshelved, and prevents patron theft. Patrons should never have unsupervised access to storage areas, even if they are well known and trusted.

Establishing procedures for retrieving and shelving materials is an important aspect of stacks maintenance. Documenting materials when they circulate in the reading room, using placeholders on shelves when boxes are in use, and having designated carts or areas for in-use and to-be-shelved materials are ways to maintain physical control over collections. One useful administrative task is to have end-of-the-day procedures, during which materials that have been used are checked in, items no longer in use are shelved, materials expected to be used by returning patrons are stored in a specific area, and materials awaiting reproduction are placed in a different area. Designating a storage area for materials that are on reserve or that will be used over several days maintains security without the added time to repeatedly page and reshelve items. If time and necessity permit, archivists can be more vigilant in monitoring and accounting for high-value materials before and after research use. Not all repositories have the capacity to designate spaces for holds, and an alternative is labeling carts with dates, patron names, or specific instructions. Further, performing shelf-reading annually or other regularly designated time period both maintains accurate inventories and ensures that anything missing will not go unnoticed.

Staff members are not exempt from adhering to security measures. Though precise statistics are elusive, it is staff members who are responsible for many thefts that occur in archival repositories. To start, personnel management is essential. Properly vetting permanent and temporary personnel, as well as creating what the Association of College and Research Libraries calls an "atmosphere of trust and concern for the collections," goes far to alleviate potential theft.[23]

Training personnel on procedures for stacks maintenance, spot-checking their work, and periodically reviewing procedures sets the expectation that the work is monitored. An incident of a student employee stealing and attempting to sell valuable items from a university prompted the institution to create a security task force to reevaluate and tighten security through enhanced supervision of student processing, placement of limitations on staff knowledge of locations of valuable items, digitization of important items to alleviate access to originals, implementation of a fob system and electronic monitoring of stacks access, and improvement of reading room security.[24] As with patrons, an option is to check employee bags during each shift change. The goal is not to create an environment of distrust but instead to set an expectation for maintaining proper security protocols.

Conducting a security assessment ensures that appropriate protective measures are in place. This assessment includes examining current procedures and policies, identifying a security officer, evaluating interior and exterior spaces for visibility and potential breaches, reviewing personnel procedures, assessing archival administrative policies, and evaluating storage areas.[25] The larger the facility, the more steps are required to create a secure environment. Not all repositories are able to implement all the measures they might want to take, but identifying those steps may be useful so that stakeholders are aware of future actions that can better protect collections. Even without an assessment, there are many actions, small and extensive, that keep collections secure.

Conclusion

The reading room and its components of registration, use and handling, staffing and hours, and security serve to create a professional research environment. The ultimate goal is to provide space for researchers to properly access and use materials in a way that supports institutional missions and goals. The extent of procedures and policies can appear overwhelming at times and perhaps turn off some users, but communicating the rationales helps patrons to understand them. While security is a vital component of use, it is also important to approach it in ways that do not deter from access and use.

NOTES

[1] *Dictionary of Archives Terminology*, s.v. "reading room," Society of American Archivists, https://dictionary.archivists.org/entry/reading-room.html, captured at https://perma.cc/8SMF-L6VH.

[2] Gregor Trinkaus-Randall, "Security," in *Archival and Special Collections Facilities: Guidelines for Archivists, Librarians, Architects, and Engineers*, ed. Michele F. Pacifico and Thomas P. Wilsted (Chicago: Society of American Archivists, 2009), 65; David Carmicheal, "Functional Spaces" in Pacifico and Wilsted, *Archival and Special Collections Facilities*, 146.

[3] Zamon, *Lone Arranger*, 9.

[4] Trinkaus-Randall, "Security" in Pacifico and Wilsted, A*rchival and Special Collections Facilities*, 66; Thomas P. Wilsted, *Planning New and Remodeled Archival Facilities* (Chicago: Society of American Archivists, 2007), 32.

[5] Carmicheal, "Functional Spaces" in Pacifico and Wilsted, *Archival and Special Collections Facilities*, 146.

[6] Jim Duran et al., "Using iPads in the Reading Room," *Archival Outlook* 4 (May/June 2013): 4, 25.

[7] Zamon, *Lone Arranger*, 8.

[8] I have personal experience with unsupervised use of collections at a small religious institution. The part-time archivist allowed me unsupervised use of the collection within the institution's small library, which was a great accommodation of my schedule.

[9] Princeton University Library, Special Collections, "Before You Visit," 2019, https://library.princeton.edu/special-collections/you-visit; Yale University, captured at https://perma.cc/X5TB-RQ58, "Guide to Using Special Collections at Yale University: Register," https://guides.library.yale.edu/specialcollections/speccoll-register, captured at https://perma.cc/PM9U-Z9F8.

[10] One example is the Multnomah County Archives in Oregon. Conversation with Terry Baxter, April 2018.

[11] American Library Association, "USA PATRIOT Act," www.ala.org/advocacy/advleg/federallegislation/theusapatriotact, captured at https://perma.cc/X3KR-VDVT.

[12] Mary Lynn Ritzenthaler, *Preserving Archives and Manuscripts* (Chicago: Society of American Archivists, 2010); University of Illinois at Urbana-Champaign, "Preservation Self-Assessment Program (PSAP)," https://psap.library.illinois.edu/; Northeast Document Conservation Center, "4.1 Storage Methods and Handling Practices," 2012, www.nedcc.org/free-resources/preservation-leaflets/4.-storage-and-handling/4.1-storage-methods-and-handling-practices, captured at https://perma.cc/SF4G-2YUS.

[13] Ritzenthaler, *Preserving Archives and Manuscripts,* 271; Alexandra K. Alvis, "No Love for White Gloves, or: The Cotton Menace," *Unbound* (blog), Smithsonian Libraries, November 21, 2019, https://blog.library.si.edu/blog/2019/11/21/no-love-for-white-gloves-or-the-cotton-menace/#.XfhgH9ZKjUo, captured at https://perma.cc/Z39Q-3RXY.

[14] Claire S. Barker, "How to Select Gloves: An Overview for Collections Staff," National Park Service, *Conserve O Gram* 1, no. 12 (September 2010): 1–5, www.nps.gov/museum/publications/conserveogram/01-12.pdf, captured at https://perma.cc/KRG7-7TXT; Ritzenthaler, *Preserving Archives and Manuscripts*, 271.

[15] Maygene Daniels, "Architectural Records," in *Museum Archives: An Introduction*, 2nd ed., ed. Deborah Wythe (Chicago: Society of American Archivists, 2004), 157–158; Waverly Lowell and Tawny Ryan Nelb, *Architectural Records: Managing Design and Construction Records* (Chicago: Society of American Archivists, 2006), 157–158.

[16] Zamon, *Lone Arranger*, 9; Ritzenthaler, *Preserving Archives and Manuscripts*, 171–172.

[17] University of Georgia Libraries, Special Collections Libraries, "Policies and Procedures," June 20, 2018, www5.galib.uga.edu/scl/research/policies.html, captured at https://perma.cc/8HXQ-AJXL; Oklahoma Historical Society, "Visiting the Research Center," www.okhistory.org/research/visitor, captured at https://perma.cc/KYM6-27SS; U.S. National Archives and Records Administration, "Finding Aids," General Information Leaflet 71, www.archives.gov/publications/general-info-leaflets/71-06-dc-area-records.html, captured at https://perma.cc/77YC-GJGS.

[18] Princeton University Library, Special Collections, "Reading Room Guidelines," 2019, https://library.princeton.edu/special-collections/policies/reading-room-guidelines, captured at https://perma.cc/9J85-HY4R; Brown University Library, John Hay Library, "Reading Room Regulations," https://library.brown.edu/hay/regulations.php, captured at https://perma.cc/XW72-BDKR; Black Archives of Mid-America, "Reading Room Guidelines and Rules," http://blackarchives.org/sites/default/files/ReadingRoomGuidelines.pdf, captured at https://perma.cc/4SMT-QGJP; Upper Iowa University Archives, "Archives Use Guidelines," https://uiu.edu/resources/archives/guidelines-for-user-access.html, captured at https://perma.cc/BJ5U-NX4X.

[19] Carmicheal, "Functional Spaces" in Pacifico and Wilsted, *Archival and Special Collections Facilities*, 147.

[20] Ritzenthaler, *Preserving Archives and Manuscripts*, 155–156; Bruce W. Dearstyne, *The Archival Enterprise: Modern Archival Principles, Practices, and Management Techniques* (Chicago: American Library Association, 1993), 184.

[21] Lisa Rein, "Altered Lincoln Pardon at National Archives to Be Taken Out of Circulation," *Washington Post*, January 26, 2011, www.washingtonpost.com/wp-dyn/content/article/2011/01/26/AR2011012605804.html, captured at https://perma.cc/GV59-2K7D.

[22] Elizabeth H. Dow, *Archivists, Collectors, Dealers, and Replevin: Case Studies on Private Ownership of Public Documents* (Lanham, MD: Scarecrow Press, 2012), 105; Association of College and Research Libraries, "ACRL/RBMS Guidelines Regarding Security and Theft in Special Collections," revised January 2019, www.ala.org/acrl/standards/security_theft, captured at https://perma.cc/TV9K-VX46; Dearstyne, *Archival Enterprise*, 185.

[23] Association of College and Research Libraries, "ACRL/RBMS Guidelines Regarding Security and Theft in Special Collections."

[24] Christopher J. Anderson, "Special Collections, Archives, and Insider Theft: A Thief in Our Midst," in *Management*, ed. Kate Theimer (Lanham, MD: Rowman & Littlefield, 2014), 45–60.

[25] Trinkaus-Randall, "Security," 5–8.

6

Intellectual Access

Intellectual access comprises written and descriptive information about the repository, collections, creators, and related resources. In other words, it encompasses all the information needed to find, use, and access collections. There are many ways, both virtually and in print, to share this information, including websites, finding aids, catalogs, inventories, databases, online collections, research guides, and indexes. Without documentation about collections, neither archivist nor patron can find and use them effectively and efficiently. Through arrangement and description activities, archivists create metadata, write finding aids, update websites, and perform other tasks with the goal of providing intellectual information about collections to patrons.

It is essential for reference archivists to understand the components of arrangement and description, particularly their repository's practices. Dennis Meissner's *Arranging and Describing Archives and Manuscripts* and a plethora of other books and articles provide extensive details about the theories and practices that are central to processing. This chapter presents an overview of the common concepts and practices as they relate to reference services and access.

Arrangement and Description

Of all archival functions, processing most influences reference and access. Archivists comprehend that arranging and describing collections is a complex endeavor. The desire to extensively process collections is mitigated by the increasing size of backlogs, restraints on staff and resources, and the motivation to facilitate access to as many holdings as possible. Many repositories have collections with varying applications of arrangement and description that span many decades of different practices. Traditional, extensible, MPLP, cataloging, accessioning, and other processing methods are interpreted and implemented differently at individual repositories.

Creating access for the user is what connects all processing methods. By keeping the user as the focal point of all processing tactics, archivists enable efficient access.[1] To that end, reference professionals must have a comprehensive understanding of, and the ability to interpret, the components and practices of both physical control (arrangement) and intellectual control (description) as means for providing effective service. The following sections do not delve into extensive definitions or examples of each type of processing method but instead provide a framework of the fundamental concepts and practices of arrangement and description as they relate to providing reference services.

Levels of Control

To establish both physical and intellectual control over collections, archives follow a common hierarchical structure. This organization provides both archivists and patrons a way to navigate the collection and understand the context in which records were created. Following is the basic hierarchy:

- Repository: The organization, institution, or department that manages the collection
- Record Group or Collection: Provenance or originating creator of the records
- Series or Record Series: Overarching organization of the collection based on original order, constructed order, or originating department
- Container or File Unit: The physical housing of materials
- Document or Item: Individual records[2]

The repository, record group or collection, and series represent the intellectual aspect of arrangement, while the file unit and document constitute the physical arrangement. The top two levels are mandatory for indicating ownership and provenance, but there is flexibility in how to approach the other levels of control.

A collection or record group is determined by provenance, which SAA's *Dictionary of Archives Terminology* defines as "1. the origin or source of something; 2. information regarding the origins, custody, and ownership of an item or collection."[3] Provenance is important because it is the initial context of who, whether a person or an organization, created or collected the materials. Because collections are discrete groups of materials, they are not intermingled, even when multiple collections revolve around similar subject-based topics.

The next step is determining what further arrangement a collection or record group requires. Small collections may need minimal arrangement, while larger ones benefit from being organized into series. The *Dictionary of Archives Terminology* defines a series as a "group of similar records that are arranged according to a filing system and that are related as the result of being created, received, or used in the same activity."[4] What constitutes "similar records" is open to interpretation. It might be based on the format of materials, such as audiovisual items or artifacts; the type of record, such as correspondence or reports; or the subject matter of the documentation, whether personal or professional. Using series presents a collection with context and an organization that assists researchers.

Within a series, archivists collate materials into an order, often again grouping similar items together, whether that order is determined by institutional practices, chronological sequence, research importance, topical classification, or other theme. Depending on the content and size of a series, an archivist can create sub-series or sub-sub-series to enhance and refine organization. More granular organizational schemes below the sub-series level find few adherents today and mainly exist in legacy collections that were processed in the distant past.

Record groups are analogous to collections and most often are used to organize institutional records in government, nonprofit, corporate, academic, or other institutional archives. A record group also relates to provenance, as it represents the originating department or organization that maintained the files when they were active. Because there are many agencies or departments within an organization, maintaining the provenance for each record group provides important contextual information that assists researchers in understanding the institution. Record groups are also sometimes organized into series or sub-groups. These can be defined by sub-departments, functions or topics, formats, transaction types, or other divisions.[5] For example, a department's record groups might include series for annual reports, correspondence, financial documents, and publications.

Physical Arrangement

Intellectual organization is the framework that creates an overall understanding of the collection. Once that has been established, the next step is to determine physical arrangement of the materials within those components. Within collections, series, and record groups, materials are arranged by container or file unit to solidify final arrangement and prepare for access. Physical arrangement involves tangibly arranging materials into a specific order within folders, containers, and collections. Because archival practices have evolved over time, most repositories have collections to which different methods were applied during different eras. Archivists have many options to choose from for how to employ physical arrangement, whether they attempt to maintain the original order, impose an order, or accept the fact that there is no order at all. Arrangement can be based on the original order that the creator intended or on an order that the processor determines best, based on activities, subjects, formats, dates, or other pertinent aspects.

After an archivist determines the arrangement of series or other groupings (if used), the next step is to decide how to physically arrange everything within each level. The ultimate goal of physical arrangement is to enable accurate retrieval of materials. With that in mind, archivists organize collections in containers, file units, and items:

- A container is the top level, such as a box, folder, shelf, drawer, cabinet, or other type of case that houses materials.
- Within containers are the file units, which can be folders, trays, partitions, smaller boxes, envelopes, or other means that organize materials within a larger container.
- Last are the individual items placed in containers or file units, which can be papers, photographs, cassettes, videos, films, disks, publications, artifacts, or any other items.

The physical arrangement occurs within the levels of control. Collections may be physically arranged to directly follow the levels assigned, with box and folder numbers in numerical order. However, a direct correlation with intellectual arrangement is not required for physical arrangement. For example, if following MPLP practices, the intellectual arrangement collates information for easier review by researchers, but the physical locations of materials may be scattered throughout the collection based on such factors as size, accession date, or format.

Physical arrangement helps with collection access. For example, if a collection has been organized at the box level, archivists can advise researchers that some materials might be unrelated to specific inquiries, thereby saving time and effort. If a collection has been organized at the file level, archivists can advise that folders contain varying amounts of materials. If a collection has been organized at the item level, archivists can explain the arrangement scheme that will help researchers pinpoint specific documents. Understanding physical arrangement schemes helps archivists guide researchers in estimating how much time it will take for research. When collections are arranged at the item level, users know they are getting the exact items needed, whereas materials organized at the folder or box levels require more time for review. Taking the time to communicate such information guides researchers on what to expect and how to use their time effectively.

The most important aspect of physical arrangement involves identifying the specific containers to retrieve for patrons. Regardless of the level at which the collection was processed, the physical arrangement indicates the box, folder, drawer, shelf, cabinet, or other container that contains the relevant information. In addition to allowing the archivist to find the proper items, precise retrieval allows patrons to assess the quantity of materials required for their research.

Description

Description unites intellectual and physical arrangement and ultimately is the most important factor of processing collections. Arrangement is important, but description guides users to materials and allows them to thoroughly grasp the contents of the collection. Finding aids, databases, inventories, collection-level records, catalog records, indexes, print guides, and other bibliographic descriptions are the means that direct users to materials.

Essentially, description is the information about the contexts and contents of collections. The contextual information describes the acquisition, title, size, date range, creator, languages, repository, and scope of the collection. Content description is the inventory of the collection that includes series descriptions, titles, date ranges of containers or items, and details about the materials. As with arrangement, there are varied levels of description, from a brief overview of a collection through item-level inventories. Reference professionals must have the ability to discern the different levels of description to appropriately guide patrons.

Archivists also become adept at interpreting strengths and omissions in the description. Processing archivists strive to create thorough descriptions, but it is nearly impossible to document every topic or item within a collection. For example, a patron may request information about activism using search terms such as *activist, activism, protest, demonstration,* or other related terms. However, an archivist may know that a certain report contains information about a certain event or demonstration, which is not specifically described in those terms.

Description is a complicated process, but it is crucial to accessing collections. As Dennis Meissner advises, description is organized information based on a structured data model, contains common meanings and characteristics, and explains the context, content, structure, and function of the collection.[6] Reference archivists must comprehend how all these components intersect to ensure that they understand and can communicate to patrons how to find and interpret relevant materials.

Access Outputs

The culmination of arrangement and description is creating guides, finding aids, inventories, indexes, catalog records, and other bibliographic resources. Through online searching or consulting reference archivists, patrons use catalogs, finding aids databases, websites, or other systems to seek information. Reference archivists play an important role as the mediator between patrons and information and must be familiar with all the resources that their institution uses to facilitate access to collection descriptions. The following sections outline the basics of common tools and systems used to create and make accessible descriptive information.

Collections Management Systems

The creation of archives-specific systems and software has enabled institutions to gain better control over collections management. Archivists' Toolkit, Archon, ArchivesSpace, PastPerfect, and Collective Access, as well as custom-built solutions, are examples of collections management systems. These systems comprehensively collate collection documentation, including accessions, donor information, copyright, restrictions, description, and stacks management. There are two primary purposes for these systems: to create consistent entry and output of collection descriptions and to enable searching across collection information.

Since their creation, these systems have already evolved in major ways. Archivists' Toolkit is a desktop application and Archon is a web application. In 2015, they merged into ArchivesSpace, which brought together features from both into a web application. Though all are open source, they require technical skills to install and maintain, and an institution can use other means that suit its needs. However, they provide many benefits for archivists and users.

Systems enable archivists to enter customized collection details. They might include accession records, collection-level records, and full inventories. Predetermined fields include general repository information, finding aid front matter, series descriptions, and container inventories. Once completed, the finding aid can be exported into various formats, such as a PDF or an .xml file, and then be uploaded to a website or finding aid portal.

An additional benefit of Archon and ArchivesSpace is an online public interface, which eliminates the steps involved in exporting files. Within the system, archivists select the fields to publish for public access. Another appealing feature is immediate updating, which keeps information current. Patrons can search across all designated public information, while archivists have access to both public and nonpublic information.

Finding Aids

Creating finding aids is a standard method of describing collections. Many repositories use *Describing Archives: A Content Standard* (DACS) as a template for their finding aids,[7] and take advantage of including elements such as biographical and historical notes, scope and content notes, provenance, processing notes, copyright statements, preferred citation, and other components that document contextual information about the origins, creators, and contents of collections. How patrons discover and use finding aids has changed. When finding aids were provided as print copies only, researchers were more likely to read the front matter before looking at the inventory. Today, online searches often lead a user directly to specific boxes, folders, or items of interest, which means they may overlook the carefully crafted contextual information. The front matter may or may not have relevant information for a researcher's inquiry, but reference archivists can point it out and direct researchers toward it nonetheless.

Once a finding aid is created, there are many ways to share it: by publishing through a collection management system's public interface; posting PDFs or Word documents on websites; emailing documents directly to patrons; making print versions available onsite; or creating private documents that are shared onsite or on a selective basis. For broader discoverability of collections, repositories also elect to participate in local, state, regional, or national finding aids portals. Some use these as the sole way to provide access to finding aids, while others use them in addition to content management systems or catalogs. Some examples include the Online Archive of California, Rocky Mountain Online Archive, and ArchiveGrid.[8] These portals enhance search engine indexing, thereby increasing the chances of researchers encountering collection information. They are also good resources for locating collections beyond the boundaries of individual institutions. There is an initiative to create a national finding aid catalog, the National Archival Finding Aid Network.[9] Although in early stages, the goal is to create a network that supports both repositories and aggregators.

Catalogs

Many patrons are used to using catalogs to find books, maps, journals, or other materials beyond archival collections through Online Public Access Catalogs (OPACs). Contributing collection-level records to an OPAC offers another avenue for discoverability. Following the standards used by libraries, archives enter information into predetermined fields that indicate titles, dates, creators, collection size, subjects, and other collection-level details. Catalog records are meant to be brief; therefore, they seldom include a full inventory of a collection. Rather, they have a space to include an abstract, list of series, and a link to a finding aid. In lieu of a library catalog, these records can be presented using collections management systems or on websites. Particularly when a finding aid is not available, catalog and collection-level records enable basic discovery.

In addition to institutional or local catalogs, there are options for adding records to national catalogs for further exposure. The Online Computer Library Center's (OCLC) WorldCat, National Union Catalog of Manuscript Collections (NUCMC), and ArchiveGrid are national interconnected catalogs. Savvy researchers use WorldCat, NUCMC, or ArchiveGrid to search for collections, and reference professionals can encourage patrons to use these catalogs to further their research.

Alternative Formats

Finding aids and catalog records are standard, but there are many instances in which other options provide more efficient output of description, such as databases, lists, indexes, or data sets.[10] Alternative formats are appropriate when creating lengthy inventories that are cumbersome in the flat structure of a finding aid, combining information from multiple collections, or compiling comprehensive holdings information. Some institutions do not have the capacity for implementation or a need for extensive collection management systems and find that alternative formats are the best fit. In particular, small repositories or ones not affiliated with a library sometimes do not have the staff or infrastructure to produce extensive finding aids or implement cataloging software. Examples of alternative formats are listed below. (See Appendix D for examples.)

Websites: A website is a powerful tool to use in providing information about archival holdings, starting with a simple list of collections. Websites can be enhanced with brief or detailed descriptions and can be organized by subject or time period or in other ways that provide information about holdings.

Documents: Word documents or PDFs are sufficient ways to share finding aids, lists, indexes, and inventories. These may be newly created or scanned from legacy print resources and can be made available for download via websites or emailed directly to patrons. Another option is using shareable file services, such as Dropbox or Google Drive. These can be set up with documents, photographs, or other materials organized in read-only folders.

Access and Excel: The standard finding aid format is often not conducive to inventories of large collections. By making those collections available through Microsoft Access, Excel, or similar tools, archivists can enhance access. Materials can be embedded or connected to websites for online searching or placed in shareable folders for downloading. Such tools have an additional benefit of filtering and sorting results in myriad ways.

Databases: Like Access and Excel, databases are conducive to collections that do not fit within a standard finding aid format. They can contain collection inventories or compiled data about subjects, people, or events. Examples include a searchable inventory of a large clippings collections at a historical society or a searchable index of the names of past faculty at an academic archives.

Data Sets: A newer format is compiled data, either concerning or from collections, which might be made available through downloading from a website. Information such as metadata of digital or analog collections provides researchers opportunities for new and advanced analysis of collection information.

Online Searching

Finding aids portals, catalogs, or other databases are intended to facilitate a focused search, but many patrons start their inquiry with Google, Bing, Yahoo, or other search engines. Whether looking for general information about a topic or specifically archival materials, online searching is a fundamental and powerful resource to lead patrons to archival materials. Search engines lead them to websites, portals, finding aids, and digital collections or even to a specific box, folder, or item. Indeed, patrons now commonly inform archivists that they have contacted the repository because of what they found online.

Search engines continually index digital information provided on the web. Recognizing this power, archivists intend that collection descriptions will be discoverable through search engines. Access is enabled through any file that can be indexed by a search engine, be it textual information, EAD, HTML, PDF, Word, photo, video, audio, or other type of file or document.[11]

Essentially, search engines index webpage text, file names, file types, and information presented in an online format.

There is a misperception that because information is available online, a researcher does not need the assistance of a professional. Archivists recognize that savvy researchers can find and interpret online information effectively. Archivists also recognize that most researchers benefit from professional assistance in explaining context and assurance that all available materials have been found. For example, a patron who comes across a historical video may not realize that it is part of a larger collection. A researcher may not review the front matter of a finding aid and so overlooks the context of a specific box or folder. Further, researchers may be surprised at the inability to click on descriptions to find the actual materials because they do not differentiate between digital information and digital content.

While some researchers do not need assistance with online searches, discoveries often lead them to contact the repository. These inquiries include requests for more details about what they found, information on how to access materials, questions regarding other related resources, and guidelines concerning permission to use. Particularly if patrons find information rather than content online, they will inquire about the ways to procure reproductions or physically access collections.

Though online searching is ubiquitous, it does not always yield the desired results. Reference archivists are aware of its limitations and must take initiative to both encourage patrons to search online to find archival content and educate them on how to do so effectively and efficiently. Archivists can offer tips, such as using advanced search options to limit to .gov, .org, or .edu sources, thereby eliminating questionable content; adding words such as *papers, records, archives,* or *digital collections* that generate more relevant archival content; or searching specifically for images or audiovisual sources.

Print Sources

Though archives strive to create accessible content online, this does not preclude the necessity or value of print sources. Some repositories may not have the resources or infrastructure to share information virtually, but instead maintain substantial print finding aids or inventories. This situation is common in small repositories, archives that are available to internal constituents only, and institutions that impose limits on collection information. For a long time, print was the only option available for descriptive access, so many archives have a trove of legacy content in the forms of card catalogs, finding aids, inventories, subject guides, or other print materials. Most repositories already have transferred—or are in the process of transferring—this content into the virtual environment, but many still have resources available in print only. Even when information is available online, repositories may elect to provide print copies of finding aids or other sources for consultation. Further, some patrons prefer a physical copy to refer to during their research.

Conclusion

Reference professionals must have core knowledge about arrangement and description, outputs for collection information, and systems and tools used to locate materials. Beyond these duties, and their obligation to serve as the intermediary between patrons and collections, they also have the opportunity to communicate with processing archivists about the effectiveness of collection arrangement and description and to suggest possible enhancements to description based on researcher feedback.

NOTES

[1] Dennis Meissner, *Arranging and Describing Archives and Manuscripts* (Chicago: Society of American Archivists, 2019), 156.

[2] Meissner, *Arranging and Describing,* 26;

[3] *Dictionary of Archives Terminology*, s.v. "provenance," Society of American Archivists, https://dictionary.archivists.org/entry/provenance.html, captured at https://perma.cc/8CUQ-B23L.

[4] *Dictionary of Archives Terminology*, s.v. "series," Society of American Archivists, https://dictionary.archivists.org/entry/series.html, captured at https://perma.cc/MH6D-P4N8.

[5] U.S. National Archives and Records Administration, "Record Group Concept," www.archives.gov/research/guide-fed-records/index-numeric/concept.html, captured at https://perma.cc/H3XB-5HTX.

[6] Meissner, *Arranging and Describing,* 36–37.

[7] Society of American Archivists, Technical Subcommittee on Describing Archives: A Content Standard (TS-DACS), "Describing Archives: A Content Standard, Second Edition (DACS)," www2.archivists.org/standards/DACS.

[8] Online Archive of California, https://oac.cdlib.org/; Rocky Mountain Online Archive, 2006, https://rmoa.unm.edu/; ArchiveGrid, https://researchworks.oclc.org/archivegrid/.

[9] "Toward a National Archival Finding Aid Network: A Planning Initiative," https://confluence.ucop.edu/display/NAFAN/Toward+a+National+Archival+Finding+Aid+Network%3A+a+Planning+Initiative, captured at https://perma.cc/9EHB-R7YF.

[10] Pam Hackbart-Dean and Elizabeth Slomba, *How to Manage Processing in Archives and Special Collections* (Chicago: Society of American Archivists, 2012), 75.

[11] Santamaria, *Extensible Processing for Archives and Special Collections*, 118–119.

7

Virtual Access

Well into the digital age, people increasingly turn to online means to search for information. Skilled researchers use the web to find specific collections that are relevant to their research, while others may unexpectedly discover archival sources. Researchers typically search online for content, but archivists remain critical mediators as they assist researchers in developing their skills in effective online research.

This focus on sharing information online has greatly affected user types and users' information-seeking behaviors. When embarking on a new research topic, users turn to search engines, online catalogs, or online databases, some of which are not necessarily archives specific, to find resources. There has been an increase in "accidental" users who do not specifically set out to find archival content but serendipitously stumble onto primary sources. Such new or "accidental" users may not recognize that digital content represents only a small fraction of holdings. Conversely, reference archivists know that online content is limited and hope that patrons will contact them directly for more information. The more that archivists make holdings information publicly discoverable, the greater the possibility that a wider variety of users will find and use archival materials.

As for physical collections, access is a core concern in the virtual environment. The core concepts of access to digital collections parallels those of physical collections, but the procedures, ways of providing access, and user responsibilities differ. Reference interviews, patron registration, and security procedures are removed, while access options, searching capabilities, and use differ. Although some patrons access online content with little or no assistance from professionals, archivists still play a key role in providing reference services for digital content.

Websites

Websites, whether available publicly or as internal intranets, act as "one-stop shopping" for information. An effective website caters the information and resources directly to patron discovery.[1] As repositories expand their holdings, audiences, policies, and means of access, a website becomes more crucial to offering users thorough information. Most institutions already have websites, but it is important to review and update the content for accuracy, relevancy, and currency. As the conduit between patrons and the repository, reference archivists play a crucial role in monitoring and assessing a website's effectiveness.

A website often is the first impression a user formulates about an archives, and designing a website that is user-friendly, engaging, and informative creates a welcoming atmosphere. In general, a good website is easy to navigate, concise, organized logically, and aesthetically pleasing and answers the classic questions of *who, what, where, when,* and *how*.[2] Users expect to easily find current information about holdings, hours, policies, searching collections, contact information,

General Information	Policies/Procedures
About the institution/library/department	ADA compliance and access
Contact info: address, phone, email	Copyright
Feedback or suggestions	Digital photography
Hours	Loans
Mission statement	Permission to use/publish
Parking/visiting	Privacy policy
Social media	Reproductions
Staff directory	
Strategic plan	**Outreach**
	Calendar of events
Collection Information	Exhibitions
Collection development policy/records management policy	Friends of the library
	Gift shop
Collection holdings and descriptions	How to get involved/volunteer
Donations	News, newsletters, or publications
	Prizes/travel funding/research grants
Using Collections	Programming
Class instruction and visits	Tours
Collections search	Virtual tour
Curriculum and teaching materials	
Digital collections	
Finding aids databases	
Forms	
Reading room guidelines	
Subject research guides	

FIGURE 7. Suggested Components of a Website

and other details helpful to visit a repository or conduct their remote research. No single standard structure exists for websites, but, as indicated in Figure 7, there are numerous components that are central to maintaining appropriate levels of information.

A key strategy for a website is to build the information based on audiences' needs. Listing reading room guidelines, reproduction policies, links to digital content and search portals, copyright regulations, security procedures, contact information, registration or other forms, and any other pertinent information informs patrons about the repository. An FAQ section can also provide answers to recurring inquiries as well as quick tips. It is also helpful to create printer-friendly options for patrons who prefer to maintain physical documentation of their research.[3]

Because websites contain extensive information, navigation ought to be clear and clean. Not all users come to the main page first; instead, they find information through Google searches, finding aids, digital collections, or other portals. Using a structure that clearly directs users to home pages and basic information regardless of where they start ensures that the website's information is comprehensive. Along those lines, a consideration is patrons' technological sophistication.[4] Although web searching is deeply entrenched in society and most users regularly navigate websites, some populations may have less familiarity with either accessing archives or using websites as their primary research tools and require additional assistance or accommodation.

The language used sets the tone and expresses how the repository views its audience. Friendly, conversational, and brief wording enables users to skim content quickly to find answers to their questions, while lengthier text is more appropriate when providing specific instructions or explaining complex policies. If possible, incorporating easy-to-understand language and avoiding, or at least limiting, archival jargon enables easier use. For example, new users may be unfamiliar with the phrase "Finding Aids," but almost everyone will understand "Search Our Collections." On the other hand, by incorporating some jargon along with definitions and explanations, archivists offer users the opportunity to gain greater familiarity with archival practices and terminology.

Photographs, images, and multimedia enhance both navigation and aesthetics. Images make pages more interesting and provide visual directions, as long as those images do not overshadow information. Multimedia presentations also enrich the visitor experience. Some archives have videos explaining instructions on use and handling of materials, highlighting collections, or giving virtual tours of a reading room or facility. Archivists must be mindful of how much visual content they include; too much can be overwhelming while too little can be more distracting than helpful.

Some patrons prefer self-service options for research assistance, which saves time for reference archivists. Creating videos, tutorials, step-by-step guides, or other tools can help patrons use finding aids or develop search strategies.[5] Research guides that collate appropriate resources into sections geared toward specific user groups, such as genealogists or educators, are also popular. Other sections might offer guides to specific formats or types of materials, such as maps, photographs, or vital records. These tools typically are created based on frequently asked questions, institutional strengths, and patrons' needs.

Assessment is part of maintaining a relevant and effective website. There are many options for gathering feedback, including pop-up surveys, lengthier comment forms, and individual conversations. Surveys and forms require thoughtful planning, as well as time to compile and analyze the results. Conversations often occur organically as part of a reference interaction. If a user specifically mentions an institution's website, whether with a compliment or a question, the archivist can engage the user in a dialogue to find out what the user found most helpful or how the presentation might be improved.

Another assessment approach is using analytics to enhance and develop online information. Engaging in a systematic approach to comprehend the effectiveness of online information leads to decisions to improve websites and therefore improve patron experiences.[6] A popular tool is Google Analytics, which provides statistics on webpage hits, the length of time that visitors stayed on pages, and the ways in which people found a website. Some website platforms, such as Wordpress, have built-in analytics that offer insights and reports to track usage and behavior over time.

Data privacy is a concern with digital assessment. Most users are aware, and perhaps expect, that some of their data is collected on websites, but they may not realize the extent to which such data is aggregated and analyzed. Coupled with changing definitions and interpretations of what constitutes "privacy," particularly among digital natives, collecting data while ethically maintaining patron privacy can be complicated.[7] At minimum, anonymizing data so it is not tied to an individual is a good approach.

What web analytics tools do not measure is an individual's thought process while exploring a website. For more comprehensive assessment, usability testing fills that gap. To capture a user's thoughts and behaviors, a study can include questions such as: Can the user find appropriate information? Is the layout effective? Is it viewable through computer and mobile devices? In addition, these studies often prove predictive of user behavior.[8] Conducting usability testing requires extensive time and planning, but the return on investment is high.

All of these suggestions also apply to intranets or internal websites. Institutions that are not open to the general public often do not have an external web presence. However, intranets provide the same information to internal constituents. The purpose is the same—to provide information about how to do research, what resources and collections are available, staff member contact information, and other necessary details. Using analytics or conducting user studies ensures that the information provided is helpful and relevant for internal audiences.

Digital Collections

Since 2005, when Mary Jo Pugh published the second edition of *Providing Reference Services for Archives and Manuscripts*, providing access to digitized and born-digital materials has grown and changed exponentially. For archivists, the concept of "digital content" is a complex landscape consisting of born-digital files; digital reproductions; files found on obsolete media, such as disks and CDs; social media; websites; emails; text messages; voicemails; audiovisual files; and hosts of other content created or reproduced in digital formats. Compounding this landscape is the necessity to use multiple systems to manage content, create metadata, and provide access.

A major obstacle of reference services for digital content is that the general public often believes or expects that "everything is online." Indeed, some users ignore nonelectronic resources, even if online sources do not adequately meet their information needs. Archives are particularly challenged by this notion. Whereas individual libraries are not solely responsible for the digitization of journals and books, archival collections are distinct and only found in one place. Archivists therefore assume the responsibility for figuring out how to provide digital access to their unique materials. Most archives strive to make original content available online, but staffing issues, limited funding, and technological challenges mean that only a very small percentage of existing materials are presented in a virtual environment.

Reference archivists frequently field questions about online availability of materials. Depending on the interest of the audience, archivists can explain that time, money, staffing, and technology required, as well as copyright, fragility, or other factors, prevent digital access to all holdings. This can be a frustrating disconnect between patrons' expectations and reference archivists' capabilities. However, reference staff members are responsible for helping patrons to navigate these realities and educating them about the digital universe.

Sometimes, researchers do not recognize the difference between digital information and digital content. When patrons access a finding aid or other description, they may expect to find the actual items online. Many archivists have had the experience of a patron asking why nothing happens after clicking on a folder title or why no files come up after a search. Because archives continually put both information and content online, this situation will continue to be a component of educating patrons.

There are already many books, articles, and other resources that provide details about managing and providing access to digital collections. What reference archivists most need to understand is the importance of metadata, the skills required to understand and manipulate digital content systems, and their institutional practices.

Digitization

Patrons have a general understanding that materials are scanned and made available online but seldom understand the complexities of how items are selected for digitization, the technology to make access possible, or the digitization process itself. In simple terms, digitization is the conversion of analog materials into electronic formats. However, as archivists know, digitization is a lengthy process with numerous and intricate components designed to optimize the integrity and quality of digital materials.

Repositories vary greatly in how they maintain digitization programs; for example, large institutions may have departments dedicated to digitization, while small repositories may approach digitization through *ad hoc* requests or small projects. Regardless of the approach, reference archivists must have familiarity with their institution's processes for selection, reformatting, metadata creation, and access systems, and how to communicate these strategies to patrons when appropriate.

There are multiple criteria used in selecting materials for digitization, such as high use, fragility, subjects and themes, and format. Some of these are determined through acquisition or processing, but reference archivists are integral to the selection process. From their direct contact with researchers, reference archivists are familiar with which collections are used, notice fragile materials or those in need of preservation, and assess which items require reformatting before access is possible. Many institutions integrate patron-driven digitization into their workflows, which initiates projects based on frequently requested collections or items. Prioritizing researchers' needs enhances any approach to digitization.

While patron-driven digitization works well for single items or small collections, it is less effective for large quantities of materials. Archivists recognize that it is mostly unrealistic to digitize the contents of dozens or hundreds of boxes but instead can evaluate the option of reproducing portions of large collections. While this is helpful for access, it may also be confusing for patrons.

Because finding aids are mostly separate from digitized content, researchers may not realize the extent of a collection if they come across only the digitized portion or they may expect to find the entire collection online. By including links to finding aids in digital object metadata and cross-referencing digitized content within the finding aid, archivists can assist patrons in understanding these issues.

Born Digital

After World War II, American archivists lamented the increasingly rapid creation of and sheer volume of paper records. Postwar archivists could never have foreseen that, by the new millennium, this problem would be compounded, though not entirely replaced, by the even more voluminous proliferation of electronic records. Born-digital records, defined by SAA's *Dictionary of Archives Terminology* as records "originating in a computer environment,"[9] require an intense focus on acquisition, processing, and long-term preservation within the context of enabling future research. In addition, archivists are corralling obsolete media, software releases, file types, and systems. Managing born-digital records remains a work in progress at present, and reference archivists must facilitate access while recognizing the needs of patrons, limitations on the archives, and connections between these two factors.

There are seemingly endless types of electronic records produced by organizations and people in everyday life, and new types emerge constantly. Archival literature traces the vast amount of developments that have occurred, from punch cards to word-processing software to web-based applications. For the first several decades, most electronic records produced and acquired were produced in the course of business functions. Once personal computers became more common in the 1980s, personal electronic records from individuals increased. Many archives now contain a wide range of such records in their collections in the forms of punch cards, floppy disks, CDs, external hard drives, or even computers themselves.

It is easy to see, and be overwhelmed by, the continual development of new types of electronic records, both functional and ephemeral. Social media, text messages, emails, mobile applications, video games, and other ephemeral content are important to capture. Organizations correspond primarily through email, but these are easily deleted and difficult to acquire. An individual may have extensive contact with friends and family through text messages but may not know how to download those messages for preservation. These are some of the issues with which repositories grapple.

Unlike analog records, which, it is always hoped, can be presented in their original condition in perpetuity, electronic records require ongoing attention. Technology and software are developed at a fast pace, and electronic files created even as recently as a decade ago may no longer be accessible because they are in outdated formats. Efforts are in place to preserve software as well as allow cultural institutions to obtain copies for preservation and access.[10] Files must be reformatted periodically and updated within the systems used to ensure ongoing access, which directly affects researchers. A researcher may download a file but may later discover that they can no longer open it. Further, because archives acquire collections in the form in which files were created, those files are not always in the formats that patrons expect or need. For example, a patron may request a high-resolution image for a publication, but if the image was initially created as a low-resolution file, archivists will be unable to reformat it. Easy solutions to this problem are not yet in place, but perhaps the future will bring more options.

Systems and Formats

Archivists are making great strides in providing access to all types of digital content through websites, content and digital asset management systems, institutional repositories, and home-grown systems. With a seemingly infinite number of types of digital records, there is no single system that facilitates access to all formats under all conditions, and archives use multiple systems to present digital items primarily based on content, format, and, especially, the availability of technical support and infrastructure. Reference archivists must be fluent in their systems to educate and assist users.

Recognizing the difference between specific formats and the reasons why content is presented in those formats gives archivists tools they need for assisting patrons. For example, placing .jpgs instead of .tiffs of photographs online facilitates quicker loading in browsers, but clarifying that a high-resolution .tiff is available for publication use educates patrons on the differences.

To increase discoverability, repositories participate in digital collections portals, which harvest metadata from institutional platforms. The Mountain West Digital Library, Montana Memory Project, Arizona Memory Project, and Digital Public Library of America (DPLA) are a few examples. The developments of these sites are changing how users find digital content. Portals enable more focused searches than search engines, and, most important, users know they are searching through authentic digital primary sources. Taking this further, some of these portals create exhibits, timelines, primary source sets, and other guides to collate information and facilitate faceted searches.

Archivists provide access to digital content through a content management system, website, onsite-only workstation in the reading room, or combination of these methods. Some repositories have records that they can make available only in-house. Access to digital content may also be restricted to an institutional logon or registration, which could involve entire collections or partial access to select content.[11] Particularly with access to internal digital collections, there are security risks to consider, such as the ability to download to a flash drive or to send material as email content.

While personal computers gave people an option for doing research in their homes, at work, or in libraries, mobile technology allows users to access content from anywhere, anytime. Archives are catching up with this technology by modifying their platforms to be adaptive and accessible on mobile phones, tablets, or other devices. As time progresses, there will be a growing need to adapt access to watches, glasses, and, no doubt, technologies that have yet to be invented.

Following are broad categories of technological options available for digital content:

Websites: Knowledge of HTML, XML, or another coding language is no longer necessary to manage a website; there are a plethora of platforms that have easy-to-use back-end interfaces. These are particularly helpful for small institutions that have little or no IT support. Websites are appropriate for sharing a small amount of content, usually low-resolution images or files with basic descriptions.

Social Media: Social media platforms are good for quick access and sharing, but they are not used for long-term management of digital content. The benefits of using, for example, blogs for written records, YouTube for videos, SoundCloud for audio, or Flickr or Instagram for photographs are that they allow for quick and easy sharing and assigning tags for sorting and searching.

Content Management Systems (CMS): CMSs, sometimes called archival management systems, are robust systems designed to manage digital content. With options such as Omeka, CONTENTdm, and Islandora, CMSs are used to create digital exhibits and showcase digital content, ranging from a few documents to hundreds of thousands of items, through structured metadata application. They have the ability to present multiple types of formats, such as files, images, and audiovisual materials.

Digital Asset Management (DAM) Systems: Similar to CMSs, DAMs facilitate the presentation, description, and management of digital content. Sometimes found in archives, they are more broadly used in corporate institutions and other settings that manage large quantities of creative content. In particular, they are used to share digital content and digital rights for internal and external constituents.

Institutional Repositories (IR): IRs are similar to CMSs and DAMs. Most often found in academic institutions, IRs are used to create and disseminate scholarship. There is crossover with library materials, as an IR is used to present electronic theses and dissertations, sometimes managed with archivist involvement. But IRs are also used for photos, textual and audiovisual materials, and other types of digital content.

Home-grown Systems: Most common in large institutions, home-grown systems are a collaboration between archivists and IT staff to build and manage systems. A repository may opt against existing software platforms if they have specific requirements or desire extensive control over customization.

Specialized Software: Some platforms are designed for specific formats, such as Stanford University's ePADD for email or the Internet Archive's Wayback Machine (using Archive-It) for websites.

Metadata

Regardless of whether materials are digitized or born digital, the crux of digital content is metadata. Metadata is structured information that describes, organizes, and manages content for retrieval and more broadly enables interoperability, preservation, and identification to ensure long-term accessibility.[12] The levels of description vary, but because of the systems and metadata schema used, item-level description is common. However, archivists are exploring ways of using minimal description to enable access to more digital materials.[13]

In the systems described above, metadata is assigned to individual digital objects according to a schema, which combines set elements into a specific structure. Like using DACS for finding aids, a metadata schema includes fields that describe the title, creator, date, collection identifier, topics and subjects, and repository as well as further components of location, item identifiers, detailed description, physical format, and copyright and use statements.[14] These details are what enable extensive searching capabilities.

Metadata is assigned to a single digital object. Often, a digital object is a single file, but it can also encompass multiple items, such as a PDF of the entire contents of a folder, box, or book, or a .zip file or data set that contains several objects. The metadata assigned can be minimal, extensive, or anywhere in between. At minimum, including the basics of title, creator, date, and subjects provides some access. If time and staffing permit, adding fields for place, original format, related resources, provenance, and any other details enhances searchability.

Archives acquire many hybrid collections, which contain both digital and analog content. Even when digital records are not made available online, metadata remains important. The finding aid can include a note about these records, the type of physical format (e.g., 3.5-inch disk), a brief description of the contents, and whether or how the records can be accessed (e.g., in-house only). Further, a metadata record can be created in an online system as a collection-level record without an attachment, like a catalog record, that enables discoverability.

Virtual Reading Room

According to SAA's *Dictionary of Archives Terminology*, a "virtual reading room" has two definitions:

> 1. an online research environment in which the discoverability and/or downloading of materials is deliberately limited, and/or access is restricted to researchers who have created a limited-term account and agreed to terms of use similar to those that apply in a physical reading room of an archives; 2. an online environment in which digital materials are made freely available.[15]

Essentially one definition simulates the physical access process within a virtual environment, while the other describes openly available digital content.[16] As the technological age advances and more patrons expect and demand remote access to archival materials, it is likely that more repositories will create virtual reading rooms.

In 2011, archivists Rachel Onuf and Tom Hyry recommended advancing digital records access systems to "mirror our reading rooms, where readers must register and agree to a set of access rules before they can use materials."[17] A pilot project conducted at the University of California, Irvine, did exactly that. To create access to born-digital records, and to forestall printing and mailing copies of files to users who were unable to visit in person, they translated their existing model of registered user access from a physical process to a virtual platform. The prerequisite to access was filling out the standard registration form to agree to terms of use. On receipt, the IT department added the individual's email address to the list of approved users. Utilizing DSpace for remote access, one collection had an item-level inventory with detailed search capabilities, while the other had downloadable .zip files with aggregated files.[18] Although the project remains in its early stages and has not yet generated extensive details about its effectiveness, this option is worth considering and implementing to provide virtual access.

Some systems already have options for mediated access. DAMs come with a built-in option to set levels of permissions, and other systems have functionality to set access by IP address, creation of user profiles, or email address.

Virtual procedures that simulate physical access offer new avenues for patrons. This is a potential solution that might provide access to digital collections while maintaining some of the same controls applied to physical collections. Further, this procedure introduces an option for access to collections that cannot be made available publicly online due to copyright, donor, or other restrictions. Although this is a newer practice for which there are no established standards, it has great potential to transform virtual access in the future.

Innovations in Digital Research

Until recently, the purpose of providing access to digital content was to allow patrons to view items for research or information, or just for fun. Increasingly, scholars view online and digital content as a continually growing and diverse resource with high research potential—in effect, more of a data source than a traditional archive.[19] An Ithaka S+R study that surveyed historians, archivists, librarians, and other supporters of historical research found that research methods have fundamentally changed, largely due to advancements in how archives provide digital access to collection information and contents. Although research trips to physically explore collections are crucial, researchers are continually challenged to find the time and funding for in-person visits and therefore rely increasingly on online resources.[20]

There are ever-increasing software options geared toward research within digital content and information: text mining, data visualization, geospatial analysis, pattern matching, and other tools are ways researchers compare files and metadata to identify relationships.[21] As the amount of content increases, so do the opportunities for new research and analysis.

The interdisciplinary field of digital humanities is an example of innovative scholarship with digital content. According to humanities and information technology professor Patrik Svensson, digital humanities merges technology with any discipline(s) within the humanities as a way of using and exploring "information technology as both a scholastic tool and a cultural object in need of analysis."[22] In other words, digital humanists seek content that exists or can be reproduced digitally and then utilize various tools to explore new interpretations or analysis of content. Although this occurs most often within academic communities, many scholars search for avenues and platforms to engage with and encourage participation from the public, including television interviews, podcasts, social media, and ebooks.[23]

One of the outputs is visualization, which compiles content and metadata into a portal that provides multiple options for viewing. For example, Yale University's Photogrammar, which contains 170,000 photographs created by the United States Farm Security Administration and Office of War Information (1935–1945), offers new options to explore the images beyond traditional item-level viewing: an interactive geotagged map, a subject heading Treemap, a metadata dashboard, and an option to view the color photographs by hue, lightness, and saturation.[24]

Geospatial information systems, which take geographical data to generate interactive maps, are increasingly popular. Maps are the foundation, but demographic, sociological, and other empirical data are often also incorporated. The Locating London's Past project website presents historical maps with options to add coroner's records, criminal records, and other data into current Google maps.[25] By using widely available software, such as Google Earth, StoryMaps, or ArcGIS, anyone can create geospatial projects.

Text mining and text encoding facilitate searching across multitudes of textual documents to find and interpret recurring words, phrases, subjects, and themes. The Largest Vocabulary in Hip Hop is a project that analyzes the first 35,000 words of an artist's lyrics to determine how many unique words the artist uses.[26] As a means for enhancing marketing strategies, Baylor University mined tweets that included the school's name to find which words were most popular.[27]

Digital research collection and production is not limited to the humanities; STEM, computer science, social sciences, and other fields also create and repurpose content. In particular, these disciplines use data sets that encompass current research or historical content. There are numerous organizations that actively collect such data sets to make them publicly accessible and downloadable, such as the Inter-University Consortium for Political and Social Research, the Association of Religion Data Archives, the Government of Canada Historic Climate Data, AidData Open Data for International Development, and Data.gov, to name a few.[28]

Archives, and government repositories in particular, also collect, create, and preserve data sets. Metadata for online content is one instance of data creation, and some platforms allow users to openly download the Application Programming Interface (API) to manipulate the data. For example, archivists used Twitter's API for an extensive analysis of the tweets from the eighteen-day revolution in Cairo, Egypt, in 2011.[29] The DPLA, Chronicling America, and National Archives are a few examples of organizations with open APIs.[30] By making this data available, archives greatly expand public use and access to online archival content.

These are only a few examples of the types of digital projects. Because this type of research exists primarily in a virtual environment, it has also influenced how an "archive" is viewed and defined. Further, as patrons amass content from various sources, they view their own curated collections as "archives," which in this context is defined by author and archivist Kate Theimer as "a grouping of materials that had been purposefully selected in order to be studied and made accessible."[31] This constitutes a fundamental difference between the digital humanities approach and the archival approach to collecting. Archivists broadly solicit materials to make them available for research, while digital humanists frequently curate around specific topics for their own interpretation and research interests.

Literary scholars offer one illustration of the ways in which scholars have moved toward creating curated collections. They frequently research a single author or specific genre and strive to obtain any or all materials related to their topics, even if those materials are scattered throughout multiple institutions. The creation of an author's digital "archive" brings together dispersed materials and/or references in portals that are accessible to others. In recent years, there has been a significant trend in the creation of such digital projects, and noteworthy examples include the Samuel Beckett: Digital Manuscript Project, Jane Austen's Fiction Manuscripts, and the Elizabeth Jennings Project.[32]

Archivists also curate digital collections that may not, at least initially, reside with a traditional archive. One example is the September 11 Digital Archive. According to its website, the project "uses electronic media to collect, preserve, and present" the event's history, including public reactions. The archive contains art, audio, video, photographs, personal accounts, and other features that document the event and its immediate aftermath and continues to collect reminiscences from anniversary events.[33]

Conclusion

Though electronic records have existed for decades, it is only more recently that technological developments have advanced access to digital content. Archives now have abundant options for sharing born-digital and digitized images, files, audio, video, and other content. This serves patrons well, as there is a growing expectation that they will find information and materials online.

Reference archivists must be adept at navigating through an increasingly electronic world. They must be familiar with their collections, know how to develop search strategies, understand metadata, understand how digital content advances research, and meet patrons' needs in the virtual environment. A seemingly tall order, some of this is acquired through education but especially through on-the-job duties. Indeed, for most professionals, using digital records and systems are daily tasks.

It is an exciting time for digital archivists because the amount of time working with digital content will only increase exponentially in the immediate future. Cutting-edge software, systems, and research encapsulate how archives can and will advance. At times, dealing with the digital realm can appear daunting, but reference archivists can embrace the potential to serve patrons in new ways. Further, archivists are also agents of change in advancing how archival content is found, used, and interpreted.

NOTES

[1] Michele M. Lavoie, "Websites," in *Public Relations and Marketing for Archives*, ed. Russell D. James and Peter J. Wosh (Chicago: Society of American Archivists, 2011), 13.

[2] Kate Theimer, *Web 2.0 Tools and Strategies for Archives and Local History Collections* (New York: Neal-Schuman Publishers, 2010), 22–23; George Plumley, *Website Design and Development: 100 Questions to Ask Before Building a Website* (Indianapolis: John Wiley & Sons, 2010), 147.

[3] Plumley, *Website Design and Development*, 106–108.

[4] Lavoie, "Websites" in James and Wosh, *Public Relations and Marketing For Archives*, 14.

[5] Dalhousie University, "Guide to Archival Research," https://dal.ca.libguides.com/c.php?g=257178&p=5022146, captured at https://perma.cc/3L46-SFAT; John F. Kennedy Presidential Library and Museum, "Basics of Archival Research," www.jfklibrary.org/archives/search-collections/basics-of-archival-research, captured at https://perma.cc/QGS2-RCCT; Denver Public Library, Genealogy, African American and Western History Resources, "Research Guides," https://history.denverlibrary.org/research; University of Manitoba Libraries, "Rare Research – How to Do Primary Research with Rare Documents," 2019, www.umanitoba.ca/libraries/units/archives/collections/rarebooks/rare_research.html.

[6] Christopher J. Prom, "Using Web Analytics to Improve Online Access to Archival Resources," *American Archivist* 74, no. 1 (2011): 160–162, https://doi.org/10.17723/aarc.74.1.h56018515230417v.

[7] Case and Given, *Looking for Information*, 234–235.

[8] Lynn Silipigni Connaway and Marie L. Radford, *Research Methods in Library and Information Science*, 6th ed. (Santa Barbara, CA: Libraries Unlimited, 2017), 278–279.

[9] *Dictionary of Archives Terminology*, s.v. "born digital," Society of American Archivists, https://dictionary.archivists.org/entry/born-digital.html, captured at https://perma.cc/Q5YQ-QCNX.

[10] Center for Media and Social Impact, "Code of Best Practices in Fair Use for Software Preservation," September 2018, https://cmsimpact.org/code/fair-use-software-preservation/, captured at https://perma.cc/LG9H-UH6Z.

[11] Aaron D. Purcell, *Digital Library Programs for Libraries and Archives: Developing, Managing, and Sustaining Unique Digital Collections* (Chicago: ALA Neal-Schuman, 2016), 147; Hackbart-Dean and Slomba, *How to Manage Processing*, 51.

[12] Purcell, *Digital Library Programs for Libraries and Archives*, 116.

13. Edward Benoit III, "#MPLP Part 1: Comparing Domain Expert and Novice Social Tags in a Minimally Processed Digital Archives," *American Archivist* 80, no. 2 (2017): 407–438, https://doi.org/10.17723/0360-9081-80.2.407; Edward Benoit III, "#MPLP Part 2: Replacing Item-Level Metadata with User-Generated Social Tags," *American Archivist* 81, no. 1 (2018): 38–64, https://doi.org/10.17723/0360-9081-81.1.38.

14. Society of American Archivists, "Guide to Implementing Rights Statements from RightsStatements.Org," www2.archivists.org/standards/guide-to-implementing-rights-statements-from-rightsstatementsorg, captured at https://perma.cc/ESJ8-28DB.

15. *Dictionary of Archives Terminology*, s.v. "virtual reading room," Society of American Archivists, https://dictionary.archivists.org/entry/virtual-reading-room.html, captured at https://perma.cc/KPQ2-2YF7.

16. Isabella Stewart Gardner Museum, "Virtual Reading Room," www.gardnermuseum.org/organization/virtual-reading-room; U.S. Department of State, "Virtual Reading Room Documents Search," https://foia.state.gov/Search/Search.aspx; University of Southampton, Special Collections, "Virtual Reading Room," www.southampton.ac.uk/archives/virtual/index.page.

17. Rachel Onuf and Tom Hyry, "Take It Personally: The Implications of Personal Records in Electronic Form," in *I, Digital: Personal Collections in the Digital Era*, ed. Christopher A. Lee (Chicago: Society of American Archivists, 2011), 253.

18. Michelle Light, "Managing Risk with a Virtual Reading Room: Two Born-Digital Projects," in *Reference and Access*, ed. Kate Theimer (Lanham, MD: Rowman and Littlefield, 2014), 17–35; see also the online application at University of California, Irvine, Special Collections and Archives, "Application for the Virtual Reading Room in UCIspace," https://special.lib.uci.edu/application-virtual-reading-room-ucispace, captured at https://perma.cc/J6X4-ACJB.

19. Meyer and Schroeder, *Knowledge Machines*, 192.

20. Jennifer Rutner and Roger C. Schonfeld, "Supporting the Changing Research Practices of Historians" (New York: Ithaka S+R, December 10, 2012), 7–11.

21. Susan Thomas, "Curating the I, Digital: Experiences at the Bodleian Library," in Lee, *I, Digital*, 300.

22. Patrik Svensson, "Humanities Computing as Digital Humanities," *Digital Humanities Quarterly* 3, no. 3 (2009): para. 1, http://digitalhumanities.org/dhq/vol/3/3/000065/000065.html.

23. Daniels and Thistlethwaite, *Being a Scholar in the Digital Era*, 95–100.

24. Yale University, "Photogrammar," http://photogrammar.yale.edu/.

25. Locating London's Past, www.locatinglondon.org/index.html.

26. Matt Daniels, "The Largest Vocabulary in Hip Hop," *The Pudding*, https://pudding.cool/projects/vocabulary/index.html, captured at https://perma.cc/R62F-AGBB.

27. Joshua Been, "Topics from Tweets Mentioning Baylor University," Baylor University Libraries, Digital Scholarship, September 1, 2018, https://blogs.baylor.edu/digitalscholarship/2018/09/01/topics-from-tweets-mentioning-baylor-university/, captured at https://perma.cc/C56Z-YAW2.

28. Inter-university Consortium for Political and Social Research, www.icpsr.umich.edu/icpsrweb/; Association of Religion Data Archives, www.thearda.com/; Government of Canada, "Historical Climate Data," last modified December 14, 2019, https://climate.weather.gc.ca/; College of William & Mary, "AidData: A Research Lab at William & Mary," www.aiddata.org/; Data.gov, www.data.gov/.

29. Timothy Arnold and Walker Sampson, "Preserving the Voices of Revolution: Examining the Creation and Preservation of a Subject-Centered Collection of Tweets from the Eighteen Days in Egypt," *American Archivist* 77, no. 2 (2014): 510–533, https://doi.org/10.17723/aarc.77.2.794404552m67024n.

30. Digital Public Library of America, "API Codex," https://pro.dp.la/developers/api-codex; Library of Congress, Chronicling America, "About the Site and API," https://chroniclingamerica.loc.gov/about/api/; U.S. National Archives and Records Administration, "National Archives for Developers," last reviewed March 18, 2020, www.archives.gov/developer.

31. Meyer and Schroeder, *Knowledge Machines*, 192; Kate Theimer, "Archives in Context and as Context," *Journal of Digital Humanities* 1, no. 2 (2012), http://journalofdigitalhumanities.org/1-2/archives-in-context-and-as-context-by-kate-theimer/, captured at https://perma.cc/U4AN-73QJ.

32. Samuel Beckett: Digital Manuscript Project," https://www.beckettarchive.org/; University of Oxford and King's College London, Jane Austen's Fiction Manuscripts, https://janeausten.ac.uk/index.html; Jane Dowson, Elizabeth Jennings, 1926–2001, "About This Website," Centre for Textual Studies, http://elizabethjennings.dmu.ac.uk/about_site.html.

33. The September 11 Digital Archive, http://911digitalarchive.org/.

8

Ethics, Patron Privacy, and Accessibility

Three overarching concepts inform reference actions beyond policies and procedures: ethics, patron privacy, and accessibility. At a glance, these topics appear to be separate concepts. However, they intersect through the primary goal of placing the user first and ensuring that all interactions between repositories and users are equal, respectful, and accommodating. Archivists must provide equal services to patrons, value their inquiries and perspectives, and perform any tasks necessary to ensure accessibility of materials.

Ethics

Since 1955, when the National Archives released its first code of ethics, archivists have engaged in ongoing dialogue regarding ethical behavior and policies toward reference and access. The goal of professional ethics is to solidify existing practices into a comprehensive and consistent approach to archival functions and services that provides equitable access, maintains authentic and reliable records, and advocates for the importance of the historical record. Although these are the overarching tenets, the ethics related to reference services are primarily geared toward equitable access and relationships with patrons.

Ethics are applicable to all aspects of reference services. Access, collection use, copyright, restrictions on materials, and patron interactions all have the potential to raise situations in which archivists must make ethical decisions. The "SAA Core Values Statement and Code of Ethics," which was last revised in 2012, specifies practices for access and use as follows:

> Recognizing that use is the fundamental reason for keeping archives, archivists actively promote open and equitable access to the records in their care within the context of their institutions'

missions and their intended user groups. They minimize restrictions and maximize ease of access. They facilitate the continuing accessibility and intelligibility of archival materials in all formats. Archivists formulate and disseminate institutional access policies along with strategies that encourage responsible use. They work with donors and originating agencies to ensure that any restrictions are appropriate, well-documented, and equitably enforced. When repositories require restrictions to protect confidential and proprietary information, such restrictions should be implemented in an impartial manner. In all questions of access, archivists seek practical solutions that balance competing principles and interests.[1]

The codes of ethics of the Association of Canadian Archivists, Australian Society of Archivists, Archives and Records Association (UK and Ireland), and Association of Records Managers and Administrators include similar tenets.[2]

Archivists promote the democratic ideal of allowing anyone to access historical records. Essentially, equitable access means that archivists cannot discriminate against anyone who has an interest in viewing records within the parameters of institutional policy. For example, some corporate, museum, tribal, or religious institutions prohibit public access to maintain legal or repository-imposed privacy, while other institutions welcome everyone. Academic archives are generally open to the public, although some (usually private) may choose to set limits on public access and focus on their campus constituents. Government archives, however, are open to all people.

Ethics apply to all aspects of access, including providing physical and virtual access, producing reproductions, granting uses and permissions, and adhering to restrictions and legal regulations. Setting appropriate policies, providing consistent services, and training staff members to adhere to standards and make informed decisions constitute the core of solid ethical practices. Archivist Elena Danielson's *The Ethical Archivist*, archivist Karen Benedict's *Ethics and the Archival Profession: Introduction and Case Studies*, and the SAA Committee on Ethics and Professional Conduct's recently developed case studies publications offer insight into and guidance for specific ethical issues.[3]

Patron Privacy

The library and archives professions have a long-standing practice of protecting the privacy of patrons. The current SAA Code of Ethics states that "Archivists respect all users' rights to privacy by maintaining the confidentiality of their research and protecting any personal information collected about the users in accordance with their institutions' policies."[4] This core principle is meant to protect patrons' identities and information about collections used, purposes of research, and any other data collected by the repository. Patron privacy is protection from initial contact through the end of the reference interaction, whether in person or via email or phone, and patrons have a right to expect that the repository will conceal their information in perpetuity.

Archivists have an ethical obligation to respect each individual's right to privacy.[5] The concept of "privacy" is subject to different interpretations. In the context of archival reference, some patrons focus primarily on not sharing their registration information, some prefer to have all conversations remain confidential, and some are unconcerned about privacy. When a reference area is an open and public space, privacy remains difficult to protect. Archivists can assess to what extent individuals desire privacy by directly asking patrons to share their comfort levels.

There are two primary aspects to maintaining confidentiality: not sharing patron registrations or data, and not sharing information about collections accessed or research topics. Archivists can take precautions to ensure confidentiality by placing distance between researchers (when possible), limiting discussions about research purposes within earshot of others, and ensuring that registration forms are not visible. Conversely, patrons have the option to grant permission to share their research or personal information. Written permission is preferable in such cases, whether noted on a registration form, through an email, or by a signed document.

Privacy begins when a patron walks into the archives. Interactions frequently occur in a public area where anyone can listen, but there are strategies for minimizing problems. Registration forms can include a statement about the repository maintaining confidentiality about patrons and their research. Designating a separate area for interviews helps maintain that privacy, but archivists cannot always offer that as an option. Archivists can take care to keep voices low, move to a quiet area, or caution patrons about possible privacy breaches. Archivists, of course, sometimes need to discuss patrons and their questions among themselves in order to solicit reference assistance from colleagues, manage shift changes, or satisfy other internal concerns.

Written documentation is also subject to confidentiality. Registration forms, driver's licenses, identification cards, credit card numbers, and any other personal information in paper or electronic form must be accessible only to staff. Generally, it is easy to keep such information out of public view by filing registration forms, returning IDs immediately, and shredding payment records. These tasks may not occur immediately, particularly if a patron is visiting over more than one day, but it is important to keep these documents out of view in a secure place.

The principles of privacy extend to virtual and phone interactions. Patrons can expect that emails will not be shared and phone conversations will be kept confidential.

Although maintaining patron confidentiality is a long-standing archival practice, one particular federal regulation tests privacy protections. As a result of the 2001 terrorist attack in the United States, the federal government passed the USA PATRIOT Act. This legislation dramatically expanded federal surveillance techniques to combat terrorism. Although much of the USA PATRIOT Act focuses on government agencies, one section authorizes law enforcement agencies to obtain business records held in private hands, such as bank records or store purchases.[6] Though not specified in the Act itself, law enforcement has used this option to obtain patron records from libraries to determine whether books borrowed influenced or contributed to criminal or terrorist acts. This intervention has appeared to nullify well-established institutional practices that have protected patron privacy and confidentiality.

A result of the USA PATRIOT Act was libraries anonymizing user data while still retaining valuable statistics. Moving registration and other information into the digital realm has changed how archives collect, monitor, and use data. Many libraries have taken action to alleviate access to this information, often by changing their systems to detach records (e.g., book checkouts) from patron information. Electronically collecting user information and use is common, and archivists must be conscious of the security, privacy, and ethics concerns that surround this digital information.

Integrated library systems, archives management software, and registration systems collect data, making it incumbent on repositories to figure out and customize procedures to maintain useful administrative data while maintaining patron privacy. For example, Aeon offers an option for anonymizing data by separating the reference transaction from the patron information.[7] Other systems, such as LibAnalytics, are customizable to exclude collecting patron information with data about transactions. Repositories need not forego using third-party systems and software but, rather, must carefully read contracts, specifications, and other information to ensure that they are fully informed about the strengths and limitations of particular products.

Accessibility

According to a 2015 report, approximately 20 percent of US adults have at least one disability, and the World Health Organization estimates about one in seven people worldwide, or more than one billion people, have a disability. The disability rights movement in the United States gained momentum in the early 1970s, eventually culminating in the 1990 Americans with Disabilities Act (ADA).[8] Since then, libraries and archives have made great strides in implementing accommodations within their services. Initially, accommodations focused on physical disabilities, such as vision or hearing impairments and mobility issues. Today, efforts to address disabilities have been expanded to include people with both physical and intellectual challenges.

Archives began to explore options for making accommodations starting in the 1970s and 1980s, when these concerns first appeared in archival literature. One researcher with a hearing disability advised providing a sign-language interpreter and communicating through written notes. In addition, he advised training staff about helping patrons with disabilities, recruiting or training staff who might be proficient in sign language, creating visual aids, providing written policies and procedures, and publicizing accessibility options.[9] Another author described situations in which patrons might not have a specific disability but could require special accommodations. She offered advice, such as staff training, keeping lists of local agencies that provide assistance when needed, and assessing physical space. Most important, the author noted that archivists should be conscious of their attitudes and behaviors. Staff members might treat people with disabilities differently or inappropriately, often without meaning to.[10]

These early articles began a broader discussion within archives of how to modify services to accommodate people with disabilities. Thanks to legislation, technology, and efforts to be proactive and inclusive, there is much more guidance available today on how to accommodate special needs. Libraries have taken an especially proactive stance in this area. The Association of Specialized Government and Cooperative Library Agencies (ASGCLA, a division of the American Library Association) continually updates resources on its website. These resources include physical space and assistive technologies toolkits that address children; persons with hearing challenges, visual impairments, physical disabilities, autism spectrum disorders, developmental and learning disabilities, and mental illnesses; and service animals. The guidelines address these needs in employees, volunteers, and patrons.[11]

SAA first approved the "Best Practices for Working with Archives Researchers and Employees with Physical Disabilities" in 2010, and published a 2019 revision titled "Guidelines for Accessible Archives for People with Disabilities." SAA's guidelines provide a solid starting point for creating institutional practices regarding values, communication, physical space, public services, exhibits, programming, workplace, and digital content.[12] In addition to these resources, archivists should consult their parent institution's legal counsel, policies, and guidelines to ensure compliance with organizational and professional standards.

Many institutions acknowledge accessibility options on their websites. Most often mentioned are parking options for people with disabilities. Some repositories also include information about elevators, computers, photocopiers, restrooms, lactation spaces, magnifying readers, retrieval services, service animals, and personal assistance.[13]

Accessibility issues are not limited to those with a physical or intellectual disability; medical concerns may require special accommodations. For example, a researcher may be allergic to mold or certain materials, and dust masks, gloves, and a lab coat can help protect from direct contact. Another researcher may need to bring a service animal into the reading room, or a medical condition may require that food or drink be in close proximity. These types of situations seldom occur, but it is important to note that flexibility and catering to the researcher instead of collections is appropriate in rare instances.

Reference archivists may not need to address these issues on a daily basis but must be aware of potential solutions for when requests arise. Consulting patrons with disabilities who can offer guidance and test effectiveness of resources is an inclusive approach to accommodations. Preparing for a variety of situations will not only help patrons but will demonstrate that the institution takes the initiative to be aware and inclusive.

Physical Accessibility

Since the passing of the ADA in 1990, new buildings have been required to offer specific options, such as ramps and aisles for wheelchairs, automatic door openers, elevators, or other features, to accommodate persons with multiple types of physical disabilities. For buildings built before 1990, many institutions have made alterations to bring the structures up to compliance. Therefore, within the past thirty years, most archives have installed and implemented the basic accessibility components for access to their buildings.

However, a building is only one aspect of physical accessibility. Many archives have, or are moving toward, ensuring that other physical components accommodate various user needs, such as adjustable table heights and chair styles and variable lighting. Most of these alterations require a financial investment, but there are low- to no-cost options as well. For example, placing props under table legs can raise the table level to accommodate a wheelchair, or a high counter can allow for patrons to stand when reviewing materials. Extra lamps provide brighter lighting, and magnifiers make materials more readable and easier to use. A repository can also furnish a separate adjustable workstation to meet researcher needs.

Patrons may self-identify a specific need and perhaps give guidance on what will help with the interaction. If appropriate, an archivist can ask for a preferred method of communication or assistance. For those who do not disclose a disability, or for those whose disability may not be noticeable, it is important to follow their lead and maintain the same standards used with all patrons.

Virtual Accessibility

Taking accessibility into account for digital content is essential for equitable access. Because users often view content remotely, it is harder to identify the individual accommodations required. By adopting broad practices that specifically serve those who have special needs, archives can offer better accommodations for everyone. There are many resources on how to make images, multimedia, websites, and other online content meet accessibility requirements.[14]

Websites and other online resources are considered accessible if anyone can use or view them in ways that do not rely on a single ability or sense. Headings, colors, links, interactive elements, images, and all other components of the infrastructure and design affect accessibility. Recommendations include adding descriptive text to images to improve comprehension, creating a clear structure for pages and documents, improving visibility and descriptions for links, offering a clear layout and readability for text, and providing captions, descriptions, and/or transcriptions for audio and video.[15] These components also apply to other systems and software that facilitate access to digital content. Archivists have less control over third-party applications when they outsource functions, but most vendors are building accessible operability into their products.[16]

Accessibility of digital content goes beyond the operating systems to the files themselves. For example, conducting optical character recognition (OCR) for textual documents enables a read-aloud capability. However, there are limitations outside the control of archivists and available technology. OCR can misread grainy originals, and there are limited technological options for handwritten documents, which often require human transcription.[17] As technology improves, archives will have more options for applying accessibility to individual files.

While visual accessibility is prominent, considering mobility or dexterity impairments is also important. For example, incorporating options that do not require extensive keyboard typing cater to such users.[18] It can be difficult to create an extensive website with this in mind, but even basic information on short and simple pages will help with accommodations.

Because integrating accessibility into workflows was not always practiced, older content may not be compliant. Although archives have the option to update legacy data, these practices are time-consuming. When extensive revisions are not possible, a sensible practice is to respond to patron requests on a case-by-case basis.

Language

An important aspect of accessibility is language. With an increased establishment of community archives and advocacy to document ethnic and underrepresented groups in the United States, it is important to be conscientious that English may not be the first language for someone visiting or working in archives. To reduce or eliminate barriers to access, hiring personnel who speak multiple languages, seeking the services of translators, or having other tools on hand, such as translation dictionaries, mobile device apps, or online translators, will be of great benefit. Sometimes, providing pencil and paper for those who write better than speak another language is helpful. Whatever the options, every effort ought to be made to make archivists and researchers feel welcome.

As patron demographics become more diverse, some institutions are producing resources, such as finding aids or catalog records, in multiple languages. For example, a grant-funded project at Arizona State University created bilingual finding aids. Another grant-funded project is Mukurtu, which focuses on including Traditional Knowledge labels for indigenous communities.[19] Further, many browsers (such as Google Chrome) have embedded features to use in translating websites and individual pages. Assessing whether to provide multilingual content is dependent on the institution's audience but also has the potential to attract new users.

Conclusion

Ethics, privacy, and accessibility are similar in that they focus on working with and respecting patrons. Archivists have a responsibility to ensure equitable access to collections, whether in person or online. It is important for archivists to treat all patrons with respect, as the goal is to connect patrons with their desired information.

Maintaining privacy about patrons, protecting their research inquiries, and keeping confidential the collections that they have accessed and the purposes of use all constitute core components of practicing good archival ethics. Archivists, who are naturally inquisitive people, sometimes find it difficult to resist sharing their excitement or frustration at patron interactions. It is common, and often helpful, for archivists to discuss patrons or interactions with their colleagues. However, these conversations must remain confidential and be conducted with decorum in private areas.

As with privacy, directly addressing and accommodating the accessibility needs of patrons is part of creating an ethical and equitable environment. Archivists must make efforts to ensure that their physical space, virtual space, and materials can be accessed by everyone. Some accommodations can be built into use policies, while others can be handled on a case-by-case basis. Integrating accessibility into long-term planning assures ongoing attention to accommodating patrons.

These aspects apply to all types of patron interactions. Incorporating ethics, privacy, and accessibility into reference services helps to advance services and demonstrates to patrons a repository's commitment to creating an accessible and inclusive environment.

NOTES

[1] Society of American Archivists, "SAA Core Values Statement and Code of Ethics," www2.archivists.org/statements/saa-core-values-statement-and-code-of-ethics#code_of_ethics, captured at https://perma.cc/4XV9-FSRP.

[2] Association of Canadian Archivists, "Code of Ethics and Professional Conduct," October 18, 2019, https://archivists.ca/resources/Documents/Governance%20and%20Structure/aca_code_of_ethics_final_october_2017.pdf, captured at https://perma.cc/2QC5-8GPG; Australian Society of Archivists, "Code of Ethics," June 17, 1993, www.archivists.org.au/about-us/code-of-ethics, captured at https://perma.cc/QT69-3QHZ; Archives and Records Association, UK and Ireland, "Code of Ethics," https://www.archives.org.uk/images/ARA_Board/2019/Code_Of_Ethics_February_2020_final.pdf, captured at https://perma.cc/CAV5-FZLY; ARMA International, "Code of Ethics," www.arma.org/page/IGP_Ethics, captured at https://perma.cc/CM2K-M289.

[3] Society of American Archivists, "Case Studies in Archival Ethics," www2.archivists.org/groups/committee-on-ethics-and-professional-conduct/case-studies-in-archival-ethics; Elena Danielson, *The Ethical Archivist* (Chicago: Society of American Archivists, 2010); Karen Benedict, *Ethics and the Archival Profession: Introduction and Case Studies* (Chicago: Society of American Archivists, 2003).

[4] Society of American Archivists, "SAA Core Values Statement and Code of Ethics."

[5] Tomas A. Lipinski, "Legal Issues Involved in the Privacy Rights of Patrons in 'Public' Libraries and Archives," in *Libraries, Museums, and Archives: Legal Issues and Ethical Challenges in the New Information Era*, ed. Tomas A. Lipinski (Lanham, MD: Scarecrow Press, 2002), 98; Laura A. Millar, *Archives: Principles and Practices* (New York: Neal-Schuman Publishers, 2010), 98.

[6] U.S. Department of Justice, "The USA PATRIOT Act: Preserving Life and Liberty," www.justice.gov/archive/ll/highlights.htm, captured at https://perma.cc/D8N3-FUHY.

[7] Email from Renee Chastain-Smith, May 28, 2019, and see also Aeon's website, https://aeon.aaa.si.edu/; Sara Juel, "Anonymizing Users," Atlas Systems, 2019, http://support.atlas-sys.com/hc/en-us/articles/360011920093-Anonymizing-Users, captured at https://perma.cc/78WX-2KSV.

[8] Carli Spina and Margaret Cohen, *Spec Kit 358: Accessibility and Universal Design* (Washington, DC: Association of Research Libraries, May 2018), 2; World Health Organization, "WHO Global Disability Action Plan 2014–2021: Better Health for All People with Disability" (Geneva, Switzerland: World Health Organization, 2015), 2, https://apps.who.int/iris/bitstream/handle/10665/199544/9789241509619_eng.pdf;jsessionid=1A18578B3A7224A616B6BFD63C99E016?sequence=1, captured at https://perma.cc/2HS8-Q927; Mary Minow, "Welcome to . . . The Legal Responsibility to Offer Accessible Electronic Information to Patrons with Disabilities," in Lipinski, *Libraries, Museums, and Archives*, 119–120; for an overview of the act, see Ronald L. Gilardi, "The Archival Setting and People with Disabilities: A Legal Analysis," *American Archivist* 56, no. 4 (1993): 704–713, https://doi.org/10.17723/aarc.56.4.68070hw410848230.

[9] Lance J. Fischer, "The Deaf and Archival Research: Some Problems and Solutions," *American Archivist* 42, no. 4 (1979): 463–464, https://doi.org/10.17723/aarc.42.4.bt681l38560032x2.

[10] Brenda Beasley Kepley, "Archives: Accessibility for the Disabled," *American Archivist* 46, no. 1 (1983): 44–46, https://doi.org/10.17723/aarc.46.1.7275k33t7817w00u.

[11] Association of Specialized Government and Cooperative Library Agencies, "Resources," www.asgcladirect.org/resources/.

[12] Society of American Archivists, "Guidelines for Accessible Archives for People with Disabilities," www2.archivists.org/standards/guidelines-for-accessible-archives-for-people-with-disabilities, captured at https://perma.cc/J2GY-7EAU.

[13] University of Georgia Libraries, Special Collections Libraries, "Accessibility," www5.galib.uga.edu/scl/visit/accessibility.html, captured at https://perma.cc/QF7W-HS5W; U.S. National Archives and Records Administration, "Accessibility," last reviewed November 20, 2019, www.archives.gov/global-pages/accessibility, captured at https://perma.cc/DUA8-Y7LZ; Wisconsin Historical Society, "Accessibility," www.wisconsinhistory.org/Records/Article/CS71, captured at https://perma.cc/YH5F-E49J; Emory Libraries and Information Technology, Stuart A. Rose Manuscript, Archives, and Rare Book Library, "Accessibility," 2020, http://rose.library.emory.edu/about/accessibility.html, captured at https://perma.cc/JLX9-2YWW.

[14] U.S. Government, General Services Administration, "18F Accessibility Guide," https://accessibility.18f.gov/index.html.

[15] Minow, "Welcome to . . ." in Lipinski, *Libraries, Museums, and Archives*, 116; Kevin Rydberg, "The Must-Have Accessibility Handbook" (Siteimprove, n.d.), http://go.siteimprove.com/hubfs/Content/eBooks_Guides_Whitepapers/EN_Accessibility_Handbook.pdf; American Foundation for the Blind, "Web Accessibility Resources," www.afb.org/about-afb/what-we-do/afb-consulting/afb-accessibility-resources/resources-2177; W3C WAI, "Making the Web Accessible," 2020, www.w3.org/WAI/; Lisa Snider, "Access for All: Making Your Archives' Website Accessible for People with Disabilities," in Theimer, *Reference and Access*, 143–151.

[16] OCLC, "Accessibility Statement," 2020, https://policies.oclc.org/en/accessibility.html; Omeka.org, "Accessibility Statement," *Omeka Classic User Manual*, https://omeka.org/classic/docs/GettingStarted/Accessibility_Statement/; ArchivesSpace, "Accessibility and VPAT," 2020, https://archivesspace.org/application/accessibility-vpat.

[17] Adobe, Inc., "Training Resources | Adobe Acrobat Accessibility," www.adobe.com/accessibility/products/acrobat/training.html. Work is advancing on OCR software for handwriting. For example, Elisa H. Barney Smith, Boise State University professor of electrical and computer engineering, develops tools to enhance and advance OCR. Boise State University, "Selected Works of Elisa H. Barney Smith," https://works.bepress.com/elisa_barney_smith/.

[18] Rosemary Musachio, "Web Accessibility from a Personal Perspective," *Access Matters Blog*, Interactive Accessibility, June 20, 2013, https://interactiveaccessibility.com/blog/web-accessibility-personal-perspective#.XfW7mdZKjUq, captured at https://perma.cc/6AR7-YSCQ.

[19] Elizabeth Dunham and Xaviera Flores, "Breaking the Language Barrier: Describing Chicano Archives with Bilingual Finding Aids," *American Archivist* 77, no. 2 (2014): 499–509, https://doi.org/10.17723/aarc.77.2.p66l555g15g981p6; Millar, *Archives*, 186; Mukurtu CMS, https://mukurtu.org/.

9

Legal Regulations

Balancing privacy and legal issues with access is a delicate process. A non-lawyer might find it overwhelming to keep current with legal information, and reference archivists need not be legal experts. However, they ought to be familiar with the most common regulations applicable to their institution's collections, where to find information concerning those issues, and how to inform patrons about access regulations.

Attorney and archivist Menzi L. Behrnd-Klodt advises archivists to draft written policies because they "provide (1) direction, continuity, and predictability for the archives and its parent; (2) accountability for standards and service; (3) standardization for compliance with any legal and regulatory requirements and ethical expectations; (4) guidelines for staff, volunteers, and visitors concerning expectations, obligations, and rights; and (5) uniformity by establishing consistency in operations."[1] As she notes, policies are for both internal staff members and external audiences. Archivists can provide basic information of how they comply with legal statutes, through finding aids, registration forms, and websites, but they also need to consult legal counsel when appropriate.

This chapter presents an introductory overview of the legal regulations and other regulations that repositories commonly follow, along with some illustrations and applications. The chapter does not provide official legal guidance, and archivists should consult their institutional policies or legal counsel for accurate interpretation and application.

Archivists' Responsibility

Archives strive to be transparent and document their access policies and restrictions based on laws, regulations, and ethics. It is through acquisition and processing that materials are evaluated within the context of laws and regulations, and reference archivists assume the responsibility for being the intersection between patrons and restrictions. They field questions related to physical and digital content, ensure that closed records are not accessed, and provide guidance on copyright, use, and reproduction.

Acquisition and processing constitute the key activities to which relevant laws are applied and access restrictions are formulated. During the acquisition process, archivists have conversations with donors to identify materials that are subject to regulations, asking specific questions about the contents of records to begin the evaluation. In the best-case scenario, the creator, whether a person or organization, can pinpoint specific records or groups of records to review for adherence to legal restrictions. At times, donors may not know how laws apply to records; this may occur, for example, when the donor is not the creator and therefore is unfamiliar with a collection's detailed contents. In these situations, archivists assume more responsibility in evaluating the contents for potential restrictions.

During the acquisition process, time and staffing limitations may keep archivists from thoroughly reviewing collections' contents. They rely on processing archivists to more comprehensively review collections and flag potential restrictions. When archivists arrange and describe collections, they use information received from donors and further assess entire record groups or individual items to determine whether materials are subject to restrictions, redactions, or deaccessioning. As a result of these assessments, records deemed inaccessible for research are removed or segregated to ensure that they remain closed to researchers. The processing archivists document whether portions of collections or entire collections are closed through internal collection information, notes in finding aids, clear labels on folders and boxes, or other means.

As the intermediaries between collections, patrons, and access limitations, reference archivists must know how to review finding aids and other documentation to verify open and closed records and learn how to elucidate the rationales to patrons. With the exception of copyright, most reference interactions do not require dealing with the intricacies of laws governing access. However, being familiar with the laws helps archivists be well prepared to handle situations as they arise. The following sections are overviews of the most common laws pertaining to archival records. Archivists may find that some of these regulations do not pertain to their collections; in that case, they should focus on those regulations that are most relevant to their situations.

Freedom of Information Act

Access to information is a fundamental principle for archives. However, for nearly two centuries, there were no federal laws in the United States specifying that the government was required to save information, much less that citizens had a right to access that data. The gradual creation of government archives throughout the twentieth century on the local, state, and federal levels helped to forward the creation of laws to preserve records for public access. Over time, these events laid the foundation that all citizens have the right to access information.

- The University of Michigan holds the papers of John Tanton, a founder of several anti-immigration groups. An immigration attorney submitted a FOIA request to access the collection, which, per donor stipulation, is closed until 2035.
- The Federation of American Scientists requested documents from the Defense Intelligence Agency about the Advanced Aerospace Threat Identification Program, which investigated instances of "odd" science such as wormholes, UFOs, and negative energy.
- The Buffalo Field Campaign (Montana) requested documents from the National Park Service and U.S. Department of the Interior about the management of bison in Yellowstone National Park to determine actions and polices about the bison population.
- The American Civil Liberties Union and the Center for Media Justice are still attempting to obtain documents about the Federal Bureau of Investigation's "Domestic Security" cases, which include surveillance of Dr. Martin Luther King Jr.

FIGURE 8. Examples of FOIA Requests

Sources: Lisa Peet, "Attorney Sues for Access to Tanton Papers in Closed Archive," *Library Journal*, September 18, 2018, www.libraryjournal.com?detailStory=180918-Tanton-Papers; Steven Aftergood, "More Light on Black Program to Track UFOs," *Secrecy News* (blog), Federation of American Scientists, https://fas.org/blogs/secrecy/2019/01/aatip-list/, captured at https://perma.cc/2UCD-MD9Y; Brett French, "Bison Group Sues to Get FOIA Fulfilled; Yellowstone Bison Population Reported," *Billings Gazette*, October 14, 2019, https://billingsgazette.com/outdoors/bison-group-sues-to-get-foia-fulfilled-yellowstone-bison-population/article_80bb8469-7e87-5789-a2c8-cd8eaa18ae0g.html; Patrick G. Eddington, "MLK and the FBI: 50 Years On, Secrets and Surveillance Still," *The Hill*, April 4, 2019, https://thehill.co/opinion/civil-rights/436437-mlk-and-the-fbi-50-years-on-secrets-and-surveillance-still.

This eventually culminated in the federal Freedom of Information Act (FOIA), which was passed by Congress in 1967. Along with several amendments passed in subsequent decades, this law stipulates that the public has the right to request documents from executive-level federal agencies. These agencies are required to describe their operations and methods for obtaining information and producing records to any person with a qualifying request.[2] There are nine exemptions to providing information under FOIA, three of which are of particular interest to archivists: confidential and privileged information, personnel and medical records, and law enforcement records.[3]

FOIA applies to federal records, but individual states have passed similar laws that apply specifically to state government agency records. The National Freedom of Information Coalition collates information about individual states' open records laws.[4] These laws mirror the federal FOIA in that they define which records are considered subject to open records laws, as well as exemptions pertaining to privacy, trade secrets, financial records, or law enforcement records. See Figure 8 for examples of FOIA requests.

Family Educational Rights and Privacy Act (FERPA)

Academic institutions, K–12 schools, and other educational organizations produce myriad records, not all of which are available for public access. This law is most relevant in education-based archives, but other repository types may hold educational institutions' records or personal papers that contain such records.

Established in 1974 and amended, most recently, in 2011, the Family Educational Rights and Privacy Act (FERPA) protects student records and information at institutions that receive federal funding.[5] The educational institution is required to inform students and parents about their rights under FERPA; the communication, which must take place annually, is transmitted through websites, handbooks, and/or in written form. The archives can use this same information to provide public statements about adhering to FERPA[6] and list which records are open and which are restricted. Schools that do not receive federal funding, such as private or parochial elementary institutions, are not obligated to comply with FERPA.

The U.S. Department of Education defines "education records" as "those records that contain information directly related to a student and which are maintained by an educational agency or institution or by a party acting for the agency or institution."[7] However, the department has not provided a precise list of what constitutes "educational records." In general, educational records are related to grades, disciplinary action, enrollment applications, or financial information. These records cannot be shared without a parent's written permission or without the permission of a student who is eighteen or older. In some cases, information can be shared without written permission, such as when requested via a subpoena or accrediting organization or for an audit or safety or health emergency.[8] Though these are allowable circumstances, the recipient is required to keep the records confidential.

Much student information is not protected under FERPA and instead is considered public record. One specific example is directory information, which includes addresses, dates of attendance, awards, and birthplace and birthdate, although students or parents can request that this information be withheld from the public.[9] Directories are sometimes available online or are published as print volumes that are sent to alumni and available in the library, archives, alumni center, or other campus offices.

Essentially, documents, photographs, ephemera, social media, or other materials that are broadly available are also not restricted under FERPA. Some examples include student newspapers published in print or online, commencement programs, and photographs and ephemera from events or student organizations. Indeed, most academic archives actively collect materials about student life to preserve organizational history and make them publicly available.

Occasionally, records not restricted under FERPA generate controversy. Individuals may request redaction or restriction of any materials that mention their names. Sometimes people are embarrassed about their college activities or fear for their personal safety, or materials are thought to be inappropriate for current viewers in light of current societal context. In one example, the administration of Hollins University chose to remove online access to yearbooks when it was publicized that the yearbooks contained photos showing faculty members and students in blackface, dressed as Native Americans, and raising the Confederate flag. The justification for removing online access to the yearbooks was to avoid causing pain or damage to those who viewed them, and some people advocated that they remain public with educational and informational contexts. Many individuals criticized this decision because they believed in maintaining access as a means to openly address the issues raised by such photographs.[10]

Health Insurance Portability and Accountability Act (HIPAA)

The Health Insurance Portability and Accountability Act of 1996 (HIPAA) and its subset Privacy Rule (2003) are federal laws that protect an individual's health and medical information within covered entities of health-care providers, health plans, and health-care clearinghouses.[11] Federal lawmakers have determined that it remains paramount to protect people's medical privacy. However, even among institutions that utilize the Privacy Rule component, interpretations vary.[12] Archives themselves may or may not be covered entities, and whether or not records are covered under these laws is murky and requires consulting legal counsel to ensure proper compliance.

Within a historical context, medical records are imperative to the history of medicine, science, and public health. Their importance goes well beyond those fields, revealing much about race, class, gender, public health, and other sociohistorical issues. Researchers find medical records vital to the study of historical trends and practices. In their study "The Practice of Privacy," archivists Emily R. Gustainis and Phoebe Evans Letocha explored interpretations, ramifications, and challenges for archivists by consulting directly with researchers to create recommended practices regarding health and medical collections. In particular, they examined archival practices for both HIPAA- and non-HIPAA-covered collections, defined restrictions and how to apply them, specified how to screen collections for private and confidential records, and explained how to properly describe those records to distinguish accessible and restricted content.[13] This study accentuates the extensive complications regarding medical records and specific tactics to address them.

Privacy Act

Prompted by the government's increased creation of automated data systems, the Privacy Act of 1974 "establishes a code of fair information practices that governs the collection, maintenance, use, and dissemination of information about individuals that is maintained in systems of records by federal agencies."[14] The government is required to maintain information about individuals, and the act's purpose is to balance that need with protection of individuals' rights. The act establishes rules about disclosure of personal information without consent, outlaws federal secret recordkeeping, permits individuals to request their information and supply corrections or amendments, and requires agencies to create secure and up-to-date recordkeeping systems.[15]

The Privacy Act concerns information created and maintained by federal agencies, and the U.S. Department of Justice provides Privacy Impact Assessment templates.[16] Though specifically intended for government agencies, any archives can use the templates to identify records held that are subject to privacy protection. It is a common practice for archives to remove Social Security numbers, financial records, and other information governed or created by federal agencies.

Public Company Accounting Reform and Investor Protection Act

Following the financial misconduct and fraud scandals of Enron, Tyco International, Arthur Anderson, and WorldCom, the Public Company Accounting Reform and Investor Protection Act of 2002 changed financial reporting and corporate governance laws. As archivist and lawyer Menzi Behrnd-Klodt writes, this act, also known as the Sarbanes-Oxley Act, requires that publicly held companies disclose whatever has a material impact on their bottom lines, set up control systems and approval levels for financial records and reports, and enhance transparency. While the act is directed at for-profit companies, recent rules established by the U.S. Securities and Exchange Commission may extend compliance to nonprofit and private businesses as well.[17]

Copyright

Of all federal laws, copyright law remains the most intricate and complex. For many institutions, assessing copyright is a daily and complicated task. Reference archivists need to know the basics of copyright law, how to read donor agreements for stipulations, and who to consult for final decisions.

Copyright exists to protect authors' rights to their works. The Copyright Act of 1976, which went into effect on January 1, 1978, stipulates that copyright begins at the time a work is created. The law protects works defined with "a degree of originality and fixation in a tangible form" and applies to both published and unpublished works. In addition, the law defines "works of authorship" as literary works; musical works; dramatic works; pantomimes and choreographic works; pictorial, graphic, and sculptural works; sound recordings; architectural works; and compiled, collective, and derivative works.[18] The 1976 law protected works for the life of the author plus fifty years. In 1998, the Copyright Term Extension Act, also known as the Sonny Bono Copyright Term Extension Act, extended these terms by twenty years.

Archivist and copyright specialist Peter Hirtle has created a handy chart as a way to quickly assess the basics of copyright status (see Figure 9). Although the copyright status of most materials is determined at the time of acquisition and/or processing, seldom can the copyright status for every item in every collection be identified.[19]

Reference archivists, in particular, are the mediators between copyright and patrons. They are responsible for explaining copyright protections, fair use considerations, the fact that online content may be protected under copyright, and other parameters that dictate use and access. The following sections specify some provisions in copyright law applicable to archival research.

Copyright Ownership

Copyright is initially assessed during the acquisition of collections. Archivists work with donors to determine whether copyright is transferred to the institution or remains with donors or their designees. Deeds of gift stipulate the extent to which the donor transfers or retains copyright permissions, which could be portions of or entire collections. Donors seldom can transfer full rights to the entire contents of a collection because they may not own rights to all materials, such as correspondence that they received or newspaper articles that they collected. Copyright remains with the individual or organization who created the document.

When donors grant copyright to an institution, that copyright applies to the works they created and other materials for which a donor owns copyright. For example, when a donor transfers copyright for a literary collection, it applies to published and unpublished drafts; copyright to correspondence remains with the person who wrote it, reviews with the original publisher, images

Cornell University Library

Copyright Term and the Public Domain in the United States

Never Published, Never Registered Works

Type of Work	Copyright Term	In the public domain in the U.S. as of 1 January 2020
Unpublished works	Life of the author + 70 years	Works from authors who died before 1950
Unpublished anonymous and pseudonymous works, and works made for hire (corporate authorship)	120 years from date of creation	Works created before 1900
Unpublished works when the death date of the author is not known	120 years from date of creation	Works created before 1900

Works Registered or First Published in the U.S.

Date of Publication	Conditions	Copyright Term
Before 1925	None	None. In the public domain due to copyright expiration
1925 through 1977	Published without a copyright notice	None. In the public domain due to failure to comply with required formalities
1978 to 1 March 1989	Published without notice, and without subsequent registration within 5 years	None. In the public domain due to failure to comply with required formalities
1978 to 1 March 1989	Published without notice, but with subsequent registration within 5 years	70 years after the death of author. If a work of corporate authorship, 95 years from publication or 120 years from creation, whichever expires first
1925 through 1963	Published with notice but copyright was not renewed	None. In the public domain due to copyright expiration
1925 through 1963	Published with notice and the copyright was renewed	95 years after publication date
1964 through 1977	Published with notice	95 years after publication date
1978 to 1 March 1989	Created after 1977 and published with notice	70 years after the death of author. If a work of corporate authorship, 95 years from publication or 120 years from creation, whichever expires first
1978 to 1 March 1989	Created after 1978 and first published with notice in the specified period	The greater of the term specified in the previous entry or 31 December 2047
From 1 March 1989 through 2002	Created 1977	70 years after the death of author. If a work of corporate authorship, 95 years from publication or 120 years from creation, whichever expires first

FIGURE 9. Copyright Status Chart
Note: This chart includes select examples and is updated as laws change.
Source: Peter B. Hirtle, Copyright Term and the Public Domain in the United States, last updated January 3, 2020, Cornell University Library.

Date of Publication	Conditions	Copyright Term
From 1 March 1989 through 2002	Created before 1978 and first published in this period	The greater of the term specified in the previous entry or 31 December 2047
After 2002	None	70 years after the death of author. If a work of corporate authorship, 95 years from publication or 120 years from creation, whichever expires first
Anytime	Works prepared by an officer or employee of the United States Government as part of that person's official duties.	None. In the public domain in the United States (17 U.S.C. §105)

Sound Recordings

(Note: The following information applies only to the sound recording itself, and not to any copyrights in underlying compositions or texts.)

Date of Fixation/Publication	Conditions	In the public domain in the U.S. as of 1 January 2020
Unpublished Sound Recordings, Domestic and Foreign		
Prior to 15 Feb. 1972	Indeterminate	Subject to state common law protection. Enters the public domain on 15 Feb. 2067
After 15 Feb. 1972	Life of the author + 70 years. For unpublished anonymous and pseudonymous works and works made for hire (corporate authorship), 120 years from the date of fixation	Nothing. The soonest anything enters the public domain is 15 Feb. 2067
Sound Recordings Published in the United States		
Before 1923	None	1 January 2022
1923 to 1946	None	100 years from publication
1947 to 1956	None	110 years from publication
1957–14 Feb 1972	None	15 Feb 2067
15 Feb 1972 to 1978	Published without notice (i.e., ©, year of publication, and name of copyright owner)	In the public domain
15 Feb. 1972 to 1978	Published with notice	95 years from publication. 2068 at the earliest
1978 to 1 March 1989	Published without notice, and without subsequent registration	In the public domain
1978 to 1 March 1989	Published with notice	70 years after death of author, or if work of corporate authorship, the shorter of 95 years from publication, or 120 years from creation. 2049 at the earliest
After 1 March 1989	None	70 years after death of author, or if work of corporate authorship, the shorter of 95 years from publication, or 120 years from creation. 2049 at the earliest

with the photographer, and interviews with the station where they were recorded and broadcast. Therefore, a donor whose materials include published and unpublished drafts, correspondence, reviews, photographs, and television interviews on videotape is unable to transfer rights to the entire collection.

A difference therefore exists between physically owning a collection and owning the copyright to materials. Having physical custody does not automatically include copyright ownership, a distinction familiar to archivists but often confusing to patrons. At times, users assume that where a collection is located directly correlates to the place from which they need to obtain permission for both access or use.

Fair Use

Copyright protects the rights of the author of the created work, but there are situations in which use does not require permission nor infringe on those rights. Section 107 of the Copyright Act, "Limitations on exclusive rights: fair use," sets the parameters for when authorization is not required to use or publish items. This is particularly advantageous to archives and libraries, as it permits access to materials for study, scholarship, research, and writing, as well as preservation, without interfering with an author's copyright.[20]

Patrons seek archivists' advice on determining whether materials fall under fair use. It is helpful if repositories have an established routine to offer appropriate guidance. Familiarity with the four factors in Section 107 are the foundation to evaluate a request for fair use:

1. Purpose and character of the use, including whether the use is of a commercial nature or is for nonprofit educational purposes
2. Nature of the copyrighted work
3. Amount and substantiality of the portion used in relation to the copyrighted work as a whole
4. Effect of the use upon the potential market for or value of the copyrighted work.[21]

As a proactive measure, repository staff members can use this framework to prepare a fair use matrix for users or develop an evaluative tool for consistent application.

There are many situations applicable within fair use, such as instances in which the resulting works remain unpublished, are for single-time use, or will not generate profits. Student papers or theses, classroom use, and presentations constitute typical examples. However, fair use may no longer apply if a paper is published or a presentation is recorded and made available online. Patrons may not be aware of this distinction, which is why having written agreements or advisements is a preferable approach.

There are recent examples of the public challenging the concept of fair use and, especially, the practice of charging fees or profiting from public domain items. Several lawsuits have been initiated against Getty Images because of its licensing fees. Most of these lawsuits are thin,[22] as Getty Images clearly stipulates materials' availability for public use, as well as permission and clearance guidelines. However, these lawsuits have brought the issues more clearly into the public view.

Another example is a recent situation at Harvard University. In 1850, a Harvard scientist used photography as a way to "prove" his racist theories about slaves' biology and the superiority of the white race. In 2019, a direct descendant of the subjects sued the university, partly because the person charged that Harvard continues to profit from the photographs owing to their use in a variety of contexts, but also owing to "the extent to which history is told and appropriated by the powerful—and denied to the powerless."[23] Unresolved at the time of this writing, this case has numerous implications that will potentially affect fair use practices.

The Getty and Harvard situations are included as examples to demonstrate the complexity of fair use. Archives can, and should, continue to encourage fair use of collections.

Digital Millennium Copyright Act (DMCA)

When the Copyright Act became law in 1976, there was little inkling of how a subsequent digital revolution would forever alter the concept of authorship and copyright. To address the changing nature of publishing formats, the World Intellectual Property Organization adopted a treaty in 1996 that protected authors' works, as well as databases and computer programs, produced in the digital environment.[24] To ensure compliance with the treaty, the U.S. federal government added a digital provision to the Copyright Act.

The passage of the Digital Millennium Copyright Act (DMCA) in 2000 gave protections to digitally produced works, including those published online. Because federal law had already made it illegal to use or reproduce analog materials without permission, the DMCA expanded this by stipulating that it is "unlawful to circumvent technological measures used to prevent unauthorized access to copyrighted works." Further, it also became illegal to create or distribute software and hardware to enable people to access works without authorization.[25]

Under the DMCA, the Librarian of Congress can issue temporary exemptions in order to permit circumvention of the law under certain limited and clearly defined circumstances. In 2018, the exemptions pertinent to archives included copies lawfully obtained for accessibility and use with assistive technologies, excerpts or derivatives of audiovisual content for educational use, and acquisition of computer software and video games for preservation.[26]

Technology, Education, and Copyright Harmonization Act (TEACH Act)

As a complement to the DMCA, and in a similar vein as fair use, the Technology, Education, and Copyright Harmonization Act (TEACH Act), passed in 2002, amended copyright law to allow "governmental bodies and accredited nonprofit educational institutions" to use materials without attaining permission from the copyright holder.[27] The act specifies that under the direction of an instructor and as part of the curriculum, materials may be transmitted digitally to students enrolled in a course, though not to any other unauthorized parties. Further, materials shared in this manner have an expiration date and cannot be retained indefinitely.

Copyright Exceptions for Libraries and Archives

While Section 107 of the Copyright Act provides stipulations for use of materials, Section 108, "Limitations on exclusive rights: Reproduction by libraries and archives," stipulates provisions for reproductions. Enacted in 1976, the law authorizes archives and other cultural heritage institutions to "reproduce and distribute certain copyrighted works without permission on a limited basis for the purposes of preservation, replacement, and research."[28]

There are three requirements for reproductions: that they not be produced for commercial use, that the institution must be open to the public for research, and that a copyright notice be included on all reproductions.[29] It is common for archives to create reproductions of fragile materials to avoid handling and provide copies to patrons for private study. This is a vital component to facilitating access to archival materials. Archivists can deliver reproductions to patrons with the stipulation that they are for personal use only and that additional permission is required for publication or other public consumption.

Rights Statements

A critical resource for both patrons and archivists, rights statements reflect institutional policy, legal regulations, and guidance on use. The proliferation of digital content has made it more important than ever for archivists to communicate with patrons about copyright. For in-person visits, it is easy to have a conversation to explain the procedures. With online resources, archivists must create rights statements to include in metadata.

Including rights statements is crucial to ensure that a patron is informed about the institution's policies and viewpoints. To help cultural heritage institutions, an international consortium created RightsStatements.org, whose goal is to look "for ways to improve access to and reuse" of digital collections. The site provides twelve statements that communicate different levels of copyright knowledge and practices (see Figure 10 for the descriptions that define situations in which each statement applies). From "in copyright" through "no known copyright," these statements provide guiding language for cultural heritage institutions to communicate the varied levels of copyright and use within their collections.

In addition to assisting with interpreting rights statements, reference archivists have an important role in communicating patrons' reactions to the statements. Because reference archivists are the connection between patrons and materials, they will hear about any confusion, challenges, or compliments about the information. Archivists can share any feedback with appropriate persons involved with metadata creation, digitization, acquisition, processing, or any other function related to providing access to digital content to inform future practices.

Takedown Statements

Though advocating for open access is important, archives must also respect the needs and concerns of creators or owners of copyright. Some repositories aggressively mount items online even if copyright has not been ascertained. One reason for doing this is to encourage researchers to notify the institution with relevant copyright information. To facilitate such a dialogue, the online copyright statement can include requests for researchers to notify the institution if they have copyright information, as well as a takedown statement if copyright owners wish to have materials removed from the site (see Figure 11 for examples). Risk-averse organizations are concerned about being sued, but it is extremely rare that a lawsuit would ensue if a repository posts materials that are copyright protected, as long as takedown statements are provided. If a copyright owner discovers that their materials have been placed online, the initial action is to request removal or issue a "cease and desist" notice. If the repository removes the items, they are in compliance and forestall lawsuit possibilities.[30]

Rights Statements for In Copyright Objects

IN COPYRIGHT
This Rights Statement can be used for an Item that is in copyright. Using this statement implies that the organization making this Item available has determined that the Item is in copyright and either is the rights-holder, has obtained permission from the rights-holder(s) to make their Work(s) available, or makes the Item available under an exception or limitation to copyright (including Fair Use) that entitles it to make the Item available.

IN COPYRIGHT—EU ORPHAN WORK
This Rights Statement is intended for use with Items for which the underlying Work has been identified as an Orphan Work in accordance with Directive 2012/28/EU of the European Parliament and of the Council of 25 October 2012 on certain permitted uses of Orphan Works. It can only be applied to Items derived from Works that are covered by the Directive: Works published in the form of books, journals, newspapers, magazines or other writings as well as cinematographic or audiovisual works and phonograms (note: this excludes photography and visual arts). It can only be applied by organizations that are beneficiaries of the Directive: publicly accessible libraries, educational establishments and museums, archives, film or audio heritage institutions and public-service broadcasting organizations, established in one of the EU member states. The beneficiary is also expected to have registered the work in the EU Orphan Works Database maintained by EUIPO.

IN COPYRIGHT—EDUCATIONAL USE PERMITTED
This Rights Statement can be used only for copyrighted Items for which the organization making the Item available is the rights-holder or has been explicitly authorized by the rights-holder(s) to allow third parties to use their Work(s) for educational purposes without first obtaining permission.

IN COPYRIGHT—NON-COMMERCIAL USE PERMITTED
This Rights Statement can be used only for copyrighted Items for which the organization making the Item available is the rights-holder or has been explicitly authorized by the rights-holder(s) to allow third parties to use their Work(s) for non-commercial purposes without obtaining permission first.

IN COPYRIGHT—RIGHTS-HOLDER(S) UNLOCATABLE OR UNIDENTIFIABLE
This Rights Statement is intended for use with an Item that has been identified as in copyright but for which no rights-holder(s) has been identified or located after some reasonable investigation. This Rights Statement should only be used if the organization that intends to make the Item available is reasonably sure that the underlying Work is in copyright. This Rights Statement is not intended for use by EU-based organizations who have identified works as Orphan Works in accordance with the EU Orphan Works Directive (they must use InC-OW-EU instead).

Rights Statements for Objects That Are Not In Copyright

NO COPYRIGHT—CONTRACTUAL RESTRICTIONS
This Rights Statement can only be used for Items that are in the Public Domain but for which the organization that intends to make the Item available has entered into contractual agreement that requires it to take steps to restrict third-party uses of the Item. In order for this Rights Statement to be conclusive, the organization that intends to make the Item available should provide a link to a page detailing the contractual restrictions that apply to the use of the Item.

NO COPYRIGHT—NON-COMMERCIAL USE ONLY
This Rights Statement can only be used for Works that are in the Public Domain and have been digitized in a public-private partnership as part of which, the partners have agreed to limit commercial uses of this digital representation of the Work by third parties. It has been developed specifically to allow the inclusion of

FIGURE 10. RightsStatements.org Rights Statements

Source: RightsStatements.org, "Rights Statements," https://rightsstatements.org/en/. These statements are licensed under a CC0 Public Domain Dedication.

FIGURE 10. *RightsStatements.org Rights Statements (continued)*

Works that have been digitized as part of the partnerships between European Libraries and Google, but can in theory be applied to Items that have been digitized in similar public-private partnerships.

NO COPYRIGHT—OTHER KNOWN LEGAL RESTRICTIONS
This Rights Statement should be used for Items that are in the Public Domain but that cannot be freely re-used as the consequence of known legal restrictions that prevent the organization that intends to make the Item available from allowing free re-use of the Item, such as cultural heritage or traditional cultural expression protections. In order for this Rights Statement to be conclusive, the organization that intends to make the Item available should provide a link to a page detailing the legal restrictions that limit re-use of the Item.

NO COPYRIGHT—UNITED STATES
This Rights Statement should be used for Items for which the organization that intends to make the Item available has determined are free of copyright under the laws of the United States. This Rights Statement should not be used for Orphan Works (which are assumed to be in-copyright) or for Items where the organization that intends to make the Item available has not undertaken an effort to ascertain the copyright status of the underlying Work.

Other Rights Statements

COPYRIGHT NOT EVALUATED
This Rights Statement should be used for Items for which the copyright status is unknown and for which the organization that intends to make the Item available has not undertaken an effort to determine the copyright status of the underlying Work.

COPYRIGHT UNDETERMINED
This Rights Statement should be used for Items for which the copyright status is unknown and for which the organization that has made the Item available has undertaken an (unsuccessful) effort to determine the copyright status of the underlying Work. Typically, this Rights Statement is used when the organization is missing key facts essential to making an accurate copyright status determination.

NO KNOWN COPYRIGHT
This Rights Statement should be used for Items for which the copyright status has not been determined conclusively, but for which the organization that intends to make the Item available has reasonable cause to believe that the underlying Work is not covered by copyright or related rights anymore. This Rights Statement should not be used for Orphan Works (which are assumed to be in-copyright) or for Items where the organization that intends to make the Item available has not undertaken an effort to ascertain the copyright status of the underlying Work.

Patron Responsibility

In simple terms, archivists guide patrons in assessing who owns the copyright to materials, but users are ultimately responsible for acquiring proper permissions. When publishing or using materials in a public forum, patrons must comply with copyright laws and ask permission from the repository or other owner. Experienced patrons know how to assess and navigate copyright, but many have little to no experience with such issues. Regardless of experience, patrons rely on archivists' knowledge and expertise when assessing copyright. While archivists maintain an active role in compliance, archivists must not assume direct responsibility for how users do or do not use materials.

In general, many researchers take the initiative and are willing to adhere to and respect copyright. To emphasize the importance of copyright, repositories publicize copyright laws on websites, in finding aids, or in metadata for digital objects. Although archives provide these explanatory notes in informational outlets about collections, not all researchers read the notes. If they do, many do not fully understand the meanings of the notes. Reference archivists offer interpretations when necessary.

Some information about copyright is not available to the public. For example, a finding aid might not include a donor's contact information even if the donor is the permission granter. This type of condition is determined on acquisition, along with a procedure for contacting the appropriate person for permission.

Overall, patrons are ultimately responsible for adhering to copyright, but they can best accomplish compliance in consultation with an archivist. Through working with patrons and collections, archivists often gain extensive knowledge that they can immediately pass on to researchers. Other times, archivists will consult the appropriate resources to assist patrons. Primarily, these

---

Living Refugee Archive Take Down Policy

In accordance with current UK law, we will endeavour to make every effort to gain copyright clearance for resources appearing on the Living Refugee Archive. We will respond promptly to any enquiries in relation to copyright compliance and, if asked, are prepared to take down content at the request of the copyright holder once we have been informed.

New York University Division of Libraries Notice and Takedown Policy

Digitized collections are made accessible for purposes of education and research. NYU Libraries have given attribution to rights holders when possible; however, due to the nature of archival collections, we are not always able to identify this information.

If you hold the rights to materials in our digitized collections that are unattributed, please let us know so that we may maintain accurate information about these materials.

If you are a rights holder and are concerned that you have found material on this website for which you have not granted permission (or is not covered by a copyright exception under US copyright laws), you may request the removal of the material from our site by submitting a notice, with the elements described below, to speccoll@nyu.edu.

Please include the following in your notice:

1. Identification of the material that you believe to be infringing and information sufficient to permit us to locate the material;
2. Your contact information, such as an address, telephone number, and email address;
3. A statement that you are the owner, or authorized to act on behalf of the owner, of an exclusive right that is allegedly infringed and that you have a good-faith belief that use of the material in the manner complained of is not authorized by the copyright owner, its agent, or the law;
4. A statement that the information in the notification is accurate and made under penalty of perjury, and
5. Your physical or electronic signature.

Upon receiving a notice that includes the details listed above, we will remove the allegedly infringing material from public view while we assess the issues identified in your notice.

FIGURE 11. Examples of Takedown Statements

Sources: Living Refugee Archive, "Take Down Policy," 2018, www.livingrefugeearchive.org/digital-library/copyright/copyright-policy/, captured at https://perma.cc/UDX6-U3S5; New York University Libraries, "Notice and Takedown Policy," http://library.nyu.edu/about/visiting/policies/notice-takedown-policy/.

interactions remain most relevant to the individual cases regarding use, but archivists can also use these situations as opportunities to educate users about how archives respect and address copyright concerns.

Restrictions

In addition to adhering to legal regulations, archives impose other types of restrictions on collections based on donor stipulations, preservation needs, or institutional mandate. Archivists typically establish these restrictions during the acquisition process and as a result of interactions with donors, but some additional restriction needs are discovered through processing. Restrictions can encompass all or parts of collections and ought to be clearly communicated, readily enforceable, and easily identifiable.[31]

Preferably, mandatory and terminal time limits for restrictions permit archivists to plan for future access. There are no set standards for imposing these limits, which can range from a few years until decades after a person's death. In select cases, restrictions may be imposed in perpetuity, especially in the case of legal collections or confidential institutional records. Particularly for the latter, archivists can consult their institutional or external legal counsel to establish any necessary restrictions.[32]

Unless processing archivists conduct item-level reviews of documents (a time-consuming and rarely undertaken effort), it is important to acknowledge that confidential information can be hidden and undiscovered in openly accessible materials.[33] To alleviate potential issues, materials might be reviewed before point of access. Alternately, the registration form can include a statement stipulating that the user does not have permission to share confidential information with others and must bring these materials to the archivist's attention. To assist staff members who retrieve materials, sealing or clearly marking boxes that contain restricted or sensitive information adds extra protection to prevent inadvertent access.

Reference archivists are both legally and ethically responsible to ensure that they do not allow access to restricted materials.[34] Even when access constraints are communicated through finding aids or websites, archivists cannot rely on patrons to review these resources thoroughly. By being familiar with the restrictions their institution typically imposes, understanding how to find that documentation, and reviewing collection information before researcher access, archivists will be well informed and consistent in adhering to appropriate regulations.

Donors

During the acquisition of a collection, archivists initiate discussions with donors to determine whether the donation includes any confidential materials. Often, archivists discourage imposing restrictions but they also recognize the necessity in certain situations. A donor might request limits on access so that they can retain intellectual property rights, stipulate that the repository can make portions or all of the collection publicly available after the donor's death, or ask that the repository not digitize or share material online without permission.[35]

The donor may ask to allow access or use only with permission from the donor or the donor's designee. In these instances, the donor must provide preferred contact information and stipulate whether they can be contacted directly by the researcher or whether the archivist will serve as the intermediary. If such a procedure is put in place, archivists must check with the donor periodically to ensure that contact information is current or updated if conditions have changed.

Two examples illustrate the complicated nature of complying with donor restrictions. In 2008, a journalist requested access to a collection at the University of Illinois at Chicago (UIC) to investigate rumors that presidential candidate Barack Obama was connected to Bill Ayers, an activist and cofounder of the Weather Underground, a radical leftist organization. Simultaneously, the university received a call from the donor, and on further investigation, discovered that there was no final deed of gift and that donor-specified restrictions to maintain privacy of certain records had not been carried out. UIC chose to temporarily close the collection to address these issues, and subsequently the journalist wrote an editorial denouncing that decision and conjecturing a cover-up. Thrown into a national spotlight, citizens, journalists, and others demanded access and bombarded UIC with emails and calls. UIC staff diligently went through the entire collection and redacted a small percentage of sensitive materials. Fourteen days after the journalist's editorial, the collection was reopened. This incident prompted UIC to evaluate policies and procedures related to reference, access, acquisition, and processing.[36]

Boston College (BC) was served with a subpoena on May 5, 2011, ordering the college to provide oral interviews from its closed Belfast Project collection to the British government. While trying to navigate both U.S. and British laws, BC was caught in an ethical and legal dilemma "with a subpoena in one hand and a donor agreement in the other." The donor-imposed restrictions closed the collection with the stipulation that access be provided only if the interviewee died or gave permission. The interviews included those of members of Northern Ireland's paramilitary group the Provisional IRA, who spoke under the condition of confidentiality because stories discussed "murder, conspiracy, and accusation." To adhere to the donor agreement, BC fought against fulfilling the initial and subsequent subpoenas, and the donors/interviewers also became involved. The legal issues lasted several years, and eventually some of the interviews were turned over to law enforcement authorities.[37] This case demonstrates the difficulties involved in situations that entail both deeds of gift and the law and that require an institution to determine to what extent they must protect donor-imposed restrictions and collections.

Institutional Policy

Organizations temporarily or permanently restrict records created as part of their daily operations. If the archives exists as part of a state or federal government agency, some of these records may be subject to FOIA requests. However, both public and private institutions reserve the right to restrict records related to administrative decisions and functions, financial or legal affairs, trademarks or proprietary information, and other reasons.[38] Archivist Bruce Dearstyne nicely summarizes examples: "A church, for instance, may be sensitive about information on relationships between clergy and church members; a company may worry about unflattering information on trade practices; associations may not want their membership lists disclosed, even if they are quite old; or an individual may not want information gained in confidence to be disclosed."[39]

The purpose of these restrictions is to protect proprietary information. These types of restrictions typically are determined by the individual repository or codified by a higher governing group. For example, an institution of worship may be governed by the larger denomination, or an academic institution may be part of a statewide university system or board of regents. Although records generally remain accessible to institutional employees when needed for job functions, some documentation may be restricted to select internal staff, such as instances in which legal information is available only to the legal department.

In one test of institutional policy, the University of Oregon in 2015 provided copies of approximately 22,000 digital files to a researcher, who subsequently posted content from an alleged confidential communication online. Questions arose about the university's records management practices, which parties had responsibility for vetting records before transfer, patron privacy, the researcher's responsibility to maintain confidentiality of records, and archivists' roles in mediating access. This resulted in a media frenzy, a demand from upper university administrators for the researcher to return the files, and the disciplining of two archivists. As noted by then-SAA President Kathleen Roe, most of what the public knew was from media stories and, because it also involved a personnel issue, many details were not shared.[40] In particular, this case highlights the immense challenges archivists have in vetting and processing born-digital records as well as the difficulties of working with an institution's administration on appraisal and acquisition.

Redactions

There are many instances in which only parts of documents or files must be restricted. When this occurs, archivists have the option of redacting portions of materials to allow patrons access to non-sensitive information. This opens avenues for access but also requires extensive work.

Verifying materials that have both confidential and nonconfidential information necessitates an item-level review. When processing archivists have restricted materials within a collection, they can perform a cursory or item-level review to determine whether redacting portions of documents is merited. Because time is often a factor, this same approach can be conducted when a research request is made rather than as a standard procedure that applies to each collection. If reviewed, specific information can be redacted or not made accessible. As with FOIA requests, reproductions of physical or digital documents can be provided with certain words, phrases, sentences, or paragraphs concealed to protect confidential information.

If redaction of physical or digital items is not feasible, another option is for archivists to review files and extract the requested information for the researcher. This is less time-consuming than concealing specific information on physical items or digital files but still requires effort. However, this also enables archivists to provide researchers with answers to inquiries while maintaining confidentiality of records.[41]

Redacting materials is a time-consuming task, but there are times when some information is better than none. Individual repositories can determine whether this is a feasible option overall or establish parameters for when redacting is an appropriate measure for access to semi-confidential materials.

Preservation

At times, restrictions are imposed because of the physical state rather than the content of materials. Many preservation tasks are handled during collection processing, but others require in-depth efforts. Examples of these include rolled-up documents that would break if flattened, torn photographs, books with bindings that are loose or falling apart, or moldy items. Limiting or withholding access to materials in need of preservation or conservation alleviates further damage from handling. Users usually understand these concerns, and archivists assess access options when discovered or on request.

Unprocessed Collections

Restricting access to unprocessed collections is a common practice. The lack of intellectual or physical control means that there is a heightened risk of theft, and more burden is placed on researchers and reference staff members to locate relevant materials. There are also benefits to opening unprocessed collections: patrons can access more materials and inform archives staff members about the contents of those collections. Many institutions have lifted or relaxed this restriction to allow greater access to more collections, particularly because not all collections pose a risk of theft. Access to unorganized materials need not be an all-or-nothing proposition but can be flexible based on institutional practices, collection contents, and/or patron demand.

There are many approaches to allow or restrict access to unprocessed collections. Small collections are conducive to access if they are not processed, unless all or most items are of high value. Users often do not mind sifting through several boxes if it means advancing their research. Indeed, they might discover materials they would not have discovered if the collection had been processed. Larger collections are more challenging, as users may not want to slog through dozens of boxes that, if processed, might be whittled down to only a few.

Access to collections that are being processed or digitized is also complicated. With in-process collections, it can be difficult to locate relevant materials or return items to their proper location. Digitization usually occurs after a collection is processed, but permitting access can disrupt the workflows or materials may not be maintained in their order if used by a researcher, which requires extra time to reorganize. Granting access in either of these situations requires further attention to document what is used. In any of these cases, repositories can still collect data about what is requested to help inform processing or digitization priorities.

Conclusion

Policies, laws, and regulations surrounding legal issues and restrictions are complex. Because few archivists are trained as lawyers, this brief introduction is intended to inform reference professionals about the possible limitations regarding access to materials. The multitude of laws, interpretations of those laws, and vast array of materials to which they are applied can seem daunting to any archivist. Reference professionals must have basic knowledge of these regulations as they apply to their repository and collections to help guide patrons. However, they ought to also recognize when it is appropriate to consult administrative staff, originating departments or agencies, or legal counsel to ensure the proper administration of access and reproductions. Further, it is imperative to regularly review professional literature and relevant legislation to ensure that staff knowledge and policies are kept current.

NOTES

[1] Menzi Behrnd-Klodt, *Navigating Legal Issues in Archives* (Chicago: Society of American Archivists, 2008), 4.
[2] U.S. Department of State, "Freedom of Information Act"; Behrnd-Klodt, *Navigating Legal Issues in Archives*, 156.
[3] For a full list, see FOIA.gov, www.foia.gov/faq.html#exemptions.
[4] National Freedom of Information Coalition, "State Freedom of Information Laws," www.nfoic.org/coalitions/state-foi-resources/state-freedom-of-information-laws.
[5] U.S. Department of Education, "FERPA Regulations," https://studentprivacy.ed.gov/node/548/.
[6] Tim Pyatt, "Balancing Issues of Privacy and Confidentiality in College and University Archives," in *College and University Archives: Readings in Theory and Practice*, ed. Christopher J. Prom and Ellen D. Swain (Chicago: Society of American Archivists, 2008), 213.
[7] U.S. Department of Education, "FERPA General Guidance for Students," www2.ed.gov/policy/gen/guid/fpco/ferpa/students.html, captured at https://perma.cc/M9XT-SGGH.
[8] U.S. Department of Education, "Family Educational Rights and Privacy Act (FERPA)," https://www2.ed.gov/policy/gen/guid/fpco/ferpa/index.html, captured at https://perma.cc/W2YG-MD6B.
[9] U.S. Department of Education, "Family Educational Rights and Privacy Act (FERPA)."
[10] Lauren Camera, "Hollins University Removes Access to Yearbooks with Racist Images," *U.S. News and World Report,* April 3, 2019, www.usnews.com/news/education-news/articles/2019-04-03/hollins-university-removes-access-to-yearbooks-with-racist-images, captured at https://perma.cc/7CKB-9JX2.
[11] U.S. Department of Health and Human Services, Office for Civil Rights, "HIPAA for Professionals," September 10, 2015, www.hhs.gov/hipaa/for-professionals/index.html?language=es, captured at https://perma.cc/9HZH-RUUT.
[12] Society of American Archivists, "Issue Brief: Health Information Portability and Accountability Act," updated September 26, 2019, www2.archivists.org/statements/issue-brief-health-information-portability-and-accountability-act, captured at https://perma.cc/4UFU-YBQE.
[13] Emily R. Gustainis and Phoebe Evans Letocha, "The Practice of Privacy," in *Innovation, Collaboration, and Models: Proceedings of the CLIR Cataloging Hidden Special Collections and Archives Symposium*, ed. Cheryl Oestreicher (Philadelphia: Council on Library and Information Resources, 2015), 163–176, www.clir.org/pubs/reports/pub169/, captured at https://perma.cc/3C2Q-P3AU.
[14] U.S. Department of Justice, "Privacy Act of 1974," updated January 15, 2020, www.justice.gov/opcl/privacy-act-1974.
[15] U.S. Department of Justice, "Privacy Act of 1974"; Behrnd-Klodt, *Navigating Legal Issues in Archives*, 159.
[16] U.S. Department of Justice, "Privacy Compliance Process," updated June 11, 2019, https://www.justice.gov/opcl/privacy-compliance-process.
[17] Behrnd-Klodt, *Navigating Legal Issues in Archives*, 190–191.
[18] Behrnd-Klodt, 224–226; Heather Briston, "Understanding Copyright Law," in *Rights in the Digital Era*, ed. Menzi Behrnd-Klodt and Christopher J. Prom (Chicago: Society of American Archivists, 2015), 15–16.
[19] Santamaria, *Extensible Processing for Archives and Special Collections*, 94.
[20] Behrnd-Klodt, *Navigating Legal Issues in Archives*, 228, 237–239; Peter B. Hirtle, Emily Hudson, and Andrew T. Kenyon, *Copyright and Cultural Institutions: Guidelines for Digitization for U.S. Libraries, Archives, and Museums* (Ithaca, NY: Cornell University Library, 2009), 90.
[21] Hirtle, Hudson, and Kenyon, *Copyright and Cultural Institutions*, 98; Behrnd-Klodt, *Navigating Legal Issues in Archives*, 234; Copyright.gov, "More Information on Fair Use," www.copyright.gov/fair-use/more-info.html, captured at https://perma.cc/JDC4-4NMU.
[22] Mike Masnick, "Getty Images Sued Yet Again for Trying to License Public Domain Images," *Techdirt*, April 1, 2019, www.techdirt.com/articles/20190329/15352641901/getty-images-sued-yet-again-trying-to-license-public-domain-images.shtml, captured at https://perma.cc/V35S-38PP.

23. Emma Pettit, "A Harvard Scientist Commissioned Photos of Slaves in 1850. A Lawsuit Says the University Is Still Profiting from Them," *Chronicle of Higher Education*, March 20, 2019, www.chronicle.com/article/A-Harvard-Scientist/245939, captured at https://perma.cc/H8RQ-V8GZ.

24. Behrnd-Klodt, *Navigating Legal Issues in Archives*, 208; World Intellectual Property Organization, "WIPO Copyright Treaty (WCT)," www.wipo.int/treaties/en/ip/wct/index.html.

25. Copyright.gov, "Section 1201 Exemptions to Prohibition Against Circumvention of Technological Measures Protecting Copyrighted Works," www.copyright.gov/1201/2018/, https://perma.cc/7M96-MH9Z; Hirtle, Hudson, and Kenyon, *Copyright and Cultural Institutions*, 76.

26. "Rules and Regulations," *Federal Register* 83, no. 208 (October 26, 2018): 54013–54019, 54023–54025, www.govinfo.gov/content/pkg/FR-2018-10-26/pdf/2018-23241.pdf, captured at https://perma.cc/A3JX-93A3.

27. Behrnd-Klodt, *Navigating Legal Issues in Archives*, 208; "Technology, Education, and Copyright Harmonization Act of 2001," Pub. L. No. 107–273 (2002), www.congress.gov/bill/107th-congress/senate-bill/487.

28. Copyright.gov, "Revising Section 108: Copyright Exceptions for Libraries and Archives | U.S. Copyright Office," https://www.copyright.gov/policy/section108/, captured at https://perma.cc/TTL9-6NFE.

29. Behrnd-Klodt, *Navigating Legal Issues in Archives*, 237–238.

30. Hirtle, Hudson, and Kenyon, *Copyright and Cultural Institutions*, 199.

31. Susan K. Anderson, "Research Use: Ethics, Restrictions, and Privacy," in Wythe, *Museum Archives*, 58; Frank Boles, *Selecting and Appraising Archives and Manuscripts* (Chicago: Society of American Archivists, 2005), 141.

32. Pyatt, "Balancing Issues of Privacy and Confidentiality," 224.

33. Pyatt, "Balancing Issues of Privacy and Confidentiality," 213.

34. Menzi Behrnd-Klodt, "Lawyers, Archivists and Librarians: United or Divided in the Pursuit of Justice?," in *Public Services Issues with Rare and Archival Law Materials*, ed. Michael Widener (New York: Haworth Information Press, 2001), 121.

35. Aaron D. Purcell, *Donors and Archives: A Guidebook for Successful Programs* (Lanham, MD: Rowman & Littlefield, 2015), 18.

36. Valerie Harris and Kathryn Stine, "Politically Charged Records: A Case Study with Recommendations for Providing Access to a Challenging Collection," *American Archivist* 74, no. 2 (2011): 663–651, https://doi.org/10.17723/aarc.74.2.f252r28174251525.

37. Christine Anne George, "Archives Beyond the Pale: Negotiating Legal and Ethical Entanglements after the Belfast Project," *American Archivist* 76, no. 1 (2013): 44–67, https://doi.org/10.17723/aarc.76.1.x34p8k7848512274; "Paramilitaries 'Misled' over Boston College Tapes Confidentiality," *News Letter,* June 28, 2016, https://www.newsletter.co.uk/news/crime/paramilitaries-misled-over-boston-college-tapes-confidentiality-1-7453552, captured at https://perma.cc/S4AN-XUUK.

38. Anderson, "Research Use" in Wythe, *Museum Archives*, 56.

39. Dearstyne, *Archival Enterprise*, 181; see also Leumas, Newcomer, and Treanor, *Managing Diocesan Archives and Records*, 7–8.

40. Kathleen Roe, "Addressing Archival Issues: University of Oregon Records Release—and Beyond," *Off the Record* (blog), February 17, 2015, https://offtherecord.archivists.org/2015/02/17/addressing-archival-issues-university-of-oregon-records-release-and-beyond/, captured at https://perma.cc/M6B6-3RTJ; Society of American Archivists, Issues and Advocacy Section, "The University of Oregon Situation," www2.archivists.org/groups/issues-and-advocacy-section/the-university-of-oregon-situation, captured at https://perma.cc/A729-MSBF.

41. Anderson, "Research Use," 60–61.

10

Use Policies

So far, this book has described preparing and providing access to collections. Once access policies have been determined and materials have been provided, the focus turns to use, whether for private or public purposes. Within this context, "use" is defined as how a researcher utilizes materials beyond the immediate control of the archives, such as for private study, publishing, exhibits, licensing, or similar purposes. Providing clear options and policies for use provides researchers with better opportunities to deeply engage and share materials with broader audiences.

Determining use policies depends primarily on repository type, purpose of use, and copyright. While the researcher is responsible for reviewing finding aids or other collection information to assess potential publication use, reference archivists conduct a final review to ensure compliance. Consulting donor agreements, specific laws or regulations, and institutional policies are the initial steps required to determine permissions for use.

Types of Uses

Permitting researchers to publicly share materials from archival collections is a common practice. Researchers often request permission to publish images or information from collections for television, print or online journalism, films, books, exhibits, research papers, and a vast array of projects. Encouraging such activities affords great benefits for the archives, as these uses expand the reach of the collections and expose materials to broader audiences.

Personal

Typically, personal use occurs when any researcher requests copies or reproductions for private reasons. Archivists need not know what that personal use is, as long as the patron agrees not to publish without permission. Often, researchers want to take time to thoroughly examine the contents of materials without the constraint of reading room hours. Some requests for personal use can also be to share materials with a small group of people, such as genealogists working on family trees or a school's alumni interested in photos of their activities.

Commercial

Commercial use is defined as materials being used to produce something with the intention of making a profit. Most commonly, these are outputs such as books, films, or articles. However, there are many other types of commercial outputs, such as advertising, memorabilia, and ephemera, which includes calendars, posters, postcards, textiles, and artwork.

Noncommercial

Noncommercial use includes use for anything that is not meant to make a profit. A few examples are exhibits, free publications such as booklets or pamphlets, presentations, events or programs, multimedia displays, and scholarly articles. These uses are different from personal uses because they are meant for public consumption.

Educational

Using materials for educational purposes is common and encompasses a wide variety of outputs. Textbooks, particularly history textbooks, include reproductions or quotes from materials as a way to introduce students to primary sources. Educators also acquire copies of materials to use in class discussions or assignments.

Internal

A parent institution, department, or affiliate group—such as a board of directors or trustees—may request to use materials in advertising, publicity, fundraising campaigns, social media promotions, institutional publications, annual reports, or other internal or external outputs focused on the institution.

Reproductions

Providing reproductions of materials is a long-standing and standard practice of archival repositories. For decades, paper photocopies or microforms were the only or primary options. As digitization technology developed, institutions added the option of digital reproductions. Institutions must balance users' needs with internal capabilities to accommodate expectations, taking into consideration staffing, technological capabilities, format and delivery, preservation, copyright, fee structure, and planned use.

Forms

Offering a separate form for reproduction requests indicates to the user that there are additional stipulations beyond normal reading room use. The basics of a reproduction agreement include user contact information, the type of reproduction (paper or electronic), preferred form of delivery (mail, email, shared drive, etc.), lists of all items desired, and a copyright notice (see Appendix E for examples of reproduction forms). For digital reproductions, users can also specify file type and file size. When applicable, the archives can specify maximum quantity allowed, fees, and other stipulations, such as a disclaimer that the repository will not reproduce items if doing so will damage the original materials.

Good forms are thorough yet simple to fill out, with clear directions on how to identify specific items for reproduction within collections. A good practice is to explain the proper procedure for identifying materials for reproduction before patrons consult collections. A clear identification process ensures accuracy in itemizing the request while maintaining the order of materials. Typical procedures include providing flags or clips to mark items, staggering items in the folder, noting box and/or folder numbers, and including accurate descriptions. Sometimes, patrons think that removing an item from a folder or box without marking the item's place is the proper procedure to request reproductions, and archivists need to correct these notions at the outset. If removals inadvertently occur, archivists need to remind patrons of proper practices and discourage them from further removing items from folders.

Formats

Part of the duplication process involves determining the format of reproductions, whether physical or digital. Although paper copies were once the norm, many institutions have reduced or eliminated paper as an option and provide digital copies. Most patrons appreciate digital copies because they can choose to view or print, but some patrons continue to prefer physical reproductions. Repositories retain the prerogative to offer only the formats that they are capable of providing. It is helpful to label or stamp both physical and digital copies with the collection name and box and folder numbers as well as a copyright statement. This information helps with citations and enables patrons to easily identify where the research was obtained.

With digital copies, it may be necessary for the archivist and patron to discuss the purpose of use to determine the appropriate file type. Low-resolution files are adequate for private study, while high-resolution copies are often necessary for publication or other public use. Digital copies can be watermarked with the same notices that are stamped on physical copies. This requires extra steps but helps prevent patrons from publishing the content without permission.

Delivery

Delivery options depend on whether reproductions are physical or digital. Physical copies can be handed directly to the patron, arranged to be picked up at a later time, or mailed. There are multiple ways to provide digital copies, such as in an email; on flash drives, CDs, or external hard drives; or via shared folders available through cloud storage (e.g., Google Drive or Dropbox). Digital reproductions can be organized into appropriately titled folders with the same designations used for physical copies. This helps staff members track progress on fulfilling the request and offers easier retrieval and organization for patrons.

Providing copies of born-digital or digitized materials inherently has unique challenges. Sometimes, users assume that if materials are already in digital format, archivists can just automatically copy and deliver them to the patron. In some instances, this may be the appropriate procedure. However, if there are copyright, privacy, or other concerns, these records are susceptible to the same parameters applied to analog collections. As an analogy, copying all the files to a folder equates to letting a patron leave the repository with a box (or more) of materials. Due to the increase in born-digital and hybrid collections, repositories must establish written policies with set parameters.

Self-Service

Traditionally, archives staff members make reproductions of materials to limit handling damage to materials and maintain control over what is reproduced. Many institutions have reduced or eliminated paper copies, which opens up more self-service options, such as overhead scanners in the reading room, personal scanners, or mobile phones and cameras to take digital images.

Some repositories provide an overhead scanner in the reading room for patron use, often for no fee. There are many benefits to this option, as patrons produce and save reproductions at the point of need while also maintaining their privacy. In addition, this option relieves staff time and allows the archives to direct resources away from the routine procedure of making reproductions. Personal scanners are becoming less common, but some repositories still allow this practice with permission. There is the chance that patrons will not adhere to proper handling procedures, but providing specific instructions goes far to alleviate potential damage.

Many users bring a mobile device or camera to take digital images. Some users install scanning apps on their mobile devices, and these apps provide more options for organizing digital content. Reference archivists can provide a slip or marker to include in each photo to document the institution, collection/box/folder, and copyright. These images are usually lower resolution, and this option is less secure because patrons could publish or use images in ways that are not allowed by the repository; however, it does allow quicker access to research for the patron. To accommodate those who do not have a device, institutions can dedicate a camera or mobile device for patron use. This option may require a staff member to download and share the images, and the images can be watermarked with proper identification.

For more information about determining procedures, a good resource is *"Capture and Release": Digital Cameras in the Reading Room*, a report by Lisa Miller, Steven K. Galbraith, and the RLG Partnership Working Group on Streamlining Photography and Scanning, which was published by the OCLC. Figure 12, which shows a chart from the report, provides a quick glance at the different facets of use, self-service, and staff-provided options.[1] Ultimately, a thorough assessment of the various risks informs institutional policies.

\multicolumn{4}{c	}{**Faceted Camera Use Grid**}
Facet	**Shutter-bug**	**Exposed**	**Camera-shy**
Traditional photocopying (possible baseline for digital camera policy)	• Self-service	• Self-service after staff review	• All copying done by staff
Equipment	• No flash, no lights • Allow flatbed scanners • Allow and/or provide copy stand, tripod, extension cords, stepstool, etc. • Repository supplies camera or self-service overhead book scanner in addition to allowing patron's camera	• Patron's camera • Limits on supporting equipment (copy stands, tripods, cords, etc.)—some pieces allowed, others not • No flatbed scanners	• Repository's camera only (and possibly other equipment supplied by repository)
Photography space	• In reading room at any station	• In reading room at designated stations, usually close to reference desk	• Separate room
Photography rules	\multicolumn{3}{l	}{• No standing on tables or chairs • No rearrangement of furniture • No materials on floor • Remain behind table, facing forward at all times • Set camera to "mute" • Do not disturb others • No photographs of reading room, staff, or patrons}
Appointments	• Appointment not required	• Appointment made during visit	• Appointment made in writing in advance
Staff review of collection materials	• Part of standard staff surveillance of patrons in reading room	• Patron must verbally notify reference attendant each time camera is used and show attendant the materials being photographed	• Patron must formally indicate and curatorial staff formally review all materials • Camera stays in locker until approval is given • Same-day approval may not be possible
Materials handling rules	\multicolumn{3}{l	}{• Preservation needs always trump photography needs • Do not manipulate materials to achieve a better image • Do not press down on materials or bindings • Manuscript materials must always be flat on the table and not held up in air • Loose materials must remain in their folder and in order at all times • Photograph materials from one folder at a time • Volumes should not be laid flat—book cradles will be provided • Weight bags and snakes are available • Do not fold pages • Do not remove fasteners—ask for staff assistance • Do not remove items from sleeves, mats, etc.}

FIGURE 12. Faceted Camera Use Grid

Source: Lisa Miller, Steven K. Galbraith, and the RLG Partnership Working Group on Streamlining Photography and Scanning, Table 1. Faceted Camera Use Grid, *"Capture and Release": Digital Cameras in the Reading Room* (Dublin, OH: OCLC Research, February 2010), 8–10, www.oclc.org/content/dam/research/publications/library/2010/2010-05.pdf, captured at https://perma.cc/MC64-XKT4.

Faceted Camera Use Grid			
Facet	**Shutter-bug**	**Exposed**	**Camera-shy**
Quantity limits	• No limits	• No more than 50 pages or 20 percent (whichever is smaller) of any manuscript or book • No entire book, manuscript box, or collection, nor substantial portions of them • Please limit number of photographs to a reasonable amount • Photographs are meant to alleviate photocopying and supplement note taking, not to create a complete personal copy	• Limit to established number of shots per day • Patron's images may be reviewed during checkout to enforce quantity limit
Other limits	• Oversize items or anything that does not safely fit on table • Fragile or damaged items • No materials received on interlibrary loan, unless lending library permits • Only materials checked out to the patron using the camera • If not allowed, staff may digitize at standard fees • Repository reserves right to deny permission for any collection materials at its discretion		
Copyright	• Copyright notice (and citation) in all shots (paper strip transparency) • Digital copies are for personal research use only • Repository displays a copyright warning where digital camera requests are accepted and on digital camera policy forms		
Paperwork (in addition to forms completed by all patrons)	• Camera use agreement included on registration form • Separate camera use agreement with copyright declaration (renewed annually/per visit/per day)	• Patron provides list of collections (plus camera use agreement)	• Patron provides list of each item (plus camera use agreement) • Written request before visit
Fees	• None	• Minimal fee (per visit, per shot) • Fees for equipment supplied by repository	• Fee equals or exceeds cost of photocopies
Publication	• Publication requires permission of the copyright holder	• Images for publication or distribution must be ordered through the library at set fees	• Images taken by patron may not be published in print or on internet • Publication requires written permission from repository
Citations	• Patron is responsible for recording complete citations for each shot • Subsequent orders for high-resolution images cannot be processed without complete citations • Source repository template in all shots (paper strip or transparency, often included with copyright notice)		
Other	• Camera privileges can be revoked at any time if rules are not followed • Provide tips on taking good images and creating complete citations • In some cases, repository receives copies of all photographs		

Preservation

An aspect of document reproduction is considering preservation needs. Including a disclaimer in reproduction policies and forms permits refusal to copy items when damage may occur. Torn, fragile, or bound items may not withstand scanning. When possible, utilizing overhead or book-edge scanners, or photographing with a digital camera, alleviates some of those issues. Some oversize or audiovisual materials may require using an outside vendor to perform duplication services.

Fees

Fees are primarily instituted to recover time and labor costs, directly contribute to the budget, deter requests for excessive quantities, and place value on materials. There are no standard rules regarding implementing fees, and determining whether to charge fees is based on a variety of conditions. If the goal is to make a profit or to contribute to operating costs, implementing an extensive fee structure makes sense. If the goal is to generally share materials within the community, perhaps lower fees or free reproductions are the best options. Regardless of how fees are structured, making them logical and communicating them clearly through forms and websites helps users determine how many reproductions to request.

Some questions to consider when establishing a fee structure include:

- Does the money help fund the institution and services?
- Do other institutional departments charge for services?
- Will fees be based on patron type, such as charging external but not internal constituents?
- Are charges meant to limit the number of reproductions requested?
- Do charges include staff time and labor, or is that extra?
- Do charges include the cost of supplies (e.g., DVDs, paper)?
- Are there different charges based on original format or final output?

These points are helpful when establishing a new fee structure or reviewing existing fees. Behind the setting of fees are deeper considerations. Although it is common practice to charge for services, a consideration is the return on investment. This is highly dependent on the institution's mission, staffing capabilities, technological infrastructure, and goals of access. For example, perhaps the institution assumes any time, labor, or materials costs in order to keep fees low. Indeed, it is good practice to review assigned fees on a regular basis to ensure that they continue to serve the intended purpose(s).

Larger repositories, in particular, take multiple factors into consideration. Generally, the larger the archives, the more materials, and the more patrons will visit and use those materials, therefore generating more reproduction requests. More requests require more staff, time, labor, technology, and operations. Some institutions have departments dedicated to copying and reproductions. Smaller institutions, particularly ones that have only one staff person, face these same considerations but often have fewer resources to offer a robust service. However, they may dedicate time and energy to research and reproduction if it fits within their mission.

Use fees can be adjusted based on requestor, purpose of use, and/or project type. A sliding scale is appropriate, such as low fees for nonprofit use and higher fees for for-profit use. The user base also informs decisions about which fees are appropriate. At times, charging lower fees or offering free services establishes greater goodwill, such as when exempting K–12 or higher education students, teachers, or the local community. For example, not charging for copying locally published books facilitates community engagement and support; not charging students supports coursework and does not add to their education costs. Charging high fees prohibits many users from requesting permission, and they will seek other sources.[2]

Practices for charging internal users can vary. While some archives may never charge internal constituents, some institutions have an organizational structure in which departments charge each other for services rendered. Charges can be applied to reproductions, research, or other projects based on the number of items, amount of time spent on research, or other factors.

Unauthorized Alterations

Another consideration is the possibility that users may manipulate digital reproductions without express permission. Whether born-digital or digitized, content downloaded or acquired from reproduction requests is subject to modification without permission. Some people believe that if they located something online, it is freely available for use or repurpose. While most users are respectful and comply with the terms of an agreement, it is impossible to fully monitor what happens to the files outside the scope of direct contact with users.

If archivists discover that material has been altered to change the meaning or content or reused with the intent of sharing it publicly, there are different levels of appropriate responses. For example, if a user amends the words in an email record, altering the email's meaning, and then publishes it in an article, that merits a correction or amendment. However, if a genealogist crops a photo to share with family members, that constitutes a benign use that is not worth the effort to correct. Although a registration form can stipulate that items cannot be altered, there are few official channels to ensure enforcement. Most infractions are minor and require little or no intervention, but others can escalate. If a researcher repurposes altered content on a public website, changes the meaning or presentation of materials that could cause harm to others, or misrepresents the institution and its holdings through publications, those merit involving legal counsel to address the situation. This is rare and unlikely to occur but merits mention as a worst-case scenario.

Copyright and Public Domain

Perhaps the most important aspect of reproduction and use is copyright. Technically, users are ultimately responsible for adhering to or securing copyright permissions. Reference professionals, however, remain heavily involved in the process. When materials protected by copyright law are requested for public use, patrons must be informed about the process for securing permission. To begin the process, archivists consult finding aids, collection files, and any existing copyright statements. At times, these steps do not sufficiently address the intricacies. In problematic situations, it is necessary to consult archives supervisors or institutional legal authorities. Although these issues are covered more extensively in Chapter 9, following is a brief overview of how copyright, fair use, and public domain affect use and reproductions specifically.

Depending on the institutional policy, materials covered by copyright may be used by researchers if those materials fall under the fair use provision of the law. Private, nonpermanent, or internal reproductions do not violate copyright law. For example, a student researcher using a copy of a newspaper article for a paper or a one-time presentation that is not recorded or published can claim fair use. Registration or reproduction forms can include a stipulation that permission is granted for that specific use only and that publishing in a public forum requires express permission from the copyright holder.

Compounding the complexity is the availability of online resources. Often, members of the general public assume that if something is available online, it is open for use and/or does not fall under copyright restrictions. When archives enable online access to digitized or born-digital content, a primary component includes evaluating copyright status and including clear and explicit rights statements to indicate whether items are in the public domain or require additional permissions.[3] These statements are meant to be informative, and there is no guarantee that researchers will read and follow stipulations.

The materials in many repositories, especially those in federal and state archives, are already in the public domain and therefore are not susceptible to copyright laws. As digitization efforts proliferate, there is potential for increased confusion about whether content is copyrighted or in the public domain. The metadata of all online content should include a rights statement that informs users of their options for use and publication. Increasingly, repositories choose to make items available for open use with the stipulation of crediting the source.

There are current discussions about the ethical practices of both requiring permission and imposing fees for materials out of copyright. Because the user need not secure permission for items in the public domain, some repositories are moving away from imposing fees in these situations. As described in one analysis, imposing fees "penalized the good citizens" while others reused content without permission or payment.[4] It ought to be noted that this fee waiver applies only to use or licensing purposes and not to scanning or reproduction.

Procedures

Once an archivist has verified that materials can be published, the patron must often sign a form stipulating an agreement to terms. This type of form specifies the patron's contact information, item(s) requested, purpose of use, conditions of use, proper citation and acknowledgement, and associated fees (see Appendix F for examples of permission to publish forms). For some institutions, forms may not be necessary and permission is granted via email or letter. It is preferable to obtain written documentation in case questions arise later.

Once reproductions are in the researcher's possession, the archives no longer has control over how the materials are used. There is no guarantee that the researcher will comply with a signed agreement with explicit stipulations, but often there are no adverse consequences. A carefully worded agreement absolves the archives of any responsibility and makes the researcher's responsibility explicit. At times, permission to use may require working with an institution's legal department, public relations department, or other departments. There also may be contingencies spelled out in donor agreements based on purpose of use. For example, a donor may allow the archives to publish materials from the collection but not allow external organizations or people to have that same privilege.

Digital content requires slightly different procedures. In addition to rights statements, repositories can use other means to protect content. Because of the risk of a patron downloading and using an image without permission, an option is to watermark items (photo, document, or other) with identifying information, such as a logo, abbreviated identification, or full citation. In the print world, most requestors and publishers are conscientious about providing credit lines. Online, however, the situation is much different and credits either disappear or get lost over time as websites change. Institutions must attend to these issues in a pragmatic manner.

Overall, institutions must create clear guidelines for users for requesting permission to publish. As user bases, digital content, and archives use expands, evaluating requirements and purposes helps to balance copyright and user needs with the ultimate goal of widely sharing content consistent with repository scope and purpose.

Loans

Loaning archival materials is a common practice. It may seem contradictory, because archivists often stipulate that items do not leave the facility, but loans increase exposure to a repository and its collections. Loans are an option for exhibits, outreach activities, administrative use, or interlibrary loan. Institutions can decide whether to loan materials and under what conditions and establish clear parameters on transfer. Respecting stipulations that are contained in gift agreements ensures that archivists follow appropriate procedures and conditions for loans.[5]

There are numerous aspects to consider before loaning materials, including cost, security, fragility, and risk. These considerations vary depending on whether loans are internal or external, the length of loan, and the underlying purpose. There are risks, such as materials being damaged or unreturned, but the benefits include facilitating relations with external institutions, internal departments, or donors. Interlibrary loans and exhibits are options for reaching broader constituencies and engaging new audiences.

In 2012, the Association of College and Research Libraries (ACRL) and Rare Books and Manuscripts Section (RBMS) of the American Library Association approved "Guidelines for Interlibrary and Exhibition Loan of Special Collections Materials." Though written for academic institutions, all repository types can refer to these guidelines. To summarize, implementing loan procedures includes writing clear policies, publicizing procedures and requirements, training staff members, establishing clear communication strategies, thoroughly documenting all transactions, designing appropriate security and handling of materials, and creating efficient workflows.[6]

Exhibits are the most common reason to loan materials, which can be circulated within an institution or provided to an external organization. By loaning materials for exhibits, repositories produce goodwill and expose their collections to new audiences. There are several steps involved with borrowing or lending materials for exhibits, including getting requests in writing, establishing manageable timetables, working with an appointed representative from the lending institution, supplying facilities reports, considering whether the original is loaned or a facsimile will suffice, and adequately preparing for packing and transportation.[7] If both the lending and borrowing institutions follow these parameters, a positive experience typically ensues.

Because some patrons are unable to travel to distant archives, interlibrary loan is a helpful service for broadening access. Some institutions will loan archival materials through interlibrary loan services under the condition that they remain in the facility and are accessed within a reading room only. Frequently, the size of collections combined with shipping costs make interlibrary loans prohibitively expensive. Collections that contain only a few items or boxes, as well as books or other singular items, are more conducive to loans.

Loans can also be interdepartmental or used as a vehicle to promote donor relations. Archivists can encourage internal users to view institutional records in the archives, but circumstances may require temporarily returning materials to originating departments for use. This also applies to manuscript collections, and organizations or people may ask to borrow materials from their collection for administrative or personal reasons. In all cases, archivists can consult the requestors to determine whether they need to review original materials in person or whether reproductions are an option.

Attributions

When archives provide materials for use, they also instruct users to identify the item, collection, and repository in all references. The preferred citation information can be posted on a website, in a finding aid, or through a permission to publish form. Generally, a citation includes a short description of the item(s), box and folder numbers, title and/or number of the collection, and repository information. There are times that users, even when instructed, choose not to include a citation. There is often little recourse to enforce this stipulation, but archivists can request updates or modifications to any publications or other outputs.

An acknowledgment is slightly different from a citation. At times, a full citation is not necessary or will not fit in the final product. There are alternatives, such as citing only the collection and repository, for uses that do not accommodate a full citation. For example, a news program may use

---

American Numismatic Society

Item identification, date (if known), collection name (if appropriate), box number, folder number, item number (if appropriate), Archives, American Numismatic Society

Mennonite Church, USA

Mennonite Central Committee Self Help Records, 1962–1972. IX-052. Mennonite Church USA Archives—Goshen. Goshen, Indiana

American Heritage Center, University of Wyoming

Letter, Dennis Allen to Stan Lee, October 26, 1976, box 13, folder 4, Coll. 8302, Stan Lee Papers, American Heritage Center, University of Wyoming

FIGURE 13. Examples of Citation Formats

Sources: American Numismatic Society, "Proper Citation Format," 2016, http://numismatics.org/archive/citationformat/, captured at https://perma.cc/Q8VC-YHCR; Mennonite Church USA, Historical Committee, "Citing Archival Sources," http://mennoniteusa.org/wp-content/uploads/2015/03/CitingMCUSAArchives.pdf; University of Wyoming, American Heritage Center, "Citing Archival Materials," www.uwyo.edu/ahc/research/citation.html.

a photograph in a story, but including a full citation is prohibitive because of how the image will be viewed on a television screen.

For processed collections or other items, it is easy to adhere to the specified format of the citation. However, for those who provide access to unprocessed collections, this can be a challenge. While access to unprocessed collections is helpful, citations will be outdated when the collection is eventually processed. In these situations, asking patrons to include more details might help, but it may not be possible to locate the specific items once the collection is processed.

Ultimately, the goal is to have patrons include an attribution to credit the work of the repository and provide information for future researchers to find materials. There are many variations of how to cite or attribute use of materials (see Figure 13). At a minimum, researchers should be required to reference the repository, but it is preferable that they also include details about the items and collections. Sometimes, an acknowledgment includes the names of the archivist(s) as an expression of gratitude for the assistance.

Conclusion

Enabling use, whether public or private, commercial or nonprofit, through any output, helps to bring positive attention to an archives. Clear procedures and policies ensure that archivists approach permission to use and publish in an equitable and consistent manner. Books, media, films, research papers, articles, and any other use brings materials to wider and new audiences. There are many steps and considerations along the way, including imposing fees, assessing copyright permissions, determining the format of projects, and assessing the outcomes.

NOTES

[1] Lisa Miller, Steven K. Galbraith, and RLG Partnership Working Group on Streamlining Photography and Scanning, *"Capture and Release": Digital Cameras in the Reading Room* (Dublin, OH: OCLC Research, February 2010), www.oclc.org/content/dam/research/publications/library/2010/2010-05.pdf, captured at https://perma.cc/MC64-XKT4.

[2] Michelle Light, "Controlling Goods or Promoting the Public Good: Choices for Special Collections in the Marketplace," *RBM: A Journal of Rare Books, Manuscripts, and Cultural Heritage* 16, no. 1 (2015): 55, https://doi.org/10.5860/rbm.16.1.435; for examples, see Wyoming State Archives, "Use Fee Schedule," 2020, https://wyoarchives.wyo.gov/index.php/get-a-copy/use-fee-schedule, captured at https://perma.cc/87XP-ZYDC; Lyman Museum and Mission House, "Archives Services and Fees," 2014, https://lymanmuseum.org/archives/archives-services-and-fees/, captured at https://perma.cc/H2M4-ZQU9.

[3] Society of American Archivists, "Guide to Implementing Rights Statements from RightsStatements.Org."

[4] Light, "Controlling Goods or Promoting the Public Good," 49.

[5] Pugh, *Providing Reference Services for Archives and Manuscripts*, 242–246.

[6] Association of College and Research Libraries, "ACRL/RBMS Guidelines for Interlibrary and Exhibition Loan of Special Collections Materials," January 2012, www.ala.org/acrl/standards/specialcollections, captured at https://perma.cc/3XG4-2TSZ.

[7] Jessica Lacher-Feldman, *Exhibits in Archives and Special Collections Libraries* (Chicago: Society of American Archivists, 2013), 61–62; Lowell and Nelb, *Architectural Records*, 164–166.

11

Outreach

A primary purpose of outreach is to connect users to resources. In the early days of the profession, archivists were typically perceived to be passive custodians who waited for patrons to find and use collections. Although some forms of outreach and programming activities date back to the early days of historical societies, outreach as a common strategy did not gain professional prominence until the 1970s when archivists started to focus more on the user perspective. Over the next few decades, outreach was elevated to a vital initiative and an integral aspect of archival functions. Today, archivists actively invest in promoting research and use of their collections.

SAA's *Dictionary of Archives Terminology* defines outreach as "the process of identifying and providing services to constituencies with needs relevant to the repository's mission and tailoring services to meet those needs."[1] Although this is largely accurate, outreach extends beyond this definition toward the greater goal of educating patrons about the purpose of archives and their broader societal role. In this respect, outreach constitutes a core component of advocacy.

In a sense, all archival tasks and activities are considered outreach: donor relations, acquisitions, processing, and reference; websites, finding aids, and digital collections; and exhibits, programs, instruction, and presentations. Ultimately, archivists undertake all of these activities to better reach their audiences. By identifying strategies that promote use, archivists build positive images about their repositories, improve public perceptions of archives, develop better relationships, directly address how and why patrons engage with archives, and foster new audiences while strengthening their bonds with existing clientele. Outreach has become more intrinsic to archival and institutional missions and daily duties.[2] This chapter offers suggestions for developing such strategies and summarizes select types of successful outreach programs.

Development and Strategy

Most archives already do outreach activities, whether as part of formal initiatives or on an *ad hoc* basis. Because of varying staffing levels, some repositories may have staff dedicated to outreach; in smaller archives, a sole staff person fulfills this task while simultaneously performing myriad other functions. If the archives is part of a larger institution, staff members might choose whether to incorporate the archives-focused programs into broader organizational outreach activities, initiate their own activities, or pursue some combination. Regardless of approach, developing an outreach and promotion plan will go far in integrating these activities into an archives program.

Overall, outreach is an investment that requires careful consideration. The initial step is deciding on a strategy based on purposes of activities, goals and outcomes, audiences, types of activities, and, especially, availability of staff and resources. Archivists should understand how outreach activities connect to their institution's mission, why those activities are important and necessary, how the activities will promote use and access, and what might be a realistic return on investment. A repository can start with small and easily accomplishable goals and then move to more extensive activities.

Ascertaining the goals of outreach is central to an effective strategy. Because there are so many options (see Figure 14), pinpointing specific purposes and outcomes provides a focus and greater opportunity for success. For example, reaching more or new audiences, promoting specific collections, fundraising and improving donor relations, or showcasing scholarship are all worthy goals. Archivists rarely have a single goal for outreach activities but, rather, try to achieve several objectives by pursuing strategies that coalesce into a cohesive purpose.

Defining the audience or audiences for outreach shapes effective tactics and directly relates to the types of activities that will be implemented. Activities that target specific groups are most valuable. For example, creating curricula for K–12 or higher education teachers, producing step-by-step guides for genealogists, or initiating social media campaigns with specific audiences in mind all have clear targets. There is often considerable crossover between audiences, or the same activity can be reconfigured for different users.

Staff and resources remain the most crucial determinants of a successful campaign. Undertaking outreach activities can be particularly challenging for archives with one staff person or a small staff, and participation is scalable to available staff and resources. Small repositories may choose to write one blog post a month, offer lectures or programs once or twice a year, or perform other activities that require less time. Larger institutions may have personnel dedicated to posting daily on social media, scheduling programming, writing and sending out newsletters, and creating curricula.

Although outreach is usually thought of as a strategy for reaching external audiences, the same principles typically apply to repositories whose primary, or only, constituents are within the organization. For example, museum, religious, corporate, and university archives have institutional staff members as a primary constituent group. Connecting with them through exhibits, newsletters, and presentations perpetuates the value of retaining institutional records.[3] Indeed, outreach is just as important to internal audiences as it is to public audiences.

As with other reference and access functions, assessing outreach activities establishes whether time and staff are used efficiently, whether activities are successful, and whether programs appear sustainable. Archivists always need to keep the original goals of the outreach activities in mind.

Programming: lectures, presentations, panel discussions, discussion groups, brown bag luncheons, symposia, conferences, and the like. These could be ongoing series, specific to events or collections, or one-time sessions open to anyone interested or targeted toward specific audiences such as donors, students, or the community.

Exhibits: digital or physical. Exhibits are a platform to share and educate audiences—not just about collections but also to fulfill an institution's mission—and an advocacy tool to share information about who archivists are and what they do. Exhibits teach, disseminate knowledge, entertain, inform, and share information about collections, anniversaries, donors, or particular subjects.* Physical exhibits can be as simple as a table in the archives reading room or as complex as a custom-built, designated exhibit room. Many exhibits are up for a specific length of time, but short-term exhibits, such as displaying college memorabilia at an alumni event, are also effective. Digital exhibits can also be small or large and need not be static but can be built continually.

Tours and open houses: impromptu or scheduled. Guided tours of closed stacks connect patrons to materials and demonstrate that the archives is not "hiding" materials but instead protecting them. Pairing tours with presentations, exhibits, anniversaries, or other events associates archives with other perceptions beyond being a storehouse.

Curricula and instruction: hands-on workshops, National History Day, semester-long studies, research contests and prizes, curricula and assignments, and information and "show-and-tell" sessions. There are seemingly endless possibilities to engage students and teachers through outreach.†

Publicity: newsletters, brochures, media coverage, and social media. Promoting collections through publicity outlets can consist of sharing new acquisitions, recently processed collections, staff accomplishments, creation of resources such as digital collections or searchable databases, upcoming events, and activities of interest to potential audiences. These can be one-time efforts or ongoing initiatives, such as a regular contribution to an organizational magazine.

FIGURE 14. Examples of Outreach Activities

*Jessica Lacher-Feldman, *Exhibits in Archives and Special Collections Libraries* (Chicago: Society of American Archivists, 2013), 7–9.

†Society of American Archivists, Reference, Access and Outreach Section, "Teaching with Primary Sources—Bibliography," updated August 1, 2016, www2.archivists.org/groups/reference-access-and-outreach-section/teaching-with-primary-sources-bibliography#.Vwbb2MfEyrU.

Statistics are easily compiled, such as how many people attended a program, how many activities have been completed each year, or how many followers have been attracted on social media. These metrics can then be used to plan programming, assess staffing levels, and evaluate whether to continue with specific activities.

However, statistics are not the sole means for assessing success, and qualitative factors also matter. For example, perhaps ten people attended a presentation. For some, that number may be low, but if the event positively affected attendees or led to unanticipated post-event activity, the lecture might well be deemed a success. Perhaps attendees were actively engaged and excited, shared their newfound knowledge with others, returned to do research, donated a collection, asked to volunteer, or asked that the presentation be repeated to an expanded group. Archivists need to document these types of results when assessing the outcome of outreach.

Another example is the ability to demonstrate learning and skills. For institutions that conduct K–12 or higher education instruction, identifying and documenting outcomes such as improved research skills, subject knowledge, and educational competencies provide solid evidence for upper administration or other interested parties that the archives has performed a worthy task. This type of assessment can also be applied to students, faculty members, or other patrons.[4] Measuring outcomes occurs at the activity's conclusion but extends far beyond the moment.

Declaring an activity as unsuccessful under identified parameters does not necessarily justify ending the initiative. Archivists can assess the reasons why the outreach effort did not meet expectations: Was it advertised and promoted? Was the time and place inconvenient for attendance? Did attendees expect something that was not delivered? Incorporating feedback surveys or engaging in conversations facilitates the assessment about activities. Archivists spend considerable time planning and developing initiatives and ought to devote the same attention to post-program assessment. Choosing to invest in specific activities does not equate to immediate success, and it often takes time to build a foundation. For example, in the case of a new lecture series, people might not hear about initial programs until extensive advertising, marketing, and a word-of-mouth wave of news have enough time to develop. Audiences may grow over time, and programs may be discontinued too soon.

Social Media

Social media platforms are an aspect of both marketing and outreach strategies. Sharing content can bring in new users or increase the frequency of existing ones, and it can also educate diverse audiences about and advocate for archives. Using social media demonstrates the relevance of collections and institutions and demonstrates how efforts to "go where they are" can achieve unanticipated benefits. Successful use of social media extends influence, not just with reshares and followers, but by connecting with stakeholders and other influential parties such as donors, funders, public policy professionals, and the media.

The potential goals of utilizing social media include stimulating collection use by both in-person and remote visitors, building recognition and brand, promoting collection contents, engaging in advocacy, and soliciting donations. More specifically, social media can be used to promote events, highlight collections, and share "behind-the-scenes" activities.

Understanding how and when users access such platforms helps archivists strategize about which tools to use, as well as how often and when to post content. Different social media options are used by different audiences and demographics. According to the Pew Research Center, Facebook remained the most popular platform in 2016, with users representing a broad range of genders, ages, incomes, and locations. Instagram and Twitter were most popular among ages 18–29, and LinkedIn and Pinterest also were prevalent.[5] Instagram and SnapChat reach younger audiences and have the potential to educate about archives and engage users who may never have visited one. Facebook, on the other hand, may more effectively reach the current user base or people who already support the institution. Indeed, the most effective strategy for most institutions likely involves utilizing multiple social networking sites.[6]

Being on the front lines, reference archivists are positioned to take advantage of social media. Processing archivists share progress and collection contents, while reference archivists can demonstrate use, research activities, and services. Reference archivists can share exciting finds, highlight finding aids from recently used collections, post about frequently asked research questions, or promote publications. In addition, reference archivists can encourage users to share their own experiences, discoveries, and research. The more users engage and share their archival activities, the broader the reach and growth of potential audiences.

Patrons also take initiative to post on Twitter, Facebook, Instagram, blogs, and other platforms. An institution can facilitate posts by providing links and buttons for patrons to easily click and share. Hopefully, users post about their positive experiences or excitement about resources that they have located in an archives, but it is also helpful to prepare for potential negative comments. It also offers a platform to show appreciation to patrons. For any posts, constructive responses encourage conversation and demonstrate that the archives considers their participation valuable. A Canadian study found that some users believed that adding users' perspectives helped to democratize archives by increasing accuracy of descriptions and building trust.[7]

Formulating goals, establishing schedules, creating content well in advance of posts, and designating one or more archivists to administer the platforms ensures consistent and continuous output. An assessment plan helps monitor and document accomplishments. Statistics offer numbers and demographics, but there are other considerations for assessing success. Visibility and influence are possible measures: How many "likes" and followers, as well as "shares," did a post generate? Has sharing increased collection or monetary donations? Can the archives demonstrate an increase in the number of users who have accessed content based on a post? Has the manner in which collections are used changed in any way? Have prominent people or stakeholders become more engaged in discussions? Other issues to consider when conducting assessments include whether an increase in user inquiries has been demonstrated, the ways in which followers interact and the substance of their comments, whether certain content has achieved an outsized level of popularity or generated consistent viewing, and whether the initiative has produced steady quantitative reference growth. There are sometimes unexpected and pleasing outcomes to social media posts, so flexibility in assessing usefulness deepens the holistic view of the benefits.[8] Determining such success typically occurs over an extended period of time and enables an institution to better consider the value of using social media.

Social media options are continually changing, and archivists must be thoughtful about strategies and outcomes for integrating social media into daily operations. Although most platforms are free to join or use, incorporating social media is an investment that requires staff time and commitment. Continuous assessment allows archivists to more thoughtfully and carefully consider discontinuing or expanding use. Those archivists who are new to social media can consult other institutions that are considered models of use. Archivists who are familiar with social media can evaluate other institutions' uses for ideas and improvements. As an outreach activity, social media is a relatively simple way to reach existing and new users, share news, and promote collections.

Crowdsourcing

Crowdsourcing is a more recent development to engage audiences online. In the past, archivists have maintained tight control over their descriptions of collections. However, as the volume of online resources has increased, archivists understandably cannot keep up with providing the details that users desire. Essentially, crowdsourcing allows any user to participate in facilitating greater access to materials by contributing to collection descriptions through tagging, transcribing, or other means. User involvement benefits an institution because users develop a stronger sense of the importance of archives, and the institution then draws on wider researcher expertise. This shift in thought process both engages users and provides archivists with knowledgeable volunteers who can supplement institutional description programs.

An advantage to online crowdsourcing projects is that volunteers need not be at the institution nor even in the vicinity to contribute their talents. These endeavors also reach both existing audiences and those unable to visit a repository in person.[9] Institutions that have instigated projects specify goals, provide detailed instructions, and place value on user involvement. For example, the New York Public Library's "What's on the Menu?" project uses conversational language—"It's a big job, so we need your help."—to encourage participation in transcribing menus. The Smithsonian's Transcription Center offers a model for engaging volunteers who select from numerous projects, operate with a friendly interface, select options to transcribe and/or review materials, and have the ability to share their accomplishments through social media.[10]

Involving the public in this way underscores the fact that users need not be doing scholarly research to access a repository; rather, archives are available to everybody. It allows institutions to advocate for their holdings, demonstrate their activities to stakeholders, and, most important, promote greater access to their materials. This greatly enhances reference services in another way. As participants contribute to crowdsourcing projects and create more detailed metadata, discoverability improves for everyone.

Friends Groups

Some institutions, particularly government archives and historical societies, have "friends" groups. Many academic and public libraries also have these groups, which may be created specifically for archives and special collections or as part of larger library operations. These groups often are incorporated as separate nonprofit organizations that advocate for archives, host events, and support programming. They typically fundraise, promote education and access, process and preserve collections, purchase supplies, and connect the archives to the community.[11]

These groups are powerful allies, and members may include donors, researchers, supporters, and other interested persons who invest and actively engage in the archives and believe in the mission and value of what the institution provides. For example, friends groups helped raise money for a new building for the Michigan Historical Collections (now Bentley Historical Library at the University of Michigan) and actively participated in demonstrations and activities to prevent the closure of the Georgia Archives.[12]

Founding a friends group requires a considerable investment of staff time and resources. The groups take a long time to build and require dedication and ongoing efforts. The return on investment may not be immediate but over time can reap great rewards.

Conclusion

Firmly embedded in archival culture and practices, outreach and promotion are foundational components of access and reference, and their importance will only continue to increase. From acquisition through access, outreach is not an isolated activity but, rather, an overarching framework that ensures the end user always remains paramount. Largely because of the proliferation of online sources and social media platforms, there are unparalleled opportunities to reach and engage with a wider variety of audiences. Capitalizing on such tools to educate and engage consumers goes far to demonstrate the significance of archives to society.

NOTES

[1] *Dictionary of Archives Terminology*, s.v. "outreach," Society of American Archivists, https://dictionary.archivists.org/entry/outreach.html, captured at https://perma.cc/RS2T-AP4V.

[2] Christie Koontz and Lorri Mon, *Marketing and Social Media: A Guide for Libraries, Archives, and Museums* (Lanham, MD: Rowman & Littlefield, 2014), 162; Joy Palmer and Jane Stevenson, "Something Worth Sitting Still For? Some Implications of Web 2.0 for Outreach," in *A Different Kind of Web: New Connections Between Archives and Our Users*, ed. Kate Theimer (Chicago: Society of American Archivists, 2011), 4.

[3] Marisa Bourgoin, "Research Use: Outreach," in Wythe, *Museum Archives*, 65–71.

[4] Peter Hernon and Robert E. Dugan, *An Action Plan for Outcomes Assessment in Your Library* (Chicago: American Library Association, 2002), 66–68.

[5] Shannon Greenwood, Andrew Perrin, and Maeve Duggan, "Social Media Update 2016," Pew Research Center, Internet and Technology, November 11, 2016, www.pewresearch.org/internet/2016/11/11/social-media-update-2016/, captured at https://perma.cc/HXG9-4UPH.

[6] Adam Crymble, "An Analysis of Twitter and Facebook Use by the Archival Community," *Archivaria* 70 (Fall 2010): 129, https://archivaria.ca/index.php/archivaria/article/view/13298.

[7] Theimer, *Web 2.0 Tools and Strategies*, 29, 207; Palmer and Stevenson, "Something Worth Sitting Still For?," 10; Koontz and Mon, *Marketing and Social Media*, 252; Sean Heyliger, Juli McLoone, and Nikki Lynn Thomas, "Making Connections: A Survey of Special Collections' Social Media Outreach," *American Archivist* 76, no. 2 (2013): 375, 381–381, 391, https://doi.org/10.17723/aarc.76.2.t820u33100443q55; Wendy M. Duff, Catherine A. Johnson, and Joan M. Cherry, "Reaching Out, Reaching In: A Preliminary Investigation into Archives' Use of Social Media in Canada," *Archivaria* 75 (Spring 2013): 88–89, https://archivaria.ca/index.php/archivaria/article/view/13434.

[8] Koontz and Mon, *Marketing and Social Media*, 252; Theimer, *Web 2.0 Tools and Strategies*, 203.

[9] Nathaniel Janick, "Heard But Not Seen: Making Hidden Oral History Collections Discoverable," in Oestreicher, *Innovation, Collaboration and Models*.

[10] NYPL Labs, "About," What's on the Menu?, http://menus.nypl.org/about; Lesley Parilla and Meghan Ferriter, "Social Media and Crowdsourced Transcription of Historical Materials at the Smithsonian Institution: Methods for Strengthening Community Engagement and Its Tie to Transcription Output," *American Archivist* 79, no. 2 (2016): 443–447, https://doi.org/10.17723/0360-9081-79.2.438.

[11] Friends of the British Columbia Archives, "Friends of the BC Archives," https://friendsofbcarchives.wordpress.com/, captured at https://perma.cc/G82M-8C63; Indiana Archives and Records Administration, "IARA: The Friends of the Indiana State Archives," www.in.gov/iara/2777.htm, captured at https://perma.cc/4DUC-8CML; Moravian Archives, "Support," 2020, www.moravianchurcharchives.org/support/, captured at https://perma.cc/C9ZL-QJ4Z; City of Camden, South Carolina, "Friends of the Archives and Museum," www.cityofcamden.org/departments/archives-museum/friends-archives-museum, captured at https://perma.cc/45F8-FZFH; Indiana University Bloomington, Libraries, "Friends of the Archives of Traditional Music," https://libraries.indiana.edu/atm-friends, captured at https://perma.cc/2XPF-VNXX; Metro Archives, "About the Friends of the Nashville Public Library," 2015, http://nashvillearchives.org/friends.html, captured at https://perma.cc/SSJ2-W4KT.

[12] Hackman, *Many Happy Returns*, 109; Kaye Lanning Minchew, "Lessons Learned While Saving the Georgia Archives," *Provenance* 31, no. 1 (2013): 16–21.

12

Assessment of Reference Programs

An effective reference program is reliant on regular assessment and evaluation. In this chapter, assessment refers to an overarching program strategy, and evaluation refers to specific aspects of it. By assessing reference services, archivists achieve a better understanding of their patrons, learn about popular research methods and topics, and gauge collection use. Collecting and evaluating data offers insights that are used to improve user services or systems, provide a better basis for practices and procedures, and serve as a foundation for planning to meet strategic plans and goals. Overall, assessment is a way to recognize and enhance the value of archival services and practices.

Comprehensive assessment practices include both quantitative and qualitative measurements. In particular, learning about users' information-seeking behaviors, technical capabilities, and research methods offers ways to adapt or create services that match the evolving needs of patrons. Regardless of how assessment is conducted, it accumulates information designed to increase repository effectiveness and demonstrate value. Whether statistics and other data are gathered daily, monthly, annually, or according to another timeframe, the time spent is a worthwhile investment.

Assessing reference and its individual services can seem daunting, but even small efforts will yield high returns. At a basic level, tracking types of users and what collections are used requires minimal effort, while developing user studies or gaining more detailed knowledge about user experiences involves time and thoughtful planning. Each institution must determine the methods best suited to reach assessment goals.

Public Services Metrics

Recognizing the necessity for guidance and consistency with assessment techniques, SAA, ACRL, and RBMS jointly approved the "Standardized Statistical Measures and Metrics for Public Services in Archival Repositories and Special Collections Libraries" (hereafter referred to as Metrics for Public Services). The purpose of this initiative was to define measures and encourage implementation of professional practices that apply across all repositories. There are metrics, examples, methods, and guidelines within each of eight domains (see Figure 15) that can be adapted to any size and type of institution. While many institutions already collect data about services, this document offers professional guidance on reviewing existing procedures or implementing new assessment practices.

The initial step is to determine the metrics that the archives desires to capture. Data is collected for specific purposes and uses, such as to identify user groups, inform staffing needs, develop processing plans, initiate digitization projects, plan collection development, improve stacks maintenance, and coordinate outreach activities. The eight areas in Figure 15 are a good foundation, and there is flexibility with what areas produce the most useful outcomes based on an individual repository's goals. For example, not all institutions have instruction programs or install exhibits, so some institutions will focus more on collection use and reference transactions. The metrics can be modified for any repository type, repository size, and institutional need.

Once desired outcomes are established, the next steps are to determine how to collect data. It is advisable that tools used to track statistics correlate to the size of the staff and be easy, convenient,

---

Following is a select overview of the eight domains of the "Standardized Statistical Measures and Metrics for Public Services in Archival Repositories and Special Collections Libraries":

User Demographics: patrons identified by internal/external, geography, and affiliation

Reference Transactions: quantity of interactions, categories of inquiries (e.g., in person, email), time spent with patron, research purpose

Reading Room Visits: quantity of in-person users, time spent on research

Collection Use: quantity of units used, type of use (e.g., reading room, reference, exhibit, instruction), reproductions, loans and publication use

Events: quantity, type, number of attendees, length of event, preparation time

Instruction: quantity of sessions, number of students/attendees, duration, preparation time

Exhibitions: quantity, visitors, type, duration, preparation time, marketing

Online Interactions: page views, sessions, session duration, downloads, traffic source

---

FIGURE 15. Standardized Statistical Measures and Metrics for Public Services in Archival Repositories and Special Collections Libraries

Source: SAA-ACRL/RBMS Joint Task Force on the Development of Standardized Statistical Measures for Public Services in Archival Repositories and Special Collections Libraries, "Standardized Statistical Measures and Metrics for Public Services in Archival Repositories and Special Collections Libraries" (Society of American Archivists, Association of College and Research Libraries, Rare Books and Manuscripts Section of the Association of College and Research Libraries, October 2017), 1–76, https://www2.archivists.org/standards/standardized-statistical-measures-and-metrics-for-public-services-in-archival-repositories, captured at https://perma.cc/LN8T-LCR6.

and helpful. Some software systems systemize data collection about patron registration, collection use, exhibits, and other features. Not all repositories need the robust features offered in these systems; many use other options to track collection use.[1] Excel spreadsheets, Access databases, or paper logs are simple and affordable options.

Archivists use the results as planning tools. By knowing which collections are used most often, archivists can undertake collection development initiatives or digitization projects. Assessment results are also used to create internal training opportunities, such as those intended to develop better subject knowledge about popular topics. Conversely, data showing which collections are seldom used may stimulate outreach activities to highlight them or lead them to become candidates for deaccessioning. Collection use statistics also contribute to donor relations. Periodic reports by the archives tell donors how often a collection is used and for what purposes, thereby maintaining contact and promoting goodwill. Last, these statistics promote more effective stacks management, such as moving high-use collections to closer proximity or moving seldom-accessed collections to off-site or remote storage.

Tracking aspects of reference inquiries, including length of time, time of day, and origin, offers a realistic assessment of staffing levels. Use statistics help plan or justify expanding reading room accommodations or adjusting staffing patterns based on busy or slow times. By looking at data on how reference archivists receive questions, whether by email, in person, over the phone, or through online chats, archivists use concrete data to make informed decisions about allocating staff resources. Further, these statistics help managers advocate for additional personnel when talking to administration or stakeholders.

By analyzing researcher demographics and collection use statistics, archivists can better understand trends and popular topics. Researcher forms and reference interviews best capture this information, and archivists can determine whether certain types of patrons use specific resources, the extent to which high-use collections contribute to current research trends, and how inquiries might shape repository description practices.

Beyond statistics, collecting qualitative data, whether formally or informally, about services is also important. Options for analysis include questionnaires and surveys, exit interviews, focus groups, and complaint reports.[2] These tools can be used for the same reasons stated previously as well as for staff development or to restructure the reference program.

Assessment of reference can be conducted in conjunction with other public services activities, such as instruction, outreach, education, or circulation. When combined with other metrics, statistics demonstrate temporal changes, trends, and developments that result in policy adjustments, priority shifts, service improvements, outreach initiatives, and collection management strategies.[3]

User Studies

Understanding the motivations, skills, behaviors, and needs of users is vital to reference services. One way to discern these aspects is through user studies, which help assess the effectiveness of how patrons find, access, and use collections, as well as offer insight into the behavior and skills of patrons. Essentially, the goal is to understand patrons, to learn, as archivist Elsie T. Freeman writes, "who they are, how they think, how they learn, how they assemble information, to what uses they put it."[4]

Laying the groundwork starts with creating a framework to determine the goals of user studies, which includes identifying the objectives and purpose of the assessment and how it will be conducted. Sheila Corrall recommends starting by addressing the following key points and questions:

1. If you have conducted customer surveys or collected other customer data over the last 12 months, either formally or informally, summarize the key findings.
2. Based on the feedback, what are you doing to meet customers' needs (e.g., projects created, process improvement undertaken)?
3. What products and services have been requested that you have not been able to provide?
4. What would need to change to be able to provide these products or services?
5. Looking to the environment beyond the library, list forces that will change the way we serve our customers (e.g., electronic publishing, copyright laws).[5]

These are good guidelines for creating a framework that establishes a comprehensive outlook on how to move forward with assessment.

User studies investigate patrons' information-seeking behaviors and their capabilities using systems and resources. User studies can be geared toward specific types of users, institutions, tools, or subjects. Most archival scholarship especially focuses on U.S. historians, genealogists, and students.[6] While these groups constitute a large portion of patrons at many institutions, there is much room to explore other audiences.

Questionnaires and surveys are simple and fairly easy to implement. There is a lot of flexibility in how these are created, developed, and used for assessment. They can be administered at the point of contact or online, used for a short period of time or as part of daily interactions, and undertaken to quickly assess thoughts or reactions or to gain more extensive data for in-depth analysis. The function of these tools ranges widely, from assessing the setup and physical space of the repository, to determining the ease of finding and using collections, to evaluating the interaction with the reference archivist. A benefit of using questionnaires and surveys is that they produce immediate results for review.

User-centered design studies address the entire patron experience through speaking with and observing researcher behaviors and needs, creating a prototype or mock-up to meet those needs, actively involving users in designing services and tools, and conducting follow-up conversations and documentation to see whether needs were met.[7] These studies take more time, but the investment can be lucrative because the studies immerse the archivist and patron in mutual behaviors and thought processes. The limits on this type of study include the difficulty in studying a larger number of patrons, but the data obtained will ultimately prove beneficial.

A less prominent technique, but another option to consider, is to study how patrons use and disseminate information from the collections. Repositories can internally track permission to publish and use statistics and use this output to determine the ways in which collections have been accessed for publications, articles, presentations, exhibits, websites, or personal needs. More recently, bibliometrics and altmetrics offer options for deeper analysis. Bibliometrics involves applying mathematics and statistical methods of counting citations in published books and journals. Altmetrics expands this to related statistics, such as downloads, views, social media hits, journal impact factors, and citations, and typically is applied to books, journals, presentations, videos, data sets, and other self-published products.[8]

Assessing user behavior and needs provides useful analytical data for generating reports, establishing goals, and lobbying administrators. Measuring data for its impact and value drives decision making about access, evaluative tools, new services, the tailoring of existing programs to specific user groups, the reorganization of departments, and the justification of ongoing practices. User testing and studies demonstrate the impact and value of services and are also an advocacy tool. By investigating and gaining insight into users' thought processes and behaviors, archivists can advance access by developing more useful tools and guiding research and use in more productive ways.

Data Ethics and Privacy

When collecting data about patrons, it is important to consider ethics and privacy. Digitally collected information requires particular care, whether gathered from patrons through collection use or via user studies and assessment techniques. This section introduces basic concepts to consider, but archivists can work with their institutions to investigate and implement appropriate techniques that align with organizational values.

Surveys, questionnaires, interviews, and other formal and informal studies all gather data, either physically or digitally, to be analyzed and interpreted. Regardless of the format, archivists must maintain data security while the data remains in existence and establish parameters for deletion once the data has served its purpose.

Data on paper is fairly easy to manage. Papers can be filed in secure containers, labeled as confidential, kept in an office or desk, relegated to secure stack areas, and shredded when no longer needed. The concepts of protecting digitally collected data are similar: keep the files on a secure server, restrict access to pertinent personnel, and delete documentation when the analysis is finished. Although the concepts are simple, protecting digital data is more involved.

As with all aspects of archival work, digital data management ultimately depends on the institutional cyberinfrastructure. Basics of cyberinfrastructure include secure servers, data encryption, backup strategies, and retention schedules.[9] Consulting with an information technology professional or someone who manages technical institutional infrastructure is a good start. When this type of data management is not an option, one can use third-party cloud storage, such as Dropbox or Google Drive. However, using a third-party system requires careful review of their security policies and thoughtful consideration of the benefits and risks. Even if data is anonymized, keeping the information secure further protects patrons' privacy.

In addition to managing the data, ethical data collection requires special attention. Archivists have a responsibility to explicitly communicate with patrons about the project details, goals, and use. It remains critical to build trust with patrons, making them comfortable with participating in the process. Some institutions, particularly academic repositories, may also have strict guidelines or policies on conducting studies or assessment.[10] For example, academic institutions have Institutional Review Boards (IRB), the members of which review proposals about collecting data that involves human subjects. Even when an institution is not required to use an IRB, reviewing such guidelines is helpful for any type of user assessment.

Essentially, good security and an ethical approach to data collection are critical components of any study. Assessments must respect the participants and value their contributions. Such tasks are not difficult to execute, but they do require thoughtful planning.

Conclusion

Evaluation and assessment are important components of any reference program. Both formal and informal assessment strengthen archival knowledge about the behaviors, needs, and intentions of users. The qualitative and quantitative data generated by such studies informs the development and expansion of services and resources, helps to determine staffing needs, contributes to collection development agendas, allows institutions to set better processing priorities, and applies to other targeted aspects of reference programs.

NOTES

[1] Zamon, *Lone Arranger*, 98.

[2] Hernon and Dugan, *Action Plan*, 121–123; St. Clair, *Total Quality Management*, 127–137.

[3] St. Clair, *Total Quality Management*, 125; Dearstyne, *Archival Enterprise*, 191.

[4] Freeman, "In the Eye of the Beholder," 112.

[5] Corrall, "Planning and Policy Making" in Melling and Little, *Building a Successful Customer-Service Culture*, 34.

[6] Alexandra Chassanoff, "Historians and the Use of Primary Source Materials in the Digital Age," *American Archivist* 76, no. 2 (2013): 135–164, https://doi.org/10.17723/aarc.76.2.lh76217m2m376n28; Helen R. Tibbo, "Primarily History in America: How U.S. Historians Search for Primary Materials at the Dawn of the Digital Age," *American Archivist* 66, no. 1 (2003): 9–50, https://doi.org/10.17723/aarc.66.1.b120370l1g718n74; Ian G. Anderson, "Are You Being Served? Historians and the Search for Primary Sources," *Archivaria* 58 (Fall 2004): 81–129, https://archivaria.ca/index.php/archivaria/article/view/12479; Wendy M. Duff and Catherine A. Johnson, "Where Is the List with All the Names? Information-Seeking Behavior of Genealogists," *American Archivist* 66, no. 1 (2003): 79–95, https://doi.org/10.17723/aarc.66.1.b120370l1g718n74; Elizabeth Yakel and Deborah A. Torres, "Genealogists as a 'Community of Records,'" *American Archivist* 70, no. 1 (2003): 93–113, https://doi.org/10.17723/aarc.70.1.ll5414u736440636; Xiaomu Zhou, "Student Archival Research Activity: An Exploratory Study," *American Archivist* 71, no. 2 (2008): 476–498, https://doi.org/10.17723/aarc.71.2.n426270367qk311l.

[7] Rosalie Lack, "The Importance of User-Centered Design: Exploring Findings and Methods," in *Archives and the Digital Library*, ed. William E. Landis and Robin L. Chandler (Binghamton, NY: Haworth Information Press, 2006), 71; Society of American Archivists, "User Experience Design and Digital Archives," www2.archivists.org/prof-education/course-catalog/user-experience-design-and-digital-archives, captured at https://perma.cc/A7NQ-ED9L.

[8] Connaway and Radford, *Research Methods*, 357; Elizabeth Joan Kelly, "Altmetrics and Archives," *Journal of Contemporary Archival Studies* 4, no. 1 (2017): 1–2, https://elischolar.library.yale.edu/jcas/vol4/iss1/1/.

[9] Matt Beckstrom, "Use, Security, and Ethics of Data Collection: Data Collection, Retention, Use, and Security," in *Protecting Patron Privacy: A LITA Guide*, ed. Bobbi Newman and Bonnie Tijerina (Lanham, MD: Rowman & Littlefield, 2017), 40–42.

[10] Andrew D. Asher, "Use, Security, and Ethics of Data Collection: Risks, Benefits, and User Privacy: Evaluating the Ethics of Library Data," in Newman and Tijerina, *Protecting Patron Privacy*, 48–49.

13

The Future of Access and Reference

As the primary service provider and public component of archives, reference and access functions are crucial to the success of any operation. After reflecting on how much has changed even in just the past twenty years, it is exciting to anticipate future developments. Professional standards already have evolved to bring access to the forefront. The potential growth of new users, new collections, new technology, new digital content, new ways of outreach, and new ideas to bring patrons and collections together will continually transform repositories and the profession.

Indeed, the concept of access will continue to change. Archivists should periodically step back from normal services and think deeply about how they define access in order to assess where they are, where they want to go, and how to get there. It is not a one-time effort; it is a continuing valuation to progress institutionally and professionally.

In the past, access involved, for the most part, physical access, but that has rapidly expanded into the virtual world. Most people today use technology to conduct many daily activities, especially on personal mobile devices, such as phones and tablets—and soon, watches and eyeglasses and other unanticipated inventions that hover on the horizon. Even further, augmented and virtual reality technologies, already used by some museums, have the potential to create experiences that go far beyond just reading and viewing materials, instead generating immersive and interactive environments.

Technology will continue to expand the archival user base. Archives are no longer limited to scholars, internal departments, or the occasional member of the public. We are a global society, where archives reach far beyond their local communities to engage patrons around the world. Archivists commonly receive inquiries from patrons in faraway countries, and this trend will only increase.

As users become more diverse, so do the collections. Many institutions actively document underrepresented groups and voices. Though this practice has occurred for decades, there is a more recent shift in how this happens. While historians previously ignored certain populations and groups, many communities scrambled to preserve their own historical records. Today, many people understand the importance of not losing these histories, and the responsibility is not solely the province of professional archivists. In particular, the growth of community archives that are established outside of traditional archival venues is a testament to how more people now believe in and actively document, make available, and promote their diverse histories.

An aspect of the diversity of users and collections is language. Indeed, many repositories already have materials in languages other than English. Due to time, staffing, and skill restraints, archivists are challenged to promote access to such materials. In the future, there will hopefully be more tools available to easily and quickly translate materials, finding aids, and other descriptions that will then reach more global audiences. Some repositories have begun this process and are models for others.

Along the same vein, many archivists are working to increase the accessibility of archives and collections to audiences in which physical and virtual barriers have proven formidable. Though many repositories have structural and financial restraints, it is likely that more resources will evolve over time to address the multitude of accessibility needs. Resources such as adjustable tables and chairs, OCR options to decode handwriting, text-to-speech devices, and many others will do much to reach people who have difficulty accessing materials in their current forms.

All of these points about the future of access directly relate to reference. Already, archivists require much knowledge and many skills to provide effective reference services. As the conduit between patrons and collections, archivists will have to develop even more skills and knowledge moving forward. It is daunting to think that reference professionals need to have deeper technical skills or the ability to speak or read other languages, but these are real possibilities for the future. It remains most important to consider the skills and knowledge that are necessary at an institution or in a profession that will continue to emphasize reference and access.

It is an exciting time to be an archivist. There are unending possibilities for advancing access, reaching new audiences, and furthering activities that prove archives are vital to society.

Postscript

In the midst of final edits for this book, there were national and global events that directly and indirectly affected access to archives. I had a strong desire to go back through this manuscript to incorporate references and suggestions addressing the extraordinary times we live in. But such an endeavor is never ending; instead, this postscript highlights a few of these events that I hope will prompt archivists to consider their effects on archives, the profession, and themselves.

First, the world was hit with the COVID-19 pandemic in early 2020. I wrote this book with the assumption that archivists worked in their facilities, had access to all their holdings, welcomed researchers in person, and hosted events. Even managing digital collections requires scanners, audiovisual equipment, and software located in physical workspaces. But as a result of the public health crisis, archives closed and many archivists began working remotely, whether temporarily or indefinitely. As a profession rooted in physical spaces working with physical materials, archivists have had to shift the concept of access and reference practices.

Archives have closed before, usually as the result of planned projects such as building renovations or moving to a new site, or because of local disasters such as a flood or fire. This pandemic was different. Archivists had little time to plan and had to swiftly reprioritize work and projects. Many did not have access to physical collections nor digital content not already online. The option for researchers to visit in person was suspended, and archivists experienced new limitations for providing remote access.

Simultaneously, other tragedies are reshaping our nation and may paradoxically lead to triumphant change. The deaths of George Floyd, Breonna Taylor, and many others at the hands of law enforcement brought calls for justice and equity to the forefront as people protested throughout the country and the Black Lives Matter movement expanded. Long-term efforts to remove symbols of oppression of Black and Indigenous people resulted in statues being taken down, buildings renamed, and sports teams rebranded with new names and mascots. Racist attacks on Asian Americans increased by those who blamed China for the pandemic, while PBS aired the first docuseries about Asian Americans on commercial television. The House of Representatives passed the National Museum of the American Latino Act, which will move on to the Senate. The U.S. Supreme Court ruled that the 1964 Civil Rights Act protects LGBTQ employees from discrimination, ruled in favor of Deferred Action for Childhood Arrivals to protect the legal status of immigrants, and ruled that about half of Oklahoma's land is within a Native American reservation. And the Americans with Disabilities Act celebrated its thirtieth anniversary of promoting equal opportunities for people with disabilities.

Many archivists have long been engaged locally, statewide, and nationally to address these concerns, on both personal and professional levels. We would be remiss if we did not consider how these events influence archives and archivists—what we collect, who our audiences are, how we serve and engage patrons, what efforts will make archives more accessible, and how we can be more diverse, equitable, and inclusive as a profession. I look forward to learning how archivists convert, rebuild, and revolutionize reference and access long into the future.

CHERYL OESTREICHER
August 2020

APPENDIX A

Examples of Reference Manuals

The Bentley Historical Library, University of Michigan

01. Reference Manual
- Aeon Documentation Google Site
- AutoText Entries
- Basic Guide to Request Materials
- Correspondence Guidelines
- Customer Service ZingTrain
- Handling Architectural Drawings Guidelines
- House Scanning Process
- Onboarding Checklist
- Paging/Retrieval
- Reading Room Security Tips and Reminders
- Reading Room Workflow

02. Policies and Procedures
- A-V materials: Access and Duplication
- Access Guide to DAAS Digital Collection
- Access to U-M Alumni Records Policy
- Access to Unprocessed Collections Policy
- Handling Administrative and the University History Group Requests—Guidelines
- Handling UM Restricted Records Guidelines
- Parking Permits Issuing Procedures
- Reading Room Guidelines
- Saturday Rules
- Security in the BHL Reading Room
- Guidelines and Procedures for Filmmakers at the Bentley Library

03. Reference Letters Workflow
- Initial Responses/Routing
- Answering letters
- Permissions
- Answering the phone
- Requests received via Aeon Client
- Instructions for adding BHL as a sender to your Google email

04. Phone and Letter Log

05. Reference Letters Templates
- General Letter Template
- Visit/How to register and Request items via Aeon

06. Basic Sources for UM Common Queries

07. Basic Sources for non-UM Common Queries

08. Orientation/Classes
- Class Logistics
- Communicating with Faculty
- Finding Information about Classes

09. Reference Forms
- Forms (other than duplication)

10. Duplication Procedures, Forms and Workflows
    Duplication and Shipping Charges
    Duplication Forms

11. Reference Orientation Training

12. Reference Schedules
    Detroit Observatory Events Schedule
    Evening Hours Schedule
    Saturday Schedule
    Weekly Schedule (3 zones)

13. Weekly Meetings

14. Reference Google Calendar

15. Loan Process Workflow
    01. Upon receipt of Loan Request
    02. Preparation for transfer of requested materials
    03. Creating Loan activity in Aeon
    04. Following up on Loans procedures

16. Additional Research Tools
    Deep Blue
    Searching Digital Daily Guidelines

Source: Courtesy of Malgosia Myc, Assistant Director of Reference Services, Bentley Historical Society, University of Michigan, Ann Arbor, Michigan

Special Collections Research Center, Southern Illinois University

Overview

Procedures
    Researcher Orientation Steps
    Monitoring the Reading Room
    Assisting Researchers
    When a Researcher Leaves
    Offsite Materials

Reference Interaction

Reftracker Deskstats: Recording Reference Questions

Collection Use Count

SCRC Collection Use Statistics Online Form

Reading Room Rules

Reproduction Requests
    Fees and Payments

APPENDIX B

Examples of Registration Forms

Maryland State Archives

MARYLAND STATE ARCHIVES

Hon. Larry Hogan
Governor
Hon. Boyd K. Rutherford
Lt. Governor
Timothy D. Baker
State Archivist
Matthew P. Lalumia
Chairman, Maryland Commission on Artistic Property

Hall of Records Commission:
Hon. Mary Ellen Barbera, *Chair*
Chief Judge, Court of Appeals
C. Gail Bassette
Ronald Daniels
Hon. Peter V. R. Franchot
William E. Kirwan, Ph.D.
Hon. Nancy K. Kopp
Burton K. Kummerow
Hon. Thomas V. Mike Miller, Jr.
Christopher B. Nelson
Del. Samuel I. Rosenberg
David Wilson, Ed.D.

Registration Form

Welcome to the State Archives, the historical agency and permanent records repository for the State of Maryland. We are pleased to be able to assist you, whether you are requesting needed governmental documents, performing historical research, or investigating your family heritage. Our friendly and capable staff will help you find your materials among the nearly four hundred years of recorded history entrusted to us.

Our first duty as public servants is to insure the safety both of the visitors to the Archives and the documents in our care. We annually review our patron registrations. As part of that review, we ask that you read, accept, and abide by the regulations governing access to the Archives, a copy of which has been provided to you. While some of the rules and fees for service may seem at first arbitrary or unusual, they are the result of experience both here and at other archives and libraries around the world. Our goal is to insure that future citizens of Maryland and the United States will enjoy the same opportunities to use these resources and learn about the past as you have. I hope your visits here are pleasant and rewarding. If you have any concerns regarding the operation of the Archives, please do not hesitate to bring them to the attention of the staff or, if necessary, to me. We look forward to serving you.

Timothy D. Baker
State Archivist and
Commissioner of Land Patents

PATRON INFORMATION - PLEASE PRINT CLEARLY

First Name: _____ Last Name: _____

Institution: _____

Address: _____

City/State/Zip: _____

Phone - Work: _____ Home: _____ Cell: _____

Email: _____

Patron # _____

ID (Including

New Registration Number: _____ **Renewal Date** _____

Maryland State Archives 350 Rowe Boulevard, Annapolis, MD 21401-1686 Telephone: 410 260-6400 MD toll free: 800-235-4045 fax: 410 974-2525 tty/voice 800 735-2258
Internet address: http://msa.maryland.gov/ email: msa.helpdesk@maryland.gov

Source: Maryland State Archives, Annapolis, Maryland

Archdiocese of Cincinnati

Archives Reading Room Registration Form

Name _____

Address _____

_____

Phone _____

Email _____

Description of Research Project

_____
_____
_____
_____

I have read and agree to abide by the rules of the Archdiocese of Cincinnati Archives.

_____   _____
Signature   Date

(over)

Reading Room Policies & Procedures

Welcome to the Archdiocese of Cincinnati Archives. The archives' services are available to all archdiocesan administrative offices, pastors and parishes, and to qualified researchers doing scholarly research. In order to provide you with quality service and to ensure the preservation of the records, the following procedures have been established.

1. Upon your first visit, researchers must fill out a **Reading Room Registration Form** and present photo identification.

2. Records in the Archdiocese of Cincinnati Archives do not circulate and may be used only in the archives. Exceptions may apply for certain archdiocesan staff.

3. No food or drink is allowed in the reading room.

4. Personal items, such as coats, bags, purses and briefcases, are not allowed near the records. A place to store your personal items is provided.

5. Notebooks, laptop computers, tablets and cameras are allowed in the reading room. Photography taken by researchers may only be used for personal reference and research purposes.

6. Only pencils may be used when working in the reading room. Pens are not allowed.

7. Handle the records with care. Do not write on the materials or rearrange the papers or folders. Place markers are provided for you.

8. If you would like to photocopy records, please consult with the archivist. Large copy orders may not be completed on the day of your visit, but will be mailed as soon as they are completed.

9. Researchers must receive permission to publish from records in the archives by submitting a **Permissions to Publish Form**. When citing records from the archives, please use the following credit: **Courtesy of the Archdiocese of Cincinnati Archives**.

10. The archives utilizes security cameras throughout the facility to enhance the protection of our resources. The cameras are monitored by archdiocesan staff, and the footage is archived.

OFFICE: 513/421-3131 FAX: 513/421-6225
100 E. EIGHTH STREET CINCINNATI, OHIO 45202

Source: The Archdiocese of Cincinnati

APPENDIX C

Examples of Online Reference Request Forms

The Museum of Modern Art

Contact the Archives

Please fill out the form below. Contact information is necessary whether you are asking a question or requesting an appointment. When you press the submit button, your request will be sent to the Archives reference desk and you will receive an email confirming receipt of the request. Asterisks (*) indicate required fields.

First name *

Last name *

Your address *

Street Address

Address Line 2

City

State/Province/Region

Postal/Zip Code

Country

Email address *

Daytime phone number (with area code) *

Occupation *

Select an occupation

Request an appointment

Before requesting an appointment, please use the Guide to the Archives' Holdings to identify the materials you wish to consult so that we may better serve your research needs.

Hours: Tuesday–Friday, 1:00–5:00 p.m. Appointment required.

The Archives is closed during the month of August and the last two weeks of December.

Preferred date

| Wednesday, February 12, 2020 | ⬆⬇ |

Alternate date

| Wednesday, February 12, 2020 | ⬆⬇ |

☐ I'd like to request additional dates.

Have you visited the Archives before?

☐ Yes
☐ No

Please list the collection(s) and folders you wish to view during your appointment.

Example: Dorothy C Miller Papers

V.1–V.4, VI.B.1

[ ]

Ask a question

Please be sure to consult our finding aids and visitor information before submitting a question, as much information about our collections and policies is readily available on our website.

Enter your question here.

[ ]

Confirmation process

Please understand that submitting a request for an appointment is NOT a confirmation of your reservation. The Archives will process each request in the order received and will contact you to confirm a scheduled date and time. Allow up to 10 business days for a response.

Source: The Museum of Modern Art, New York, New York

Appendix C: Examples of Online Reference Request Forms

University of California, San Francisco Library

≡ Hours

UCSF Library

≡ Menu

Library facilities will be closed until further notice, but see Teaching and Learning Continuity for help with remote instruction and learning.

Home / Archives and Special Collections / Ask an Archivist

Ask an Archivist

Due to coronavirus (COVID-19), starting Monday, March 16 and until further notice, the UCSF Archives & Special Collections reading room is CLOSED to all researchers. The archives staff will be able to provide limited online reference service during this closure.

Do not send personal health information with this form. To request medical records, contact UCSF Medical Records.

Name *

E-mail *

Affiliation *

Department

Phone *

What is your topic? *

How can we help you? *

APPENDIX D

Examples of Access Outputs, Alternative Formats

Websites
Ramsey County Historical Society

Source: Ramsey County Historical Society, St. Paul, Minnesota

Appendix D: Examples of Access Outputs, Alternative Formats

Bachman Collection 1935-1954
[1995.15.1]
1 box
Material consists of musical programs for Johnson High School Alumni Chorus and the St. Paul Civic Opera Association, and Johnson High School Alumni Chorus attendance records.
Available for consultation and duplication.

Baker (John and Elizabeth) Collection 1951
[2004.3.1]
1 box
Handwritten correspondence to John from Elizabeth, his wife, during his time at a tuberculosis clinic in Noperning, Minnesota, September to October 1951.
Available for consultation and duplication.

Bleier (Harold B.) Scrapbook Collection 1912-1974
2 boxes
Material includes newspaper clippings, programs, and other paper documents and photographs documenting Dr. Bleier's sporting and civic activities. He was a well-known and recognized golfer, dentist, and member of the Osman Temple.
Available for consultation and duplication.

Boss (Wallace) Collection 1926-1961
[1996.3.1]
2 boxes
Material includes Winter Carnival materials of Wallace Boss as King Boreas: scrapbooks, correspondence, programs, magazines, and certificates.
Available for consultation and duplication.

Source: Ramsey County Historical Society, St. Paul, Minnesota

South Asian American Digital Archive

SAADA
South Asian American Digital Archive

About | Events | **Browse the Archive**

Browse the Archive

There are **3,897** unique items available online in SAADA.

Themes
Broad categories into which many of the materials in the archive are organized, i.e. Arts, Early Immigration, Gender & Sexuality, Political Engagement, etc.

Collections
A group of materials that were assembled by an individual, family, organization, or repository from a variety of sources.

Sources
A list of publications (journals, periodicals, etc.) from which items in the archive originate.

Creators
A list of the individuals and/or organizations that are primarily responsible for an items' creation, production, or compilation.

Time Periods
A categorization of materials according to landmark moments in South Asian American history, such as the 1923 U.S. Supreme Court decision that barred South Asians from becoming American citizens.

States
The U.S. state where an item was created.

Types
The nature or genre of an item, i.e. Correspondence, Oral History, Newspaper Clipping, etc.

Languages
The language of an item.

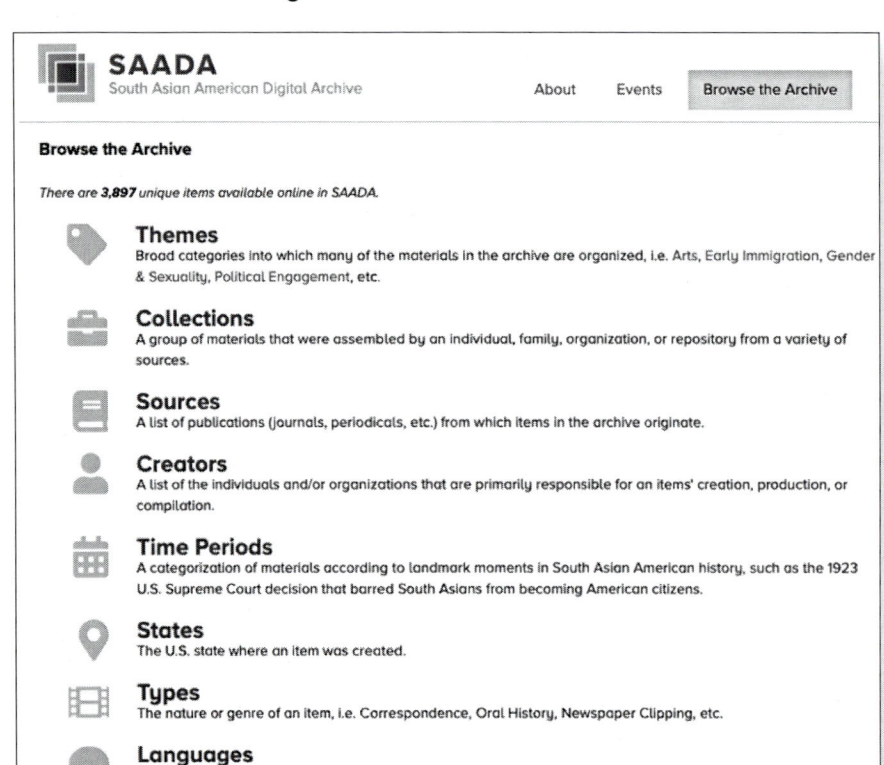

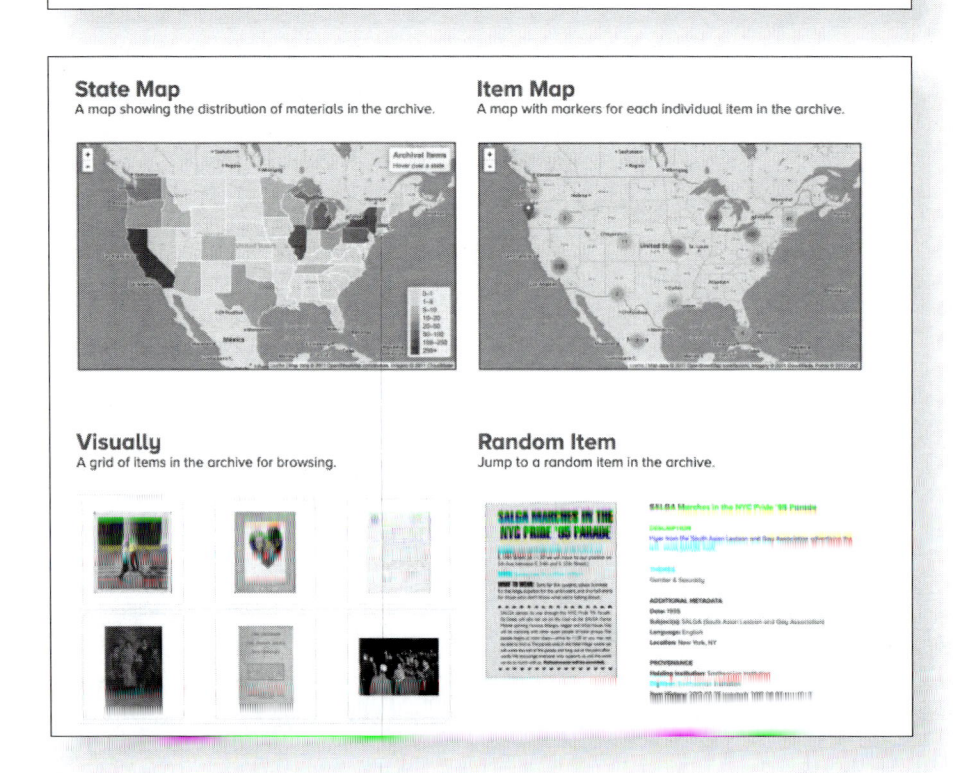

State Map
A map showing the distribution of materials in the archive.

Item Map
A map with markers for each individual item in the archive.

Visually
A grid of items in the archive for browsing.

Random Item
Jump to a random item in the archive.

Source: South Asian American Digital Archive, www.saada.org

Appendix D: Examples of Access Outputs, Alternative Formats

Access/Excel
Boise State University

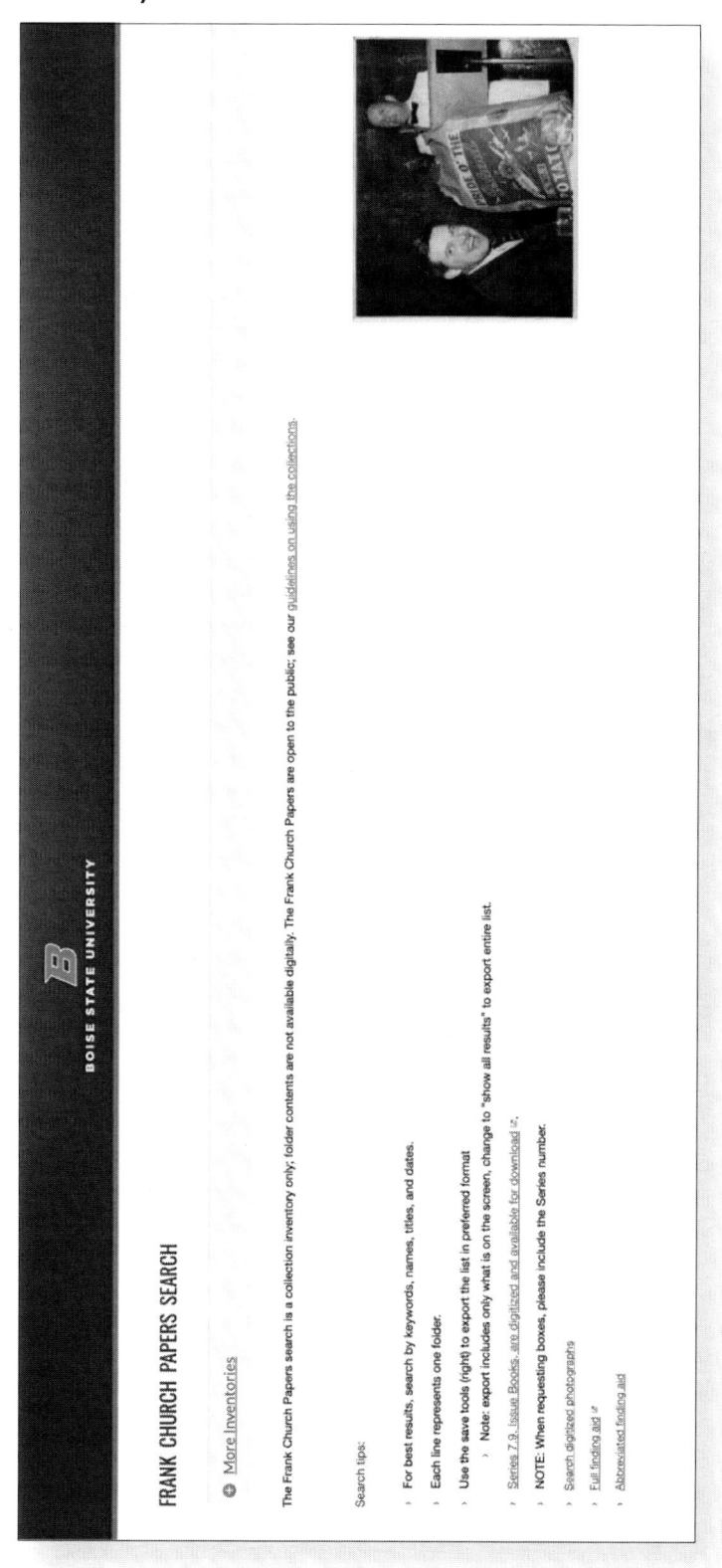

Source: Boise State University, Boise, Idaho

Title:	Keyword:	Names:	Date:	Series Name:	Subseries:
FBI	Keyword	Names	Date	Series Name	Subseries

Box: Box
Folder: Folder

⚙ Columns 🖶 Print 📊 Excel 📋 CSV 📄 Copy 📄 PDF

Show 100 ▼ entries   Search:

Title ▲	Keyword ▲	Names ▲	Date ▲	Series Name ▲	Series ▲	Subseries ▲	Box ▲	Folder ▲
Cedar Rapids, IA/Federal Court FBI vs. Aim	Federal Court FBI vs. Aim	Howard W. Cannon	1976 July 10	Speeches/Trips/Articles/...	8.20	Trips	18	16
CIA/FBI Investigation	CIA/FBI Investigation: Staff Matters: Integrity, Rules Parking, Reports; Letters Re Committee Activities; Press Releases Sent to Frank Church Re Committee Activities and What Committee Would Release; Intelligence Oversight Act of 1976	John Kenneth Galbraith; William P. Bundy; John G. Tower; John Levi; Barry M. Goldwater; Leo Ryan; Henry M. Jackson; Thomas Downing; Mike Wetherell; Richard S. Schweiker; Walter F. Mondale, Gerald R. Ford; William E. Colby; Kelley, Clarence M	1975 1977 #1	Personal	10.60	Special Files	1	21
CIA/FBI Investigation	Central Intelligence Agency; Federal Bureau of Investigation;		1975 1977 #1	Personal	10.60	Special Files	1	21
CIA/FBI Investigation	CIA/FBI Investigation (See Folder 21); Central Intelligence Agency; Federal Bureau of Investigation;		1975 1977 #2	Personal	10.60	Special Files	1	22
CIA/FBI Investigation	CIA/FBI Investigation (See Folder 21); Central Intelligence Agency; Federal Bureau of Investigation;		1977	Personal	10.60	Special Files	1	23

Showing 1 to 5 of 5 entries (filtered from 11,072 total entries)   1

Source: Boise State University, Boise, Idaho

Appendix D: Examples of Access Outputs, Alternative Formats

Data Sets
National Archives

Open Government at the National Archives
Home > Open Government > White House Tapes of the Nixon Administration, 1971-1973

White House Tapes of the Nixon Administration, 1971–1973
- What is the data?
- How do I access the data?
- What high value criteria does it meet?
- Is this the first time the data is available?
- Who may be interested in this information?
- Who do I contact if I have questions about this data?

What is the data?
This dataset provides information about the Nixon Administration's White house Tapes. The White House Tapes contain sound recordings of President Richard Nixon's telephone calls recorded at the White House in Washington, D.C. and the Presidential retreat at Camp David, Maryland. The Tapes also contain sound recordings of meetings held in the White House's Oval Office and Cabinet Room, the President's office in the Old Executive Office Building, and Aspen Lodge at Camp David. These recordings document many of the major events, decisions, and discussions of the Nixon Administration from February 16, 1971 to July 18, 1973.

This dataset contains metadata about the meetings and telephone calls recorded by the White House taping system. The metadata offers details for all 22,723 conversations, including title, time and date of recording, audiotape, recording device, geographic coordinates, participants, and a brief descriptive statement.

The Richard Nixon Presidential Library and Museum, part of the National Archives and Records Administration, is working to fully digitize the White House Tapes. For digitized audio recordings and more information about the White House Tapes, please visit: http://www.nixonlibrary.gov/forresearchers/find/tapes/index.php

How do I access the data?
This dataset is available for download in one comma-separated values (CSV) file, as well as a zipped file containing seven JavaScript Object Notation (JSON) files. The data dictionary outlines and defines the fields available in the CSV file.
- Nixon White House Tapes, 1971–1973 (CSV) (33.3 MB) [Updated 09/22/2015]
    - 37-wht-dataset-conversationlist-2015-09-22.csv
- Nixon White House Tapes Data Dictionary (PDF) [Updated 08/25/2015]
    - 37-wht-dataset-conversationlist-csv-datadictionary-2015-09-28
- Nixon White House Tapes, 1971–1973 (ZIP) (1.7 MB) [Updated 09/22/2015]
    - 37-wht-dataset-conversationlist-json-2015-09-22.zip This file contains:
        - 37-wht-dataset-conversationlist-cab-2015-08-25.json
        - 37-wht-dataset-conversationlist-cdhw-2015-08-25.json
        - 37-wht-dataset-conversationlist-cdsd-2015-08-25.json
        - 37-wht-dataset-conversationlist-cdst-2015-08-25.json
        - 37-wht-dataset-conversationlist-eob-2015-08-25.json
        - 37-wht-dataset-conversationlist-oval-2015-08-25.json
        - 37-wht-dataset-conversationlist-wht-2015-08-25.json

What high value criteria does it meet?
- Access to the government's permanent records:
- can be used to increase agency accountability and responsiveness
- improves public knowledge of the agency and its operations
- furthers the core mission of the agency
- creates economic opportunity
- responds to need and demand as identified through public consultation

Is this the first time the data is available?
This is the first time that the information about White House Tapes conversations is publicly available in a standardized, integrated, and open format. The data has been improved and refined through human analysis and machine scripting. For examples, NARA staff added value by identifying, reconciling, and creating over 4,700 individual conversation participant names across more than 61,900 participant entries.

This is the first time the data is available in CSV and JSON format.

Who may be Interested in this Information?
Historians, political scientists, academics, researchers, archivists, foreign policy analysts, journalists, and citizens.

Who do I contact if I have questions about this data?
Tapes Team, Richard Nixon Presidential Library and Musuem
E-mail: nixon@nara.gov

Source: National Archives, Washington, DC

APPENDIX E

Examples of Reproduction Request Forms

New Orleans Public Library

NEW ORLEANS PUBLIC LIBRARY
SPEAKING VOLUMES

Louisiana Division/City Archives
New Orleans Public Library
219 Loyola Avenue | New Orleans, LA | 70112 | 504.596.2610
neworleanspubliclibrary.org

Release Form for Reproduction of Materials

Date: _____

Name of Requesting Party: _____

Address: _____

Phone: _____ E-mail: _____

Please check appropriate items:

☐ Digital file(s) provided by the Louisiana Division/City Archives   (Burn to CD/DVD ☐; FTP ☐)

☐ Outside photographer or scanner used (provide name & address below)

_____
_____

USE TO BE MADE OF MATERIAL REPRODUCED (check the statement that applies):

☐ These reproductions are for personal use only or for use in research, teaching, or private study. I agree to take responsibility for any unauthorized copy or public display of the reproduction.

☐ These reproductions are for publication, broadcast and/or public display. I have read and agree to comply with the TERMS OF USE stated below. Further, I am aware of my responsibility in the case of copyright infringement.

DESCRIBE THE SPECIFIC USE TO BE MADE OF THE REPRODUCTION(S):

_____
_____
_____
_____

TERMS OF USE

Permission to reproduce items from Louisiana Division/City Archives special collections is granted for personal use or for use in research, teaching, and/or private study.

Permission to reproduce items for *ANY OTHER USE* is subject to the following conditions:

1. Permission to publish, broadcast, or display is granted only insofar as the rights of the Louisiana Division/City Archives are concerned. In many cases the Louisiana Division/City Archives claims only physical ownership of material in its collections and does not own copyright or other intellectual property rights to this material. In such cases, all responsibility for possible copyright infringement arising from use of reproductions of this material will be assumed by the requesting party.

2. Permission to reproduce materials is granted for one-time use only. Any re-use of the materials without permission of the Louisiana Division/City Archives is forbidden. This permission is not transferable to any other party.

3. Negatives or digital files supplied by the Louisiana Division/City Archives or produced by the requestor or the requestor's designee may not be transferred to any party for any use not stated in this agreement.

Source: New Orleans Public Library, New Orleans, Louisiana

Appendix E: Examples of Reproduction Request Forms

4. Any negatives made in the process of reproduction will be returned to the Louisiana Division/City Archives immediately upon completion of the reproduction process. A copy of any digital file produced by an outside party (in-house or off-site) will be supplied to the Louisiana Division/City Archives.

5. Reproduction (whether digital or otherwise) may be done only by an individual, a photographer or reproduction company approved in advance by the Louisiana Division/City Archives, whether material is reproduced off-site or in-house.

6. Alterations to the original image are not allowed in the publication of the Louisiana Division/City Archives materials without permission.

7. All published, broadcast or displayed reproductions of Louisiana Division/City Archives material must be properly credited as follows: **Louisiana Division/City Archives, New Orleans Public Library.**

8. A copy of any publication, documentary, CD/DVD, etc. containing reproductions of Louisiana Division/City Archives materials will be sent without charge to the Louisiana Division/City Archives.

_____   _____
Signature of requesting party   Date

_____   _____
Approved by   Date

DESCRIPTION OF MATERIALS TO BE REPRODUCED

(To be filled in by the Louisiana Division/City Archives. Off-site users, please attach copies of the items requested, printed from our website, or supply the URL for each image, as the URL appears on the website.)

COLLECTION:	IMAGE NAME/DESCRIPTION
_____	_____
_____	_____
_____	_____
_____	_____
_____	_____
_____	_____
_____	_____
_____	_____
_____	_____
_____	_____
_____	_____
_____	_____
_____	_____
_____	_____

FEES:

_____ scan(s) @ $5.00 each . . . . $_____   (i.e., material already available in high resolution)

_____ scan(s) @ $10.00 each . . . . $_____   (i.e., material that has not yet been scanned or must be rescanned)

Total amount due . . . . $_____

[NOPL use: _____Paid _____Cash _____Check]   Revised 10/2010

Source: New Orleans Public Library, New Orleans, Louisiana

Wyoming State Archives

Wyoming State Archives Photo Order Form

Name _____ Company Name _____
Address _____ Email Address _____
City _____ State _____ Zip Code _____ Phone Number _____

File Name or Collection	Negative Number/ Identifier	Item Description	Print		Scan		Price
			Qty	Size	File Type: tiff, jpeg	Resolution 96, 300, 600 dpi	

Prints can be mailed or held for pickup. Scans will be emailed using a link to a Google Drive.
See Copy Fee Schedule and Photo Use Fee Schedule for pricing

Use Agreement Needed? Yes ☐ No ☐   Total for photo print(s) & scan(s) $0 _____
Special Instructions _____   Commercial use fees (if applicable) $ _____
_____   Order Total $0 _____

Office Use Only: Date Order Rec'd _____ Payment Rec'd _____ UA Rec'd _____ Completed _____

Rev. 1/2019

Source: Wyoming State Archives, Cheyenne, Wyoming

APPENDIX F

Examples of Permission to Publish Forms

Willamette University

WILLAMETTE UNIVERSITY

Permission to Publish or Use Reproductions of Materials Archives and Special Collections

Please type or print the following information:

Name: _____

Organization (if applicable): _____

Address: _____

_____

Telephone number: _____ Email: _____

    I hereby request authorization to publish or to use in facsimile reproduction the material(s) identified below from Willamette University Archives and Special Collections. The permission granted is for a single use of the material(s) in a publication, exhibit, or other medium. Subsequent use of the material(s), including reprints or new editions of a publication, requires a separate request for permission to publish. By signing this form I acknowledge that I understand and agree to the following stipulations:

    I understand and agree that in giving its permission Willamette University retains its right to publish the materials identified below or to grant permission to others to do so, and that I am responsible for publishing or for using in facsimile reproduction these materials in accordance with the copyright protections established in the United States Copyright Law. I also agree not to alter the image in any way when publishing or displaying the reproduction.

    I understand and agree that this authorization does not grant license to make any of the materials identified below part of any other institution or organization's archives, photographic collections or special collection. Nor does this authorization by Willamette University remove the author's and publisher's responsibility to guard against the infringement of rights that may be held by others.

Material to be published or used in facsimile reproduction (please include collection title, box number, image number, etc.):

Intended use of materials (list type of publication, title of work, publisher, anticipated date of publication):

Source: Willamette University, Salem, Oregon

I agree to use the following credit line when I publish or use in facsimile reproduction the material(s) listed above:

Image courtesy of Willamette University Archives and Special Collections

I agree to the conditions above and will provide to Willamette University Archives and Special Collections a gratis copy of the final publication or other product that utilizes these reproductions.

Signature: _____ Date: _____

Send or fax completed form to:
Willamette University Archives and Special Collections
900 State Street
Salem, OR 97301
503.370.6141 (fax) · 503-370-6764 (phone)

(Staff Use Only below this line)

Willamette University Authorization

Willamette University Archives and Special Collections hereby authorizes the requester to publish or use in facsimile reproduction the material(s) identified above. In authorizing the publication or use of these materials Willamette retains its right to publish these materials and to grant permission to others to do so. This authorization does not remove the requestor's responsibility to guard against the infringement of rights that may be held by others.

Signature: _____ Date: _____
Title: _____

Additional comments:

Source: Willamette University, Salem, Oregon

Appendix F: Examples of Permission to Publish Forms 163

Connecticut State Library

Permission to Publish, Exhibit, Broadcast or Other Use Request Form
(For items the State Library owns all or a part of the copyright)

Name: _____
Institution: _____
Address: _____
City: _____ State: _____ Zip: _____
Phone No.: _____ Email: _____

Materials Requested (check all that apply)

☐ Artifacts ☐ Manuscripts ☐ Images ☐ Digital File ☐ Printed Materials

Other: _____

If from an archival Record Group, please include RG, series, box, and folder numbers; call number and title if from classified collections; artifact accession number, or other appropriate designation.

_____

(Attach a separate List of Materials Requested if necessary.)

Use to be Made of Material Requested (check all that apply)

☐ Article ☐ Book ☐ Broadcast ☐ Digital ☐ Exhibition ☐ Family History ☐ MA Thesis
☐ Ph.D. Dissertation ☐ Internet ☐ Promotional Other Use: _____

Title of Publication/Display/Film, etc.: _____

(Brief description of use, size of printing, display etc.): _____

(Anticipated Date or Duration of Use): _____

I/We have read the Connecticut State Library's Permission to Publish, Exhibit, or Broadcast policies and procedures and agree to abide by its restrictions and requirements. I/We certify that I/we are vested with full authority to execute this request and agreement, that the information entered is true and accurate, and that I have read and agree to all stated terms and conditions.

Signature: _____ Print Name: _____ Date: __/__/__

Please e-mail completed form to CSL.collserv@ct.gov or mail to
Connecticut State Library, 231 Capitol Ave., Hartford, CT 06106
Attn: Collection Services

LIBRARY STAFF USE ONLY
Permission is granted for publication of the items and use described on this form.

Name: _____ Title: _____ Date: _____

Revised July 24, 2018

Source: Connecticut State Library, Hartford, Connecticut

Permission to Publish, Exhibit, Broadcast, or Other Use
Reproductions of Materials From the Connecticut State Library or Museum of Connecticut History

(Note: In general, this policy concerns the use of Connecticut State Library collections that go beyond the "fair use" provisions in copyright law. For example, reproducing materials for personal and educational use usually does not require permission. For all other uses, however, you will need permission from the copyright holder.)

The Connecticut State Library encourages the use of its collections for publication and welcomes requests to reproduce its materials. All those requesting permission to publish, exhibit, or broadcast materials held by the Connecticut State Library should follow the policies and procedures outlined below.

1. By providing access to materials, or by supplying a reproduction of materials, the State Library does not authorize publication of this material. Except in cases where items are already in the public domain, researchers must obtain the permission of the copyright holder before publishing, exhibiting, or broadcasting items found in State Library collections. Also, some materials may be protected by other intellectual property or privacy laws. Though the State Library will sometimes assist researchers in determining the rights relating to specific library material, responsibility for determining copyright ownership or other rights rests solely with the researcher.

2. In cases where the Connecticut State Library holds copyright of the material reproduced, the State Library will consider providing a non-exclusive right to publication, exhibition, or broadcast. Researchers should fill out and submit the form below. Permission to publish is granted for the mutually agreed upon use as described on this form. In giving such permission, the State Library does not surrender its own right to publish, exhibit, or broadcast the material. It is the responsibility of the researcher to determine if the item reproduced requires copyright permission from other copyright holders.

3. The Connecticut State Library sometimes labels material produced by the State Library with a Creative Commons license. In these cases, researchers may use the materials according to the license included with the material. Any use not covered by the license, however, will require submission of a permission to publish form and the State Library will consider providing a non-exclusive right to publication, exhibition, or broadcast.

4. When publishing, exhibiting, or broadcasting any material from the Connecticut State Library or Museum of Connecticut History (regardless of copyright status), researchers should use the following credit line: "collection name, Connecticut State Library" or "Museum of Connecticut History." For items in the Archives, use: "title of item, record or picture group, State Archives, Connecticut State Library." Example 1: [Name or description of photo], PG 460, Colt Firearms Industry Collection, ca, 1864-1926, State Archives, Connecticut State Library. Example 2: "Signed Labor/Management Agreement Not to Strike During the War," Record Group 005, Governor Robert Hurley, State Archives, Connecticut State Library.

5. In cases where the Connecticut State Library holds copyright of the material reproduced and has given permission for its reproduction, the applicant must provide attribution (as outlined in #4 above) and must provide the State Library with a copy of the item in which the material appears.

6. Also, any time there is a significant amount of material from Connecticut State Library or Museum of Connecticut History collections used in a publication, exhibit or broadcast, the State Library should receive a copy of the item in which the material appears.

7. If approved by the Connecticut State Library, the completed and signed permission request form contains the full and complete agreement between the applicant and the State of Connecticut, Connecticut State Library and it cannot be altered or amended except in writing, signed by the applicant and a duly authorized representative of the Connecticut State Library.

8. The laws of the State of Connecticut shall govern any disputes arising under this agreement.

Revised May, 2012

Source: Connecticut State Library, Hartford, Connecticut

Bibliography

Abraham, Terry, Stephen E. Balzarini, and Anne Frantilla. "What Is Backlog Is Prologue: A Measurement of Archival Processing." *American Archivist* 48, no. 1 (1985): 31–44. https://doi.org/10.17723/aarc.48.1.m677m48014427332.

Academy of Certified Archivists. "Role Delineation Statement for Professional Archivists." www.certifiedarchivists.org/get-certified/role-delineation-statement/#domain3, captured at https://perma.cc/SB33-JQDW.

Adobe, Inc. "Training Resources | Adobe Acrobat Accessibility." www.adobe.com/accessibility/products/acrobat/training.html.

Aftergood, Steven. "More Light on Black Program to Track UFOs." *Secrecy News* (blog). Federation of American Scientists, January 17, 2019. https://fas.org/blogs/secrecy/2019/01/aatip-list/, captured at https://perma.cc/2UCD-MD9Y.

Alvis, Alexandra K. "No Love for White Gloves, or: The Cotton Menace." *Unbound* (blog). Smithsonian Libraries, November 21, 2019. https://blog.library.si.edu/blog/2019/11/21/no-love-for-white-gloves-or-the-cotton-menace/#.XfhgH9ZKjUo, captured at https://perma.cc/Z39Q-3RXY.

American Association of Museums. *National Standards and Best Practices for U.S. Museums.* Washington DC: American Association of Museums, 2008.

American Foundation for the Blind. "Web Accessibility Resources." www.afb.org/about-afb/what-we-do/afb-consulting/afb-accessibility-resources/resources-2177.

American Library Association. *Archives and Libraries. Papers Presented at the 1939 Conference of the American Library Association, Representing the Joint Program of the Committee on Archives and Libraries of the A.L.A., the Pacific Coast Members of the Society of American Archivists and the Historical Records Survey.* Chicago: American Library Association, 1939.

———. "USA PATRIOT Act." www.ala.org/advocacy/advleg/federallegislation/theusapatriotact, captured at https://perma.cc/X3KR-VDVT.

American Library Association, Reference and User Services Association. "Guidelines for Behavioral Performance of Reference and Information Service Providers." www.ala.org/rusa/resources/guidelines/guidelinesbehavioral, captured at https://perma.cc/VR5R-FR9T.

American Numismatic Society. "Proper Citation Format." 2016. http://numismatics.org/archive/citationformat/, captured at https://perma.cc/Q8VC-YHCR.

Anderson, Christopher J. "Special Collections, Archives, and Insider Theft: A Thief in Our Midst." In *Management: Innovative Practices for Archives and Special Collections*, edited by Kate Theimer, 45–60. Lanham, MD: Rowman & Littlefield, 2014.

Anderson, Ian G. "Are You Being Served? Historians and the Search for Primary Sources." *Archivaria* 58 (Fall 2004): 81–129. https://archivaria.ca/index.php/archivaria/article/view/12479.

Anderson, Susan K. "Research Use: Ethics, Restrictions, and Privacy." In *Museum Archives: An Introduction*, 2nd ed., edited by Deborah Wythe, 55–64. Chicago: Society of American Archivists, 2004.

ArchiveGrid. https://researchworks.oclc.org/archivegrid/.

Archives and Records Association, UK and Ireland. "Code of Ethics." https://www.archives.org.uk/images/ARA_Board/2019/Code_Of_Ethics_February_2020_final.pdf, captured at https://perma.cc/CAV5-FZLY.

Archives for Black Lives in Philadelphia, Anti-Racist Description Working Group. *Anti-Racist Description Resources.* Philadelphia, 2019. https://archivesforblacklives.files.wordpress.com/2019/10/ardr_final.pdf, captured at https://perma.cc/5HWG-64D9.

ArchivesSpace. "Accessibility and VPAT." 2020. https://archivesspace.org/application/accessibility-vpat.

Arizona State Library, Archives, and Public Records. "Continuing Education." https://azlibrary.gov/libdev/continuing-education.

ARMA International. "Code of Ethics." www.arma.org/page/IGP_Ethics, captured at https://perma.cc/CM2K-M289.

Arnold, Timothy, and Walker Sampson. "Preserving the Voices of Revolution: Examining the Creation and Preservation of a Subject-Centered Collection of Tweets from the Eighteen Days in Egypt." *American Archivist* 77, no. 2 (2014): 510–533. https://doi.org/10.17723/aarc.77.2.794404552m67024n.

Bibliography

Asher, Andrew D. "Use, Security, and Ethics of Data Collection: Risks, Benefits, and User Privacy: Evaluating the Ethics of Library Data." In *Protecting Patron Privacy: A LITA Guide*, edited by Bobbi Newman and Bonnie Tijerina, 43–56. Lanham, MD: Rowman & Littlefield, 2017.

Association of Canadian Archivists. "Code of Ethics and Professional Conduct." October 18, 2017. https://archivists.ca/resources/Documents/Governance%20and%20Structure/aca_code_of_ethics_final_october_2017.pdf, captured at https:// perma.cc/2QC5-8GPG.

Association of College and Research Libraries. "ACRL Standards, Guidelines, and Frameworks." www.ala.org/acrl/standards/alphabetical.

———. "ACRL/RBMS Guidelines for Interlibrary and Exhibition Loan of Special Collections Materials." January 2012. www.ala.org/acrl/standards/specialcollections, captured at https://perma.cc/3XG4-2TSZ.

———. "ACRL/RBMS Guidelines Regarding Security and Theft in Special Collections." Revised January 2019. www.ala.org/acrl/standards/security_theft, captured at https://perma.cc/TV9K-VX46.

———. "Guidelines: Competencies for Special Collections Professionals." Revised March 6, 2017. www.ala.org/acrl/standards/comp4specollect, captured at https://perma.cc/3T6K-DEDE.

Association of Religion Data Archives. "Quality Data on Religion." www.thearda.com/.

Association of Research Libraries. "Hidden Collections, Scholarly Barriers: Creating Access to Unprocessed Special Collections Materials in North America's Research Libraries." White Paper. June 6, 2003. https://www.arl.org/wp-content/uploads/2003/06/hidden-colls-white-paper-jun03.pdf, captured at https://perma.cc/ZZ3R-4W2A.

Association of Specialized Government and Cooperative Library Agencies. "Resources." www.asgcladirect.org/resources/.

Australian Society of Archivists. "Code of Ethics." June 17, 1993. www.archivists.org.au/about-us/code-of-ethics, captured at https://perma.cc/QT69-3QHZ.

Bahde, Anne, Heather Smedberg, and Mattie Taormina, eds. *Using Primary Sources: Hands-On Instructional Exercises*. Santa Barbara, CA: Libraries Unlimited, 2014.

Barker, Claire S. "How to Select Gloves: An Overview for Collections Staff." National Park Service. *Conserve O Gram* 1, no. 12 (September 2010): 1–3. www.nps.gov/museum/publications/conserveogram/01-12.pdf, captured at https://perma.cc/ KRG7-7TXT.

Bastian, Jeannette, Megan Sniffin-Marinoff, and Donna Webber. *Archives in Libraries: What Librarians and Archivists Need to Know to Work Together*. Chicago: Society of American Archivists, 2015.

Batterham, Ian. *The Copying Revolution: History, Identification and Preservation: A Manual for Conservators, Archivists, Librarians and Forensic Document Examiners*. Canberra, Australia: National Archives of Australia, 2008.

Baucom, Erin. "An Exploration into Archival Descriptions of LGBTQ Materials." *American Archivist* 81, no. 1 (2018): 65–83. https://doi.org/10.17723/0360-9081-81.1.65.

Bearman, David. "Archival Strategies." *American Archivist* 58. no. 4 (1995): 380–413. https://doi.org/10.17723/aarc.58.4.pq71240520j31798.

Beckstrom, Matt. "Use, Security, and Ethics of Data Collection: Data Collection, Retention, Use, and Security." In *Protecting Patron Privacy: A LITA Guide*, edited by Bobbi Newman and Bonnie Tijerina, 35–42. Lanham, MD: Rowman & Littlefield, 2017.

Been, Joshua. "Topics from Tweets Mentioning Baylor University." Baylor University Libraries. Digital Scholarship. September 1, 2018. https://blogs.baylor.edu/digitalscholarship/2018/09/01/topics-from-tweets-mentioning-baylor-university/, captured at https://perma.cc/C56Z-YAW2.

Behrens, Shirley J. "A Conceptual Analysis and Historical Overview of Information Literacy." *College and Research Libraries* 55, no. 4 (1994): 309–322. https://doi.org/10.5860/crl_55_04_309.

Behrnd-Klodt, Menzi. "Lawyers, Archivists and Librarians: United or Divided in the Pursuit of Justice?" In *Public Services Issues with Rare and Archival Law Materials*, edited by Michael Widener, 113–133. New York: Haworth Information Press, 2001.

———. *Navigating Legal Issues in Archives*. Chicago: Society of American Archivists, 2008.

Benedict, Karen. *Ethics and the Archival Profession: Introduction and Case Studies*. Chicago: Society of American Archivists, 2003.

Bennett, Stephanie, Stephanie Bayless, Chrystal Carpenter, Stacey Flores Chandler, and Krista Ferrante. "I Second That Emotion: Working with Emotionally Challenging Collections." Presented at the Society of American Archivists Annual Meeting, Atlanta, GA, August 4, 2016.

Benoit, Edward III. "#MPLP Part 1: Comparing Domain Expert and Novice Social Tags in a Minimally Processed Digital Archives." *American Archivist* 80, no. 2 (2017): 407–438. https://doi.org/10.17723/0360-9081-80.2.407.

———. "#MPLP Part 2: Replacing Item-Level Metadata with User-Generated Social Tags." *American Archivist* 81, no. 1 (2018): 38–64. https://doi.org/10.17723/0360-9081-81.1.38.

Berger, Sidney E. *Rare Books and Special Collections*. Chicago: ALA Neal-Schuman, 2014.

Bernard, Sheila Curran, and Kenn Rabin. *Archival Storytelling: A Filmmaker's Guide to Finding, Using, and Licensing Third-Party Visuals and Music*. New York: Focal Press, 2016.

Bishop, Wade, and Tony H. Grubesic. *Geographic Information Organization, Access, and Use*. Cham, Switzerland: Springer International Publishing, 2018.

Black Archives of Mid-America. "Reading Room Guidelines and Rules." http://blackarchives.org/sites/default/files/ReadingRoomGuidelines.pdf, captured at https://perma.cc/4SMT-QGJP.

Boise State University. "Selected Works of Elisa H. Barney Smith." https://works.bepress.com/elisa_barney_smith/.

Boles, Frank. *Selecting and Appraising Archives and Manuscripts.* Chicago: Society of American Archivists, 2005.

Bordin, Ruth B., and Robert M. Warner. *The Modern Manuscript Library.* New York: Scarecrow Press, 1966.

Bourgoin, Marisa. "Research Use: Outreach." In *Museum Archives: An Introduction*, 2nd ed., edited by Deborah Wythe, 55–64. Chicago: Society of American Archivists, 2004.

Bourne, Charles P., and Trudi Bellardo Hahn. *A History of Online Information Services: 1963–1976.* Cambridge, MA: MIT Press, 2003.

Brichford, Maynard, Harriet Ostroff, John P. Butler, and Richard H. Lytle. "Intellectual Control of Historical Records." *American Archivist* 40, no. 3 (1977): 307–313. https://doi.org/10.17723/aarc.40.3.30436v4722504547.

Briston, Heather. "Understanding Copyright Law." In *Rights in the Digital Era*, edited by Menzi Behrnd-Klodt and Christopher J. Prom, 10–71. Chicago: Society of American Archivists, 2015.

Brown University Library, John Hay Library. "Reading Room Regulations." https://library.brown.edu/hay/regulations.php, captured at https://perma.cc/XW72-BDKR.

Burgess, John T. F., and Emily J. M. Knox, eds. *Foundations of Information Ethics.* Chicago: ALA Neal-Schuman, 2019.

Burke, Frank G. "The Application of Automated Techniques in the Management and Control of Source Materials." *American Archivist* 30, no. 2 (1967): 255–278. https://doi.org/10.17723/aarc.30.2.a427563789262223.

Burton, Antoinette, ed. *Archive Stories: Facts, Fictions, and the Writing of History.* Durham, NC: Duke University Press, 2005.

Cairn, Rich. "Primary Sources: At the Heart of the Common Core State Standards." *TPS Journal* 1, no. 2 (Fall 2012). http://www.loc.gov/teachers/tps/journal/common_core/article.html.

Camera, Lauren. "Hollins University Removes Access to Yearbooks with Racist Images." *U.S. News and World Report,* April 3, 2019. www.usnews.com/news/education-news/articles/2019-04-03/hollins-university-removes-access-to-yearbooks-with-racist-images, captured at https://perma.cc/7CKB-9JX2.

Carmicheal, David. "Functional Spaces." In *Archival and Special Collections Facilities: Guidelines for Archivists, Librarians, Architects, and Engineers*, edited by Michele F. Pacifico and Thomas P. Wilsted, 127–148. Chicago: Society of American Archivists, 2009.

Case, Donald O., and Lisa M. Given. *Looking for Information: A Survey of Research on Information Seeking, Needs, and Behavior*, 4th ed. Bingley, UK: Emerald Group Publishing Limited, 2016.

Center for Media and Social Impact. "Code of Best Practices in Fair Use for Software Preservation." September 2018. https://cmsimpact.org/code/fair-use-software-preservation/, captured at https://perma.cc/LG9H-UH6Z.

Chalou, George. "Reference." In *A Manual of Archival Techniques*, edited by Roland M. Baumann, 47–53. Harrisburg, PA: Pennsylvania Historical and Museum Commission, 1979.

Chassanoff, Alexandra. "Historians and the Use of Primary Source Materials in the Digital Age." *American Archivist* 76, no. 2 (2013): 458–480. https://doi.org/10.17723/aarc.76.2.lh76217m2m376n28.

Chosky, Carol E. B. "Leading a Successful Records Management Program." In *Leading and Managing Archives and Records Programs: Strategies for Success*, edited by Bruce W. Dearstyne, 69–90. New York: Neal-Schuman Publishers, 2008.

Christopher, Henry George Thomas. *Palaeography and Archives: A Manual for the Librarian, Archivist and Student*. London: Grafton & Co., 1938.

City of Camden, South Carolina. "Friends of the Archives and Museum." www.cityofcamden.org/departments/archives-museum/friends-archives-museum, captured at https://perma.cc/45F8-FZFH.

Cloonan, Michèle Valerie, ed. *Preserving Our Heritage: Perspectives from Antiquity to the Digital Age*. Chicago: ALA Neal-Schuman, 2015.

College of William and Mary. "AidData: A Research Lab at William & Mary." www.aiddata.org/.

Connaway, Lynn Silipigni, and Marie L. Radford. *Research Methods in Library and Information Science*, 6th ed. Santa Barbara, CA: Libraries Unlimited, 2017.

Conway, Paul. "Modes of Seeing: Digitized Photographic Archives and the Experienced User." *American Archivist* 73, no. 2 (2010): 425–462. https://doi.org/10.17723/aarc.73.2.mp275470663n5907.

Copyright.gov. "More Information on Fair Use." www.copyright.gov/fair-use/more-info.html, captured at https://perma.cc/JDC4-4NMU.

———. "Revising Section 108: Copyright Exceptions for Libraries and Archives." www.copyright.gov/policy/section108/, captured at https://perma.cc/TTL9-6NFE.

———. "Section 1201 | U.S. Copyright Office." www.copyright.gov/1201/2018/, captured at https://perma.cc/7M96-MH9Z.

Corrall, Sheila. "Planning and Policy Making." In *Building a Successful Customer-Service Culture: A Guide for Library and Information Managers*, edited by Maxine Melling and Joyce Little, 27–52. London: Facet Publishing, 2002.

Cox, Richard J. *Archives and Archivists in the Information Age*. New York: Neal-Schuman Publishers, 2005.

Craven, Louise. *What Are Archives?: Cultural and Theoretical Perspectives: A Reader*. London: Routledge, 2017.

Crittendon, Christopher, ed. *Historical Societies in the United States and Canada: A Handbook.* Washington DC: American Association for State and Local History, 1944.

Crymble, Adam. "An Analysis of Twitter and Facebook Use by the Archival Community." *Archivaria* 70 (Fall 2010): 125–151. https://archivaria.ca/index.php/archivaria/article/view/13298.

Dalhousie University. "Guide to Archival Research." https://dal.ca.libguides.com/c.php?g=257178&p=5022146, captured at https://perma.cc/3L46-SFAT.

Daniels, Jessie, and Polly Thistlethwaite. *Being a Scholar in the Digital Era: Transforming Scholarly Practice for the Public Good.* Bristol, UK: Policy Press, 2016.

Daniels, Matt. "The Largest Vocabulary in Hip Hop." *The Pudding.* https://pudding.cool/projects/vocabulary/index.html, captured at https://perma.cc/R62F-AGBB.

Daniels, Maygene. "Architectural Records." In *Museum Archives: An Introduction*, 2nd ed., edited by Deborah Wythe, 153–159. Chicago: Society of American Archivists, 2004.

Danielson, Elena. *The Ethical Archivist.* Chicago: Society of American Archivists, 2010.

Dearstyne, Bruce W. *The Archival Enterprise: Modern Archival Principles, Practices, and Management Techniques.* Chicago: American Library Association, 1993.

Decker, Juliee, ed. *Engagement and Access: Innovative Approaches for Museums.* Lanham, MD: Rowman & Littlefield, 2015.

Delsalle, Paul. *A History of Archival Practice.* Translated and revised by Margaret Procter. New York: Routledge, 2017.

Denver Public Library, Genealogy, African American and Western History Resources. "Research Guides." https://history.denverlibrary.org/research.

Desnoyers, Megan Floyd. "When Is a Collection Processed?" *Midwestern Archivist* 7, no. 1 (1982): 5–23. https://minds.wisconsin.edu/handle/1793/44721.

Dictionary of Archives Terminology, s.v. "appraisal," Society of American Archivists. https://dictionary.archivists.org/entry/appraisal.html, captured at https://perma.cc/B2QL-53UT.

———. s.v. "born digital." https://dictionary.archivists.org/entry/born-digital.html, captured at https://perma.cc/Q5YQ-QCNX.

———. s.v. "outreach." https://dictionary.archivists.org/entry/outreach.html, captured at https://perma.cc/RS2T-AP4V.

———. s.v. "provenance." https://dictionary.archivists.org/entry/provenance.html, captured at https://perma.cc/8CUQ-B23L.

———. s.v. "reading room." https://dictionary.archivists.org/entry/reading-room.html, captured at https://perma.cc/8SMF-L6VH.

———. s.v. "reference interview." https://dictionary.archivists.org/entry/reference-interview.html, captured at https://perma.cc/D8XS-MW8V.

———. s.v. "series." https://dictionary.archivists.org/entry/series.html, captured at https://perma.cc/MH6D-P4N8.

———. s.v. "user." https://dictionary.archivists.org/entry/user.html, captured at https://perma.cc/RN59-MP8C.

———. s.v. "virtual reading room." https://dictionary.archivists.org/entry/virtual-reading-room.html, captured at https://perma.cc/KPQ2-2YF7.

Digital Public Library of America. "API Codex." https://pro.dp.la/developers/api-codex.

Dow, Elizabeth H. *Archivists, Collectors, Dealers, and Replevin: Case Studies on Private Ownership of Public Documents*. Lanham, MD: Scarecrow Press, 2012.

Dowson, Jane. "Elizabeth Jennings, 1926–2001: About This Website." Centre for Textual Studies. http://elizabethjennings.dmu.ac.uk/about_site.html.

Duckett, Kenneth W. *Modern Manuscripts: A Practical Manual for Their Management, Care, and Use*. Nashville: American Association for State and Local History, 1975.

Duff, Wendy M., and Catherine A. Johnson. "Where Is the List with All the Names? Information-Seeking Behavior of Genealogists." *American Archivist* 66, no. 1 (2003): 79–95. https://doi.org/10.17723/aarc.66.1.b120370l1g718n74.

Duff, Wendy M., Catherine A. Johnson, and Joan M. Cherry. "Reaching Out, Reaching In: A Preliminary Investigation into Archives' Use of Social Media in Canada." *Archivaria* 75 (2013): 77–96. https://archivaria.ca/index.php/archivaria/article/view/13434.

Duff, Wendy M., Elizabeth Yakel, and Helen R. Tibbo. "Archival Reference Knowledge." *American Archivist* 76, no. 1 (2013): 68–94. https://doi.org/10.17723/aarc.76.1.x9792xp27140285g.

Dunham, Elizabeth, and Xaviera Flores. "Breaking the Language Barrier: Describing Chicano Archives with Bilingual Finding Aids." *American Archivist* 77, no. 2 (2014): 499–509. https://doi.org/10.17723/aarc.77.2.p66l555g15g981p6.

Dunlap, Leslie W. *American Historical Societies, 1790–1860*. Philadelphia: Porcupine Press, 1974.

Eastwood, Terry and Heather MacNeil. *Currents of Archival Thinking*. Santa Barbara, CA: Libraries Unlimited, 2010.

Eddington, Patrick G. "MLK and the FBI: 50 Years On, Secrets and Surveillance Still." *The Hill*, April 4, 2019. https://thehill.com/opinion/civil-rights/436437-mlk-and-the-fbi-50-years-on-secrets-and-surveillance-still.

Eichhorn, Kate. *The Archival Turn in Feminism: Outrage in Order*. Philadelphia: Temple University Press, 2013.

Emory Libraries and Information Technology. Stuart A. Rose Manuscript, Archives, and Rare Book Library. "Accessibility." 2020. http://rose.library.emory.edu/about/accessibility.html, captured at https://perma.cc/JLX9-2YWW.

Fair, Bethany, Hannah Abelbeck, Stacey Flores Chandler, Marta Crilly, and Nadia Dixson. "Lumos Maxima! Illuminating Controversial or Restricted Records through Outreach." Presented at the Society of American Archivists Annual Meeting, Washington, DC, August 18, 2019.

Farge, Arlette. *The Allure of the Archives*. Translated by Thomas Scott-Railton. New Haven: Yale University Press, 2013.

Fischer, Lance J. "The Deaf and Archival Research: Some Problems and Solutions." *American Archivist* 42, no. 4 (1979): 463–464. https://doi.org/10.17723/aarc.42.4.bt681l38560032x2.

Fisher, Barbara. "Byproducts of Computer Processing." *American Archivist* 32, no. 3 (1969). https://doi.org/10.17723/aarc.32.3.y7x58648782q6720.

Foscarini, Fiorella. *Engaging with Archives and Records: Histories and Theories*. London: Facet Publishing, 2017.

Freeman, Elsie T. "In the Eye of the Beholder: Archives Administration from the User's Point of View." *American Archivist* 47, no. 2 (1984): 111–123. https://doi.org/10.17723/aarc.47.2.a373340078502136.

French, Brett. "Bison Group Sues to Get FOIA Fulfilled; Yellowstone Bison Population Reported." *Billings Gazette*, October 14, 2019. https://billingsgazette.com/outdoors/bison-group-sues-to-get-foia-fulfilled-yellowstone-bison-population/article_80bb8469-7e87-5789-a2c8-cd8eaa18ae06.html.

Friends of the British Columbia Archives. "Friends of the BC Archives." https://friendsofbcarchives.wordpress.com/, captured at https://perma.cc/G82M-8C63.

Frisch, Scott A., Douglas B. Harris, Sean Q. Kelly, et al., eds. *Doing Archival Research in Political Science*. Amherst, NY: Cambria Press, 2012.

Gaillet, Lynée Lewis. "(Per)Forming Archival Research Methodologies." *College Composition and Communication* 64, no. 1 (September 2012): 35–58.

Gaillet, Lynée Lewis, and Michelle F. Eble. *Primary Research and Writing: People, Places, and Spaces*. New York: Routledge, 2016.

Galbraith, V. H. *Introduction to the Use of the Public Records*. Oxford: Clarendon Press, 1934.

George, Christine Anne. "Archives Beyond the Pale: Negotiating Legal and Ethical Entanglements after the Belfast Project." *American Archivist* 76, no. 1 (2013): 47–67. https://doi.org/10.17723/aarc.76.1.x34p8k7848512274.

Gilardi, Ronald L. "The Archival Setting and People with Disabilities: A Legal Analysis." *American Archivist* 56, no. 4 (1993): 704–713. https://doi.org/10.17723/aarc.56.4.68070hw410848230.

Gilliland, Anne J. *Conceptualizing 21st-Century Archives*. Chicago: Society of American Archivists, 2014.

Gilliland, Anne J., Sue McKemmish, and Andrew J. Lau, eds. *Research in the Archival Multiverse*. Clayton, Victoria, Australia: Monash University Publishing, 2017.

Gilliland-Swetland, Anne J. "An Exploration of K–12 User Needs for Digital Primary Source Materials." *American Archivist* 61, no. 1 (1998): 136–157. https://doi.org/10.17723/aarc.61.1.w851770151576l03.

Gottlieb, Peter. "Strategic Leadership." In *Leading and Managing Archives and Manuscripts Programs*, edited by Peter Gottlieb and David Carmicheal, 25–39. Chicago: Society of American Archivists, 2019.

Government of Canada. "Historical Climate Data." December 4, 2019. https://climate.weather.gc.ca/.

Greene, Mark A., and Dennis Meissner. "More Product, Less Process: Revamping Traditional Archival Processing." *American Archivist* 68, no. 2 (2005): 208–263. https://doi.org/10.17723/aarc.68.2.c741823776k65863.

Greenwood, Shannon, Andrew Perrin, and Maeve Duggan. "Social Media Update 2016." Pew Research Center, Internet and Technology, November 11, 2016. www.pewresearch.org/internet/2016/11/11/social-media-update-2016/, captured at https://perma.cc/HXG9-4UPH.

Griffith, Sally Foreman. *Serving History in a Changing World: The Historical Society of Pennsylvania in the Twentieth Century*. Philadelphia: Historical Society of Pennsylvania, 2001.

Gustainis, Emily R., and Phoebe Evans Letocha. "The Practice of Privacy." In *Innovation, Collaboration, and Models: Proceedings of the CLIR Cataloging Hidden Special Collections and Archives Symposium*, edited by Cheryl Oestreicher. Philadelphia: Council on Library and Information Resources, 2015. www.clir.org/pubs/reports/pub169/, captured at https://perma.cc/3C2Q-P3AU.

Guthrie, Kevin M. *The New-York Historical Society: Lessons from One Nonprofit's Long Struggle for Survival*. Houston, TX: Long Tail Press/Rice University Press, 2008.

Hackbart-Dean, Pam, and Elizabeth Slomba. *How to Manage Processing in Archives and Special Collections*. Chicago: Society of American Archivists, 2012.

Hackman, Larry, ed. *Many Happy Returns: Advocacy and the Development of Archives*. Chicago: Society of American Archivists, 2011.

Handbook of Procedures. Washington, DC: National Archives and Records Service, 1952.

Hamer, Philip M., ed. *A Guide to Archives and Manuscripts in the United States, Compiled for the National Historical Publications Commission*. New Haven: Yale University Press, 1961.

Harris, Valerie, and Kathryn Stine. "Politically Charged Records: A Case Study with Recommendations for Providing Access to a Challenging Collection." *American Archivist* 74, no. 2 (2011): 633–651. https://doi.org/10.17723/aarc.74.2.f252r28174251525.

Harris, Verne, ed. *Archives and Justice*. Chicago: Society of American Archivists, 2007.

Hernon, Peter, and Robert E. Dugan. *An Action Plan for Outcomes Assessment in Your Library*. Chicago: American Library Association, 2002.

Hershey Community Archives. "About Us." https://hersheyarchives.org/about-us/.

Heyliger, Sean, Juli McLoone, and Nikki Lynn Thomas. "Making Connections: A Survey of Special Collections' Social Media Outreach." *American Archivist* 76, no. 2 (2013): 374–414, https://doi.org/10.17723/aarc.76.2.t820u33100443q55.

Hinchliffe, Lisa Janicke. "Instruction." In *Reference and Information Services: An Introduction*, 4th ed., edited by Richard E. Bopp and Linda C. Smith, 221–260. Santa Barbara, CA: Libraries Unlimited, 2011.

Hirtle, Peter B., Emily Hudson, and Andrew T. Kenyon. *Copyright and Cultural Institutions: Guidelines for Digitization for U.S. Libraries, Archives, and Museums*. Ithaca, NY: Cornell University Library, 2009.

Hubbard, Melissa A., Robert H. Jackson, and Arnold Hirshon, eds. *Forging the Future of Special Collections*. Chicago: ALA Neal-Schuman, 2016.

Hunter, Gregory. *Developing and Maintaining Practical Archives: A How-To-Do-It Manual*, 2nd ed. New York: Neal-Schuman Publishers, 2003.

Huth, Geof. "Appraising Digital Records." In *Appraisal and Acquisition Strategies*, edited by Michael Shallcross and Christopher J. Prom, 10–66. Chicago: Society of American Archivists, 2016.

Indiana Archives and Records Administration. "The Friends of the Indiana State Archives." www.in.gov/iara/2777.htm, captured at https://perma.cc/4DUC-8CML.

Indiana University Bloomington, Libraries. "Friends of the Archives of Traditional Music." https://libraries.indiana.edu/atm-friends, captured at https://perma.cc/2XPF-VNXX.

Inter-university Consortium for Political and Social Research. www.icpsr.umich.edu/icpsrweb/.

Isaacson, David. "Pleasures and Pitfalls That Can Make or Break a Reference Encounter." In *Philosophies of Reference Service*, edited by Celia Hales Mabry, 59–66. New York: Haworth Press, 1997.

Isabella Stewart Gardner Museum. "Virtual Reading Room." www.gardnermuseum.org/organization/virtual-reading-room.

Janick, Nathaniel. "Heard But Not Seen: Making Hidden Oral History Collections Discoverable." In *Innovation, Collaboration and Models: Proceedings of the CLIR Cataloging Hidden Special Collections and Archives Symposium*, edited by Cheryl Oestreicher. Philadelphia: Council on Library and Information Resources, 2015. www.clir.org/pubs/reports/pub169/, captured at https://perma.cc/3C2Q-P3AU.

Jenkinson, Sir Hilary. "The English Archivist: A New Profession." In *Selected Writings of Sir Hilary Jenkinson*, edited by Roger H. Ellis and Peter Walne, 236–259. Chicago: Society of American Archivists, 2003.

Jimerson, Randall C. *Archives Power: Memory, Accountability, and Social Justice*. Chicago: Society of American Archivists, 2009.

John F. Kennedy Presidential Library and Museum. "Basics of Archival Research." www.jfklibrary.org/archives/search-collections/basics-of-archival-research, captured at https://perma.cc/QGS2-RCCT.

Jones, Arnita A., and Philip L. Cantelon. *Corporate Archives and History: Making the Past Work*. Malabar, FL: Krieger Publishing Company, 1993.

Juel, Sara. "Anonymizing Users." Atlas Systems. 2019. http://support.atlas-sys.com/hc/en-us/articles/360011920093-Anonymizing-Users, captured at https://perma.cc/78WX-2KSV.

Kaplan, Louis. *The Growth of Reference Service in the United States from 1876 to 1893*. Chicago: Publications Committee of the Association of College and Reference Libraries, 1952.

Kelly, Elizabeth Joan. "Altmetrics and Archives." *Journal of Contemporary Archival Studies* 4, Article 1 (2017). https://elischolar.library.yale.edu/jcas/vol4/iss1/1/.

Kepley, Brenda Beasley. "Archives: Accessibility for the Disabled." *American Archivist* 46, no. 1 (1983): 42–51. https://doi.org/10.17723/aarc.46.1.7275k33t7817w00u.

Kepley, David R. "Reference Service and Access." In *Managing Archives and Archival Institutions*, edited by James Gregory Bradsher, 161–173. Chicago: The University of Chicago Press, 1989.

Kern, M. Kathleen, and Beth S. Woodard. "The Reference Interview." In *Reference and Information Services: An Introduction*, 4th ed., edited by Richard E. Bopp and Linda C. Smith, 57–94. Santa Barbara, CA: Libraries Unlimited, 2011.

Kiesling, Kris. "EAD as an Archival Descriptive Standard." *American Archivist* 60, no. 3 (1997): 344–354. https://doi.org/10.17723/aarc.60.3.r7v8555610121244.

Koontz, Christie, and Lorri Mon. *Marketing and Social Media: A Guide for Libraries, Archives, and Museums*. Lanham, MD: Rowman & Littlefield, 2014.

Krause, Magia. "Undergraduates in the Archives: Using an Assessment Rubric to Measure Learning." *American Archivist* 73, no. 2 (2010): 507–534. https://doi.org /10.17723/aarc.73.2.72176h742v20l115.

Lacher-Feldman, Jessica. *Exhibits in Archives and Special Collections Libraries*. Chicago: Society of American Archivists, 2013.

Lack, Rosalie. "The Importance of User-Centered Design: Exploring Findings and Methods." In *Archives and the Digital Library*, edited by William E. Landis and Robin L. Chandler, 69–86. Binghamton, NY: Haworth Information Press, 2006.

Lavoie, Michele M. "Websites." In *Public Relations and Marketing for Archives*, edited by Russell D. James and Peter J. Wosh, 9–54. Chicago: Society of American Archivists, 2011.

Lawrence, Susan C. *Privacy and the Past: Research, Law, Archives, Ethics*. New Brunswick, NJ: Rutgers University Press, 2016.

Lawson, Murray G. "The Machine Age in Historical Research." *American Archivist* 11, no. 2 (1948): 141–149. https://doi.org/10.17723/aarc.11.2.k10wv0736708370q.

Leopold, Robert. "The Second Life of Ethnographic Fieldnotes." *Ateliers d'anthropologie* 32 (2008), https://doi.org/10.4000/ateliers.3132.

Leumas, Emilie G., Audrey P. Newcomer, and John J. Treanor. *Managing Diocesan Archives and Records: A Guide for Bishops, Chancellors, and Archivists*. Chicago: Association of Catholic Diocesan Archivists, 2012.

Library of Congress, "Primary Sources and the Common Core State Standards." *TPS Journal* 5, no. 2 (Fall 2012). www.loc.gov/teachers/tps/journal/common_core/index.html.

Library of Congress, Chronicling America. "About the Site and API." https://chroniclingamerica.loc.gov/about/api/.

Light, Michelle. "Controlling Goods or Promoting the Public Good: Choices for Special Collections in the Marketplace." *RBM: A Journal of Rare Books, Manuscripts, and Cultural Heritage* 16, no. 1 (2015): 48–63. https://doi.org/10.5860/rbm.16.1.435.

———. "Managing Risk with a Virtual Reading Room: Two Born-Digital Projects." In *Reference and Access: Innovative Practices for Archives and Special Collections*, edited by Kate Theimer, 17–35. Lanham, MD: Rowman & Littlefield, 2014.

Lipinski, Tomas A. "Legal Issues Involved in the Privacy Rights of Patrons in 'Public' Libraries and Archives." In *Libraries, Museums, and Archives: Legal Issues and Ethical Challenges in the New Information Era*, edited by Tomas A. Lipinski, 95–111. Lanham, MD: Scarecrow Press, 2002.

Living Refugee Archive. "Take Down Policy." 2018. www.livingrefugeearchive.org/digital-library/copyright/copyright-policy/, captured at https://perma.cc/UDX6-U3S5.

Locating London's Past. December 2011. www.locatinglondon.org/index.html.

Lord, Clifford L. *Keepers of the Past*. Chapel Hill, NC: University of North Carolina Press, 1965.

Lowe, Meredith. *Archives Gig* (blog). https://archivesgig.wordpress.com/tag/reference-services/.

Lowell, Waverly, and Tawny Ryan Nelb. *Architectural Records: Managing Design and Construction Records*. Chicago: Society of American Archivists, 2006.

Lule, Irene, Carla O. Alvarez, Brendan Coates, Kelly Kerbow Hudson, and Teague Schneiter. "Transforming the Archive: Increasing Inclusivity Through Language." Presented at the Society of American Archivists Annual Meeting, Austin, TX, August 4, 2019.

Lyman Museum and Mission House. "Archives Services and Fees." 2014. https://lymanmuseum.org/archives/archives-services-and-fees/, captured at https://perma.cc/H2M4-ZQU9.

Mackey, Thomas P., and Trudi E. Jacobson, eds. *Metaliterate Learning for the Post-Truth World*. Chicago: ALA Neal-Schuman, 2019.

MacNeil, Heather. *Trusting Records: Legal, Historical, and Diplomatic Perspectives*. London: Springer, 2011.

Martin, Kristin E. "Analysis of Remote Reference Correspondence at a Large Academic Manuscripts Collection." *American Archivist* 64, no. 1 (2001): 17–42. https://doi.org/10.17723/aarc.64.1.g224234uv117734p.

Masnick, Mike. "Getty Images Sued Yet Again for Trying to License Public Domain Images." *Techdirt*, April 1, 2019. www.techdirt.com/articles/20190329/15352641901/getty-images-sued-yet-again-trying-to-license-public-domain-images.shtml, captured at https://perma.cc/V35S-38PP.

Massachusetts Historical Society. "Mission, Vision, and Values." 2020. www.masshist.org/mission.

McCulloch, Gary. *Documentary Research in Education, History, and the Social Sciences*. New York: Routledge, 2004.

Meissner, Dennis. *Arranging and Describing Archives and Manuscripts*. Chicago: Society of American Archivists, 2019.

Melling, Maxine, and Joyce Little, eds. *Building a Successful Customer-Service Culture: A Guide for Library and Information Managers*. London: Facet Publishing, 2002.

Mennonite Church USA. "Mennonite Church USA Archives." http://mennoniteusa.org/what-we-do/archives/.

Mennonite Church USA, Historical Committee. "Citing Archival Sources." http://mennoniteusa.org/wp-content/uploads/2015/03/CitingMCUSAArchives.pdf.

Metro Archives. "About the Friends of the Nashville Public Library." 2015. http://nashvillearchives.org/friends.html, captured at https://perma.cc/SSJ2-W4KT.

Meyer, Eric T., and Ralph Schroeder. *Knowledge Machines: Digital Transformations of the Sciences and Humanities*. Cambridge, MA: MIT Press, 2015.

Millar, Laura A. *Archives: Principles and Practices*. New York: Neal-Schuman Publishers, 2010.

Miller, Lisa, Steven K. Galbraith, and RLG Partnership Working Group on Streamlining Photography and Scanning. *"Capture and Release": Digital Cameras in the Reading Room*. Dublin, OH: OCLC Research, February 2010. www.oclc.org/content/dam/research/publications/library/2010/2010-05.pdf, captured at https://perma.cc/MC64-XKT4.

Miller, Page Putnam. "Developing a Premier National Institution: A Report from the User Community to the National Archives." National Coordinating Committee for the Promotion of History, 1989.

Minchew, Kaye Lanning. "Lessons Learned While Saving the Georgia Archives." *Provenance* 31, no. 1 (2013): 16–21. https://digitalcommons.kennesaw.edu/provenance/vol31/iss1/6/.

Minow, Mary. "Welcome to . . . The Legal Responsibility to Offer Accessible Electronic Information to Patrons with Disabilities." In *Libraries, Museums, and Archives: Legal Issues and Ethical Challenges in the New Information Era*, edited by Tomas A. Lipinski, 113–157. Lanham, MD: Scarecrow Press, 2002.

Mitchell, Eleanor, Peggy Seiden, and Suzy Taraba, eds. *Past or Portal? Enhancing Undergraduate Learning Through Special Collections and Archives*. Chicago: Association of College and Research Libraries, 2012.

Mitchell, Thornton. "The State of Records Management." *American Archivist* 24, no. 3 (1961): 259–266. https://doi.org/10.17723/aarc.24.3.f4285k8x40516158.

Mooradian, Norman A. *Ethics for Records and Information Management*. Chicago: ALA Neal-Schuman, 2018.

Moravian Archives. "Support." 2020. www.moravianchurcharchives.org/support/, captured at https://perma.cc/C9ZL-QJ4Z.

Musachio, Rosemary. "Web Accessibility from a Personal Perspective." *Access Matters Blog.* Interactive Accessibility, June 20, 2013. https://interactiveaccessibility.com/blog/web-accessibility-personal-perspective#.XfW7mdZKjUq, captured at https://perma.cc/6AR7-YSCQ.

National Archives and Records Service. "The Archivist's Code." *American Archivist* 18, no. 4 (1955): 307–308. https://doi.org/10.17723/aarc.18.4.g027u80688293012.

National Freedom of Information Coalition. "State Freedom of Information Laws." www.nfoic.org/coalitions/state-foi-resources/state-freedom-of-information-laws.

Nesmith, Tom. "Documenting Appraisal as a Societal-Archival Process: Theory, Practice, and Ethics in the Wake of Helen Willa Samuels." In *Controlling the Past: Documenting Society and Institutions, Essays in Honor of Helen Willa Samuels*, edited by Terry Cook, 31–50. Chicago: Society of American Archivists, 2011.

"News Notes," in "Shorter Features." *American Archivist* 1, no. 3 (1938): 149–152. https://doi.org/10.17723/aarc.1.3.633w7541151113h8.

Newsome, Albert Ray. "Uniform State Archival Legislation." *American Archivist* 2, no. 1 (1939): 1–16. https://doi.org/10.17723/aarc.2.1.32tk6267g256l5n8.

New York Public Library. Labs. "About." What's on the Menu? http://menus.nypl.org/about.

New York University Libraries. "Notice and Takedown Policy." http://library.nyu.edu/about/visiting/policies/notice-takedown-policy/.

Northeast Document Conservation Center. "4.1 Storage Methods and Handling Practices." 2012. www.nedcc.org/free-resources/preservation-leaflets/4.-storage-and-handling/4.1-storage-methods-and-handling-practices, captured at https://perma.cc/SF4G-2YUS.

Norton, Margaret Cross. "The Comparison of Archival and Library Techniques." In *Norton on Archives: The Writings of Margaret Cross Norton on Archival and Records Management*, edited by Thornton W. Mitchell, 86–105. Chicago: Society of American Archivists, 2003.

Nutt, Timothy G., and Diane F. Worrell. "Planning for Archival Repositories: A Common-Sense Approach." *American Archivist* 78, no. 2 (2015): 317–338. https://doi.org/10.17723/0360-9081.78.2.31.

OCLC. "Accessibility Statement." 2020. https://policies.oclc.org/en/accessibility.html.

Oestreicher, Cheryl, Julia Stringfellow, and Jim Duran. "Going Mobile: Using iPads to Improve the Reading Room Experience." Kate Theimer, ed. *Reference and Access: Innovative Practices for Archives and Special Collections.* Lanham: Rowman & Littlefield. 2014. p. 109–122.

Oklahoma Historical Society. "Visiting the Research Center." www.okhistory.org/research/visitor.

O'Meara, Erin, and Kate Stratton. "Preserving Digital Objects." In *Digital Preservation Essentials*, edited by Christopher J. Prom, 8–77. Chicago: Society of American Archivists, 2016.

Omeka.org. "Accessibility Statement." *Omeka Classic User Manual.* https://omeka.org/classic/docs/GettingStarted/Accessibility_Statement/.

ONE Archives Foundation. "History." 2018. www.onearchives.org/about/history/.

Online Archive of California. https://oac.cdlib.org/.

Onuf, Rachel, and Tom Hyry. "Take It Personally: The Implications of Personal Records in Electronic Form." In *I, Digital: Personal Collections in the Digital Era*, edited by Christopher A. Lee, 241–256. Chicago: Society of American Archivists, 2011.

Oregon State University Libraries, Special Collections and Archives. 2020. http://scarc.library.oregonstate.edu/about-us.html.

Osmond, Gary, and Murray G. Phillips. *Sport History in the Digital Era*. Urbana, IL: University of Illinois Press, 2015.

O'Toole, James M. "The Future of Archival History." *Provenance* 13, no. 1 (1995): 1–24. https://digitalcommons.kennesaw.edu/provenance/vol13/iss1/2/.

Palmer, Joy, and Jane Stevenson. "Something Worth Sitting Still For? Some Implications of Web 2.0 for Outreach." In *A Different Kind of Web: New Connections Between Archives and Our Users*, edited by Kate Theimer, 1–21. Chicago: Society of American Archivists, 2011.

"Paramilitaries 'Misled' over Boston College Tapes Confidentiality." *News Letter,* June 28, 2016. www.newsletter.co.uk/news/crime/paramilitaries-misled-over-boston-college-tapes-confidentiality-1-7453552, captured at https://perma.cc/S4AN-XUUK.

Parilla, Lesley, and Meghan Ferriter. "Social Media and Crowdsourced Transcription of Historical Materials at the Smithsonian Institution: Methods for Strengthening Community Engagement and Its Tie to Transcription Output." *American Archivist* 79, no. 2 (2016): 438–460, https://doi.org/10.17723/0360-9081-79.2.438.

Peet, Lisa. "Attorney Sues for Access to Tanton Papers in Closed Archive." *Library Journal,* September 18, 2018. www.libraryjournal.com?detailStory=180918-Tanton-Papers.

Peterson, Trudy Huskamp. "Archival Principles and Records of the New Technology." *American Archivist* 47, no. 4 (1984): 383–393, https://doi.org/10.17723/aarc.47.4.30u45640617n2184.

Pettit, Emma. "A Harvard Scientist Commissioned Photos of Slaves in 1850. A Lawsuit Says the University Is Still Profiting from Them." *Chronicle of Higher Education*, March 20, 2019. www.chronicle.com/article/A-Harvard-Scientist/245939, captured at https://perma.cc/C59Z-Q4V8.

Plumley, George. *Website Design and Development: 100 Questions to Ask Before Building a Website*. Indianapolis: John Wiley & Sons, 2010.

Pojmann, Wendy A., Barbara Reeves-Ellington, and Karen Ward Mahar. *Doing History: An Introduction to the Historian's Craft: With Workbook Activities*. New York: Oxford University Press, 2016.

Prentice, Ann E. *Public Libraries in the 21st Century*. Santa Barbara, CA: Libraries Unlimited, 2011.

Primary Research Group Inc. *International Survey of Research University Faculty: Use of Academic Library Special Collections*. New York: Author, 2017.

Princeton University Library, Special Collections. "Before You Visit." 2019. https://library.princeton.edu/special-collections/you-visit, captured at captured at https://perma.cc/X5TB-RQ58.

———. "Reading Room Guidelines." 2019. https://library.princeton.edu/special-collections/policies/reading-room-guidelines, captured at https://perma.cc/9J85-HY4R.

Prom, Christopher J. "Using Web Analytics to Improve Online Access to Archival Resources." *American Archivist* 74, no. 1 (2011): 158–184. https://doi.org/10.17723/aarc.74.1.h56018515230417v.

_____, and Lisa Janicke Hinchliffe, eds. *Teaching with Primary Sources*. Chicago: Society of American Archivists, 2016.

Pugh, Mary Jo. *Providing Reference Services for Archives and Manuscripts*. Chicago: Society of American Archivists, 2005.

Purcell, Aaron D. *Digital Library Programs for Libraries and Archives: Developing, Managing, and Sustaining Unique Digital Collections*. Chicago: Neal-Schuman Publishers, 2016.

———. *Donors and Archives: A Guidebook for Successful Programs*. Lanham, MD: Rowman & Littlefield, 2015.

Pyatt, Tim. "Balancing Issues of Privacy and Confidentiality in College and University Archives." In *College and University Archives: Readings in Theory and Practice*, edited by Christopher J. Prom and Ellen D. Swain, 211–226. Chicago: Society of American Archivists, 2008.

Redwine, Gabriela, Megan Barnard, Kate Donovan, Erika Farr, Michael Forstrom, Will Hansen, Jeremy Leighton John, Nancy Kuhl, Seth Shaw, and Susan Thomas. *Born Digital: Guidance for Donors, Dealers, and Archival Repositories*. Washington, DC: Council on Library and Information Resources, 2013.

Reedy, Katharine, and Jo Parker, eds. *Digital Literacy Unpacked*. London: Facet Publishing, 2018.

Rein, Lisa. "Altered Lincoln Pardon at National Archives to Be Taken Out of Circulation." *Washington Post*, January 26, 2011. www.washingtonpost.com/wp-dyn/content/article/2011/01/26/AR2011012605804.html, captured at https://perma.cc/GV59-2K7D.

RightsStatements.org. "Rights Statements." https://rightsstatements.org/page/1.0/?language=en.

Ritzenthaler, Mary Lynn. *Preserving Archives and Manuscripts*. Chicago: Society of American Archivists, 2010.

Rocky Mountain Online Archive. 2006. https://rmoa.unm.edu/.

Roe, Kathleen D. "Addressing Archival Issues: University of Oregon Records Release—and Beyond." *Off the Record* (blog), February 17, 2015. https://offtherecord.archivists.org/2015/02/17/addressing-archival-issues-university-of-oregon-records-release-and-beyond/, captured at https://perma.cc/M6B6-3RTJ.

———. *Advocacy and Awareness for Archivists*. Chicago: Society of American Archivists, 2019.

Rosenberg, Jane Aikin. *The Nation's Great Library: Herbert Putnam and the Library of Congress, 1899–1939*. Urbana, IL: University of Illinois Press, 1993.

Ross, Catherine Sheldrick, Kirsti Nilsen, and Marie L. Radford. *Conducting the Reference Interview: A How-To-Do-It Manual for Librarians*, 3rd ed. Chicago: ALA Neal-Schuman, 2019.

Rothstein, Samuel. *The Development of Reference Services Through Academic Traditions, Public Library Practice and Special Librarianship*. Chicago: Association of College and Reference Libraries, 1955.

Rubin, Rhea Joyce. *Defusing the Angry Patron: A How-To-Do-It Manual for Librarians*. New York: Neal-Schuman Publishers, 2011.

———. *Planning for Library Services to People with Disabilities*. Chicago: Association of Specialized and Cooperative Library Agencies, 2001.

"Rules and Regulations." *Federal Register* 83, no. 208 (October 26, 2018): 54010–54031. www.govinfo.gov/content/pkg/FR-2018-10-26/pdf/2018-23241.pdf, captured at https://perma.cc/A3JX-93A3.

Rutner, Jennifer, and Roger C. Schonfeld. "Supporting the Changing Research Practices of Historians." Ithaka S+R, December 10, 2012.

Rydberg, Kevin. "The Must-Have Accessibility Handbook." Siteimprove, n.d. http://go.siteimprove.com/hubfs/Content/eBooks_Guides_Whitepapers/EN_Accessibility_Handbook.pdf. https://hello.siteimprove.com/en/the-must-have-web-accessibility-handook/download.

Saffady, William. "Reference Service to Researchers in Archives." *RQ* 14, no. 2 (Winter 1974).

Samuel Beckett: Digital Manuscript Project. www.beckettarchive.org/.

Samuels, Helen Willa. *Varsity Letters: Documenting Modern Colleges and Universities*. Metuchen, NJ: Scarecrow Press, 1992.

San Diego Air and Space Museum. "Library and Archives Overview." http://sandiegoairandspace.org/research/.

Santamaria, Daniel A. *Extensible Processing for Archives and Special Collections: Reducing Processing Backlogs*. Chicago: ALA Neal-Schuman, 2015.

Schellenberg, T. R. *Modern Archives: Principles and Techniques*. Chicago: The University of Chicago Press, 1956.

Schultz, Lucille M. "Foreword." In *Beyond the Archives: Research as a Lived Process*, edited by Gesa E. Kirsch and Liz Rohan, vii–x. Carbondale, IL: Southern Illinois University Press, 2008.

The September 11 Digital Archive. http://911digitalarchive.org/.

Shipton, Clifford K. "The Reference Use of Archives." In *University Archives: Papers Presented at an Institute Conducted by the University of Illinois Graduate School of Library Science*, edited by Rolland E. Stevens, 68–81. Champaign, IL: Board of Trustees of the University of Illinois, 1965.

Slate, John H., and Kaye Lanning Minchew. *Managing Local Government Archives*. Lanham, MD: Rowman & Littlefield, 2016.

Slotkin, Helen W., and Karen T. Lynch. "An Analysis of Processing Procedures: The Adaptable Approach." *American Archivist* 45, no. 2 (1982): 155–163, https://doi.org/10.17723/aarc.45.2.63q172t634g386l4.

Smith-Yoshimura, Karen. "Strategies for Alternate Subject Headings and Maintaining Subject Headings." *Hanging Together* (blog), October 29, 2019. http://hangingtogether.org/?p=7591, captured at https://perma.cc/A94X-8NTP.

Snider, Lisa. "Access for All: Making Your Archives' Website Accessible for People with Disabilities." In *Reference and Access: Innovative Practices for Archives and Special Collections*, edited by Kate Theimer, 137–153. Lanham, MD: Rowman & Littlefield, 2014.

Society of American Archivists, Accessibility and Disability Section, Reference, Access and Outreach Section, Task Force to Revise Best Practices on Accessibility. "Guidelines for Accessible Archives for People with Disabilities." www2.archivists.org/standards/guidelines-for-accessible-archives-for-people-with-disabilities, captured at captured at https://perma.cc/J2GY-7EAU.

———, Education Department. "Real-World Reference: Moving Beyond Theory." www2.archivists.org/prof-education/course-catalog/real-world-reference-moving-beyond-theory, captured at https://perma.cc/2KQP-ZLN8.

———, Education Department. "User Experience Design and Digital Archives." www2.archivists.org/prof-education/course-catalog/user-experience-design-and-digital-archives, captured at https://perma.cc/A7NQ-ED9L.

———, Issues and Advocacy Section. "The University of Oregon Situation." www2.archivists.org/groups/issues-and-advocacy-section/the-university-of-oregon-situation, captured at https://perma.cc/A729-MSBF.

———, Reference, Access and Outreach Section. "Teaching with Primary Sources—Bibliography." www2.archivists.org/groups/reference-access-and-outreach-section/teaching-with-primary-sources-bibliography#.Vwbb2MfEyrU.

———, SAA-ACRL/RBMS Joint Task Force on the Development of Standardized Statistical Measures for Public Services in Archival Repositories and Special Collections Libraries. "Standardized Statistical Measures and Metrics for Public Services in Archival Repositories and Special Collections Libraries." Society of American Archivists. October 2017. https://www2.archivists.org/sites/all/files/SAA-ACRL-RBMS-HoldingsCountsMetrics_2019.pdf, captured at https://perma.cc/WQ3N-896B.

———, SAA-ACRL/RBMS Joint Task Force on Primary Source Literacy; Partner Organizations: Association of College and Research Libraries/Rare Books and Manuscripts Section. "Guidelines for Primary Source Literacy: Final Draft." www2.archivists.org/groups/saa-acrlrbms-joint-task-force-on-primary-source-literacy/guidelines-for-primary-source-lite-0, captured at at https://perma.cc/NC3P-JXVW.

———, Technical Subcommittee on *Describing Archives: A Content Standard* (TS-DACS). "Describing Archives: A Content Standard, Second Edition (DACS)." www2.archivists.org/standards/DACS

———. "GPAS Curriculum." Updated December 14, 2016. www2.archivists.org/prof-education/graduate/gpas/curriculum, captured at https://perma.cc/L7LQ-6GWJ.

———. "Guide to Implementing Rights Statements from RightsStatements.Org." www2.archivists.org/standards/guide-to-implementing-rights-statements-from-rightsstatementsorg, captured at https://perma.cc/ESJ8-28DB.

———. "Issue Brief: Health Information Portability and Accountability Act." www2.archivists.org/statements/issue-brief-health-information-portability-and-accountability-act, captured at https://perma.cc/4UFU-YBQE.

———. "SAA Core Values Statement and Code of Ethics." January 2012. www2.archivists.org/statements/saa-core-values-statement-and-code-of-ethics#code_of_ethics, captured at https://perma.cc/4XV9-FSRP.

———. "Strategic Plan 2020–2022." May 2019. www2.archivists.org/governance/strategic-plan/2020-2022, captured at https://perma.cc/DU9J-7DVN.

Spina, Carli, and Margaret Cohen. *SPEC Kit 358: Accessibility and Universal Design.* Washington, DC: Association of Research Libraries, May 2018.

St. Clair, Guy. *Total Quality Management in Information Services.* London: Bowker-Sauer, 1997.

Stead, Lisa. "Introduction." In *The Boundaries of the Literary Archive: Reclamation and Representation*, edited by Carrie Smith and Lisa Stead, 1–12. London: Routledge, 2013.

Steedman, Carolyn. *Dust: The Archive and Cultural History.* New Brunswick, NJ: Rutgers University Press, 2011.

Stoler, Ann Laura. *Along the Archival Grain: Epistemic Anxieties and Colonial Common Sense.* Princeton, NJ: Princeton University Press, 2009.

Stone, Amy L., and Jaime Contrell. *Out of the Closet, into the Archives: Researching Sexual Histories.* Albany: SUNY Press, 2015.

Svensson, Patrik. "Humanities Computing as Digital Humanities." *Digital Humanities Quarterly* 3, no. 3 (2009). http://digitalhumanities.org/dhq/vol/3/3/000065/000065.html.

Taylor, Robert S. "Question-Negotiation and Information Seeking in Libraries." *College and Research Libraries* 29, no. 3 (May 1968): 178–194. https://doi.org/10.5860/crl_29_03_178.

Technology, Education, and Copyright Harmonization Act of 2001. Pub. L. No. 107–273 (2002). www.congress.gov/bill/107th-congress/senate-bill/487.

Theimer, Kate. "Archives in Context and as Context." *Journal of Digital Humanities* 1, no. 2 (2012). http://journalofdigitalhumanities.org/1-2/archives-in-context-and-as-context-by-kate-theimer/.

———. *Web 2.0 Tools and Strategies for Archives and Local History Collections.* New York: Neal-Schuman Publishers, 2010.

Thomas, Lynne M., and Beth M. Whittaker, eds. *New Directions for Special Collections: An Anthology of Practice.* Santa Barbara, CA: Libraries Unlimited, 2017.

Thomas, Susan. "Curating the I, Digital: Experiences at the Bodleian Library." In *I, Digital: Personal Collections in the Digital Era*, edited by Christopher A. Lee, 280–306. Chicago: Society of American Archivists, 2011.

Tibbo, Helen R. "Primarily History in America: How U.S. Historians Search for Primary Materials at the Dawn of the Digital Age." *American Archivist* 66, no. 1 (2003): 9–50. https://doi.org/10.17723/aarc.66.1.b12037011g718n74.

Totleben, Kristen, and Lori Birrell, eds. *Collaborating for Impact: Special Collections and Liaison Librarian Partnerships*. Chicago: Association of College and Research Libraries, 2016.

Trinkaus-Randall, Gregor. "Security." In *Archival and Special Collections Facilities: Guidelines for Archivists, Librarians, Architects, and Engineers*, edited by Michele F. Pacifico and Thomas P. Wilsted, 61–68. Chicago: Society of American Archivists, 2009.

———, and Kaari Mai Tari. "The Massachusetts Municipal Clerks Archival Education Project: A Study in Collaboration." Presented at the CoSA Member Webinar, May 26, 2016. www.statcarchivists.org/files/8714/6774/5531/CoSAMemberWebinar_May_2016_05_26.pdf, captured at https://perma.cc/96BM-ACF7.

Tucker, Louis Leonard. *The Massachusetts Historical Society: A Bicentennial History, 1791–1991*. Boston: Massachusetts Historical Society, 1995.

Turton, Alison. *The International Business Archives Handbook: Understanding and Managing the Historical Records of Business*. New York: Routledge, 2017.

Tyckoson, David A. "History and Functions of Reference Service." In *Reference and Information Services: An Introduction*, 4th ed., edited by Richard E. Bopp and Linda C. Smith, 3–28. Santa Barbara, CA: Libraries Unlimited, 2011.

University of California, Irvine, Special Collections and Archives. "Application for the Virtual Reading Room in UCIspace." https://special.lib.uci.edu/application-virtual-reading-room-ucispace, captured at https://perma.cc/J6X4-ACJB.

University of Georgia Libraries, Special Collections Libraries. "Accessibility." www5.galib.uga.edu/scl/visit/accessibility.html, captured at https://perma.cc/QF7W-HS5W.

———. "Policies and Procedures." June 20, 2018. www5.galib.uga.edu/scl/research/policies.html, captured at https://perma.cc/8HXQ-AJXL.

University of Illinois at Urbana-Champaign. "Preservation Self-Assessment Program." https://psap.library.illinois.edu/.

University of Manitoba Libraries. "Rare Research – How to Do Primary Research with Rare Documents." 2019. www.umanitoba.ca/libraries/units/archives/collections/rarebooks/rare_research.html.

University of Oxford and King's College London. "Jane Austen's Fiction Manuscripts." https://janeausten.ac.uk/index.html.

University of Southampton, Special Collections. "Virtual Reading Room." 2020. www.southampton.ac.uk/archives/virtual/index.page.

University of Wyoming, American Heritage Center. "Citing Archival Materials." www.uwyo.edu/ahc/research/citation.html.

Upper Iowa University. "Guidelines for Archives Use." https://uiu.edu/resources/archives/guidelines-for-user-access.html, captured at https://perma.cc/BJ5U-NX4X.

U.S. Department of Education. "Family Educational Rights and Privacy Act (FERPA)." www2.ed.gov/policy/gen/guid/fpco/ferpa/index.html, captured at https://perma.cc/W2YG-MD6B.

———. "FERPA General Guidance for Students." Last modified June 26, 2015. www2.ed.gov/policy/gen/guid/fpco/ferpa/students.html, captured at https://perma.cc/M9XT-SGGH.

———. "FERPA Regulations." https://studentprivacy.ed.gov/node/548/.

U.S. Department of Health and Human Services, Office for Civil Rights. "HIPAA for Professionals." www.hhs.gov/hipaa/for-professionals/index.html?language=es, captured at https://perma.cc/9HZH-RUUT.

U.S. Department of Justice. "Privacy Act of 1974." Updated January 15, 2020. www.justice.gov/opcl/privacy-act-1974.

———. "Privacy Compliance Process." Updated June 11, 2019. www.justice.gov/opcl/privacy-compliance-process.

———. "The USA PATRIOT Act: Preserving Life and Liberty." www.justice.gov/archive/ll/highlights.htm, captured at https://perma.cc/D8N3-FUHY.

U.S. Department of Justice, Freedom of Information Act (FOIA). FOIA.gov. www.foia.gov/faq.html#exemptions.

U.S. Department of State. "Virtual Reading Room Documents Search." https://foia.state.gov/Search/Search.aspx.

———. "The Freedom of Information Act." https://foia.state.gov/Learn/FOIA.aspx.

U.S. General Services Administration. Data.gov., www.data.gov/.

U.S. Government, General Services Administration. "18F Accessibility Guide." https://accessibility.18f.gov/index.html.

U.S. National Archives and Records Administration. "Accessibility." Last reviewed November 20, 2019. www.archives.gov/global-pages/accessibility, captured at https://perma.cc/DUA8-Y7LZ.

———. "Finding Aids." General Information Leaflet 71. Last reviewed October 31, 2016. www.archives.gov/publications/general-info-leaflets/71-06-dc-area-records.html, captured at https://perma.cc/77YC-GJGS.

———. "Mission, Vision and Values." Last reviewed February 5, 2019. www.archives.gov/about/info/mission.

———. "National Archives for Developers," Last reviewed January 17, 2018. www.archives.gov/developer.

———. "Record Group Concept." www.archives.gov/research/guide-fed-records/index-numeric/concept.html, captured at https://perma.cc/H3XB-5HTX.

———. "Strategic Plan 2018–2022." February 2018. https://www.archives.gov/files/about/plans-reports/strategic-plan/2018/strategic-plan-2018-2022.pdf, captured at https://perma.cc/98NA-TMJ6.

Vaknin, Judy, Karyn Stuckey, and Victoria Lane, eds. *All This Stuff: Archiving the Artist*. Faringdon, UK: Libri Publishing. 2013.

Varlejs, Jana. *Information Seeking: Basing Services on Users' Behaviors*. Jefferson, NC: McFarland, 1987.

Varnum, Kenneth J., ed. *Exploring Discovery: The Front Door to Your Library's Licensed and Digitized Content*. Chicago: ALA Editions, 2016.

Verma, Henrietta. *Reviews Are In: Read, Write, and Expand Your Career*. Santa Barbara, CA: Mission Bell Media, 2016.

W3C Web Accessibility Initiative. "Making the Web Accessible." 2020. www.w3.org/WAI/.

Walch, Victoria Irons. "Part 3. A*CENSUS: A Closer Look (Expanded Version)." Chicago: Society of American Archivists, 2006.

Wallace, Margo. *Writing for Museums*. Lanham, MD: Rowman & Littlefield. 2014.

Weideman, Christine. "Accessioning as Processing." *American Archivist* 69, no. 2 (2006): 274–283. https://doi.org/10.17723/aarc.69.2.g270566u745j3815.

Weingand, Darlene E. *Customer Service Excellence: A Concise Guide for Librarians*. Chicago: American Library Association, 1997.

Weiss, Debra Cassens. "Innocence Project Sues Museum for Access to Archives on 'Tragically Flawed' Bite-Mark Evidence." *ABA Journal*, February 21, 2019. www.abajournal.com/news/article/innocence-project-files-first-amendment-suit-over-denied-access-to-museums-bite-mark-archives, captured at https://perma.cc/GFF5-Z8V8.

Whalen, Lucille, ed. *Reference Services in Archives*. New York: Haworth Press, 1986.

Whaley, John H. Jr. "Digitizing History." *American Archivist* 57, no. 4 (1994): 660–672. https://doi.org/10.17723/aarc.57.4.6w4443523781g154.

Whitehill, Walter Muir. *Independent Historical Societies: An Enquiry into Their Research and Publication Functions and Their Financial Future*. Boston: Boston Athenaeum, 1962.

Wilsted, Thomas P. *Planning New and Remodeled Archival Facilities*. Chicago: Society of American Archivists, 2007.

Wisconsin Historical Society. "Accessibility." www.wisconsinhistory.org/Records/Article/CS71, captured at https://perma.cc/YH5F-E49J.

World Health Organization. "WHO Global Disability Action Plan 2014–2021: Better Health for All People with Disability." Geneva, Switzerland: World Health Organization, 2015. https://www.who.int/disabilities/actionplan/en/.

World Intellectual Property Organization. "WIPO Copyright Treaty (WCT)." www.wipo.int/treaties/en/ip/wct/index.html.

Wosh, Peter J. "Research and Reality Checks: Change and Continuity in NYU's Archival Management Program." *American Archivist* 63, no. 2 (2000): 271–283. https://doi.org/10.17723/aarc.63.2.n00l0588g6157373.

"Writings on Records Management: A Select List." *American Archivist* 36, no. 3 (1973): 367–482, https://doi.org/10.17723/aarc.36.3.m737p55318011656.

Wyoming State Archives. "Use Fee Schedule." 2020. https://wyoarchives.wyo.gov/index.php/get-a-copy/use-fee-schedule, captured at https://perma.cc/87XP-ZYDC.

Yakel, Elizabeth, and Doris Malkmus. "Contextualizing Archival Literacy." In *Teaching with Primary Sources*, edited by Christopher J. Prom and Lisa Janicke Hinchliffe, 8–140. Chicago: Society of American Archivists, 2016.

Yakel, Elizabeth, and Deborah Torres. "AI: Archival Intelligence and User Expertise." *American Archivist* 66, no. 1 (2003): 51–78. https://doi.org/10.17723/aarc.66.1.q022h85pn51n5800.

———. "Genealogists as a 'Community of Records.'" *American Archivist* 70, no. 1 (2003): 93–113. https://doi.org/10.17723/aarc.70.1.ll5414u736440636.

Yale University. Photogrammar. http://photogrammar.yale.edu/.

Yale University Library. "Guide to Using Special Collections at Yale University: Register." Updated January 2, 2020. https://guides.library.yale.edu/specialcollections/speccoll-register, captured at https://perma.cc/PM9U-Z9F8.

Zamon, Christina. *The Lone Arranger: Succeeding in a Small Repository*. Chicago: Society of American Archivists, 2012.

Zhou, Xiaomu. "Student Archival Research Activity: An Exploratory Study." *American Archivist* 71, no. 2 (2008): 476–498. https://doi.org/10.17723/aarc.71.2.n426270367qk311l.

About the Author

CHERYL OESTREICHER is the head of Special Collections and Archives and associate professor at Boise State University. She has a PhD in modern history and literature from Drew University and an MLIS from Dominican University. She previously worked at Auburn Avenue Research Library on African American Culture and History at Emory University, the University of Chicago, Drew University, and Princeton University. Oestreicher has taught introduction to archives, archives management, reference, and research methods at Georgia State University, Clayton State University, and Boise State University. She has been actively involved in SAA by serving on the Publications Board, Manuscripts Section Steering Committee, 2016 Annual Meeting Program as co-chair, and the SAA-ACRL/RBMS Joint Task Force to Revise Statement on Access. She was the 2015 recipient of the Emerging Leaders Award. For the Academy of Certified archivists, she was a member of the Recertification Review Task Force and Nominating Committee and serves on the Exam Development Committee focusing on Domain 3: Reference Services and Access. She has served as a grant reviewer for the Council on Library and Information Resources, National Historical Publications and Records Commission, and the National Endowment for the Humanities. She is a former editor of *Provenance*, the journal of the Society of Georgia Archivists.

Index

A

Academy of Certified Archivists (ACA), 22
access
    defined, 1–2
    equitable, 88, 91
    future of, 140–141
    historical influences, 2–4, 6–8
    intellectual. *See* intellectual access
    physical. *See* physical access
    to reference manual, 27
    restrictions, 61, 82, 109–112
    technology and, 4, 8
    virtual. *See* virtual access
access policies, 4
access restrictions, 61, 82, 109–112
accessibility, 90–92, 141
"accessioning as processing," 7
acknowledgements, 125
acquisition, 15–17, 96
active listening, 40
advocacy, 19–20
Aeon, 89
alteration, unauthorized, 122
American Archivist, 5, 33
American Library Association (ALA), 40, 58, 90
Americans with Disabilities Act (ADA), 53, 75, 90, 91
Anglo-American Cataloging Rules (AACR), 6
appraisal, 15–17
archival intelligence, 33
archival literacy, 32–34
ArchiveGrid, 43, 70

archives
    changes in content of, 3
    libraries vs, 5, 32–33
    role of, 1–2
    users view of, 35, 83, 84
Archives, Personal Papers, and Manuscripts (Library of Congress), 6
Archives and Manuscripts: Reference and Access (Holbert), xiii
Archives and Records Association (UK and Ireland), 88
ArchivesSpace, 9, 41, 69
archivists
    defined, xiii, 1
    as finding aids, 26
    as researchers, 37
"The Archivist's Code" (National Archives), 5, 87
Archivists' Toolkit, 9, 69
Archon, 9, 69
arrangement, 6–8, 17, 65–68
Arranging and Describing Archives and Manuscripts (Meissner), 65
assessment
    of archive websites, 76–77
    of outreach activities, 128, 129–130
    of reference programs, 134–139
    of security, 62
    of social media activities, 131
Association of Canadian Archivists (ACA), 88
Association of College and Research Libraries (ACRL), 7, 22, 33, 62, 124, 135

Association of Records Managers and Administrators (ARMA), 88
Association of Specialized Government and Cooperative Library Agencies (ASGCLA), 90
attribution, 125–126
audiovisual materials, 59
Australian Society of Archivists (ASA), 88

B
backlogs, 7
Baylor University, 84
Behrnd-Klodt, Menzi L., 95, 100
Belfast Project, 110
Benedict, Karen, 88
"Best Practices for Working with Archives Researchers and Employees with Physical Disabilities" (SAA), 90–91
book cradles, 59
born-digital records
    appraisal of, 15, 17
    challenges of, 9–10
    confidentiality and, 111
    historical, 4
    managing, 19
    metadata for, 81–82
    preservation issues, 79
    processing, 8
    reproduction of, 118
    systems, 80–81
    See also electronic records; virtual access
Boston College, 110

C
camera use grid, 119–120
"Capture and Release": Digital Cameras in the Reading Room (Miller and Galbraith), 118
Case, Donald O., 31–32
cataloging, 6, 70
catalogs, 69, 70
chairs, 53
Chalou, George, 26, 39
chat reference, 47
citations, 125–126
collection development policies, 15
collection management systems, 9, 17, 69
collection use metrics, 135, 136
Collective Access, 69
Committee on Ethics and Professional Conduct (SAA), 88
communication, 40–41, 45–46, 76
community archives, 92, 141
confidentiality, 40–41, 88–89, 111. *See also* access restrictions
connectivity, internet, 53
content management systems (CMS), 81

cooperation, eliciting, 49, 59–60
copies. *See* reproductions
copyright, 100–109, 122–123
copyright status chart, 101–102
Corrall, Sheila, 26
COVID-19, 142
cross-training, 29
crowdsourcing, 131–132
curatorial model, 54–55
customer service, 15, 36

D
Danielson, Elena, 88
data ethics, 138
data privacy, 77, 89
data sets, 71, 84, 156
databases, 71
Dearstyne, Bruce, 110
Defusing the Angry Patron: A How-To-Do-It Manual for Librarians (Rubin), 48
Describing Archives: A Content Standard (DACS), 17, 69
description
    forms of, 68–72
    historical overview, 6–8
    involving users in, 131–132
    metadata, 25, 81–82
    reference and, 17
    technology's effect on, 8–9
Desnoyers, Megan, 17
"Developing a Premier National Institution: A Report from the User Community to the National Archives" (Miller et al.), 4
Dictionary of Archives Terminology (SAA), 41, 52, 66, 79, 82
digital archives, 84, 153
digital asset management systems (DAMS), 81, 82
digital camera policies, 118–120
digital collections, 77–78
digital collections portals, 80
digital content. *See* born-digital records; electronic records; virtual access
digital humanities, 83–84
Digital Millennium Copyright Act (DMCA), 104
digitization, 4, 8, 18–19, 59, 78–79, 112, 118
donors, 109–110
Dublin Core, 41

E
education records, 97–98
electronic records, 9–10, 19, 79. *See also* born-digital records; virtual access
email, access to, 81
email inquiries, 45–46

emotions, as reference component, 44
Encoded Archival Description (EAD), 9, 41
ePADD, 81
equitable access, 88
The Ethical Archivist (Danielson), 88
ethics, 87–88, 138
Ethics and the Archival Profession (Benedict), 88
Excel files, 71, 154
exhibit metrics, 135
exhibits, 124, 129
Extensible Processing for Archives and Special Collections: Reducing Processing Backlogs (Santamaria), 8

F
Facebook, 130
fair use, 103–104, 122
Family Educational Rights and Privacy Act (FERPA), 97–98
feedback, 29
fees, 121–122, 123
file formats, 80
film, photographic, 59
finding aids, 9, 26, 69–70
finding aids portals, 70
forms
    permission to publish, 123–124, 161–164
    reference request, 149–151
    registration, 56–57, 82, 89, 109, 146–149
    reproduction request, 117, 122, 123, 158–160
Freedom of Information Act (FOIA), 3, 96–97, 110
"friends" groups, 132
functional model, 55–56

G
Galbraith, Steven K., 118
Galbraith, V. H., 5
geospatial systems, 83
Gilliland, Anne J., 1
Gilliland-Swetland, Anne, 33
Given, Lisa M., 31–32
gloves, 58–59
Google Analytics, 77
Gottlieb, Peter, 13
Greene, Mark, 7, 17
"Guidelines for Behavioral Performance of Reference and Information Service Providers" (ALA), 40
"Guidelines for Interlibrary and Exhibition Loan of Special Collections Materials" (ACRL/RBMS), 124
Gustainis, Emily R., 99

H
handling procedures, 58–60, 112
Health Insurance Portability and Accountability Act (HIPAA), 99

health records, 99
hierarchy of control, 66
Holbert, Sue, xiii
hybrid collections, 82
Hyry, Tom, 82

I
in-process collections, 112
inclusivity, 25, 58, 90
information literacy, 32
information-seeking behavior, 31–32
Instagram, 130
institutional policies, 110–111
institutional repositories (IRs), 81
Institutional Review Boards (IRBs), 138
instruction, 76, 129
instruction metrics, 135
intellectual access
    alternate formats, 71–72
    arrangement, 6–8, 17, 65–68
    catalogs, 69, 70
    collection management systems, 9, 69
    finding aids, 9, 26, 69–70
    online searches, 71–72
    print sources, 72
    See also description
intellectual organization, 65–67
interlibrary loan, 124–125
the internet, 9
interpersonal skills, 25–26, 47–50

J
jargon, 41, 76
Jenkinson, Hilary, 5
job postings, sample, 23
Joint Task Force on the Development of Guidelines for Primary Source Literacy (SAA), 33

K
knowledge
    archival, 23–24
    collection, 24
    interaction, 23–24
    legal, 24, 96
    research, 24

L
language accessibility, 92, 141
The Largest Vocabulary in Hip Hop, 83–84
legal issues
    archivists' responsibility, 24, 96
    copyright, 100–109
    corporate records, 99–100
    education records, 97–98
    fair use, 103–4

federal data, 99
health/medical records, 99
subpoenas, 110
See also Family Educational Rights and Privacy Act (FERPA); Freedom of Information Act (FOIA); Health Insurance Portability and Accountability Act (HIPAA)
Letocha, Phoebe Evans, 99
levels of control, 66
LibAnalytics, 89
libraries, vs archives, 5, 32–33, 77
Library of Congress, 6
lighting, 53
loans, 124–125
Locating London's Past, 83
"lone arrangers," 54, 61

M

Machine-Readable Cataloging (MARC), 6, 17
medical records, 99
Meissner, Dennis, 7, 17, 65, 68
metadata, 25, 81–82
metrics, 129, 131, 135–136
"Metrics for Public Services" (SAA, ACRL, and RBMS), 135
Miller, Lisa, 118
Miller, Page Putnam, 4
mission statements, 13–14
monitoring, 60–61
"More Product, Less Process" (MPLP), 7, 8, 17, 41
multimedia, for reference instruction, 76

N

National Archival Finding Aid Network, 70
National Archives and Records Administration (NARA), 3, 5, 15, 26, 61
National Freedom of Information Coalition, 97
National Union Catalog of Manuscript Collections (NUCMC), 70
Newsome, Albert Ray, 3
Nilsen, Kirsti, 42
Norton, Margaret Cross, 3, 5

O

Obama, Barack, 110
online searches, 4, 19, 71–72, 74
Onuf, Rachel, 82
open houses, 129
outlets, electrical, 53
outreach, 19–20, 127–133
outreach activities, 129
outreach metrics, 128–129, 135
oversize items, 59

P

PastPerfect, 69
patrons. *See* users
PDF documents, 9, 25, 69, 70–71, 81
permission to publish, 123–124, 161–164
Photogrammar (Yale), 83
photographs, 7, 27, 44, 59, 80, 98, 103, 112
    patron self-service, 118–120
physical access
    handling procedures, 58–60, 112
    reading rooms. *See* reading rooms
    security, 60–62
    virtual vs., 74
physical organization, 67–68
"The Practice of Privacy" (Gustainis and Letocha), 99
preservation, 18, 58–59, 112, 121
primary source literacy, 33
print sources, 72
privacy, 58, 77, 88–90, 99, 138
Privacy Act, 99
Privacy Impact Assessment templates, 99
processing, 6–7, 17, 19, 65–68, 96, 109
professional development, 29
programming, 129
programming metrics, 135
proprietary information, 111
provenance, 66
Providing Reference Services for Archives and Manuscripts (Pugh), xiii, 77
"the public," xiv, 36
Public Company Accounting Reform and Investor Protection Act, 99–100
public domain, 101–102, 106–107, 123
public services metrics, 135–136
publicity, 129
Pugh, Mary Jo, xiii, 77

Q

qualitative data, 131, 136, 137
quantitative data, 57, 58, 77, 129, 135–136
questionnaires, 137, 138

R

Radford, Marie L., 42
Rare Books and Manuscripts Section (RBMS), 33, 124, 135
reading rooms
    accessibility, 53, 92
    handling procedures, 58–60
    metrics, 135
    physical requirements, 52–53
    registration, 56–58
    rules (sample), 57
    security, 60–62
    staffing, 54–56
    virtual, 82–83

redactions, 111
reference
    defined, 2
    historical influences, 4–8
    self-service, 19, 76
    technology and, 6, 140
    See also remote reference; virtual reference
reference archivist. *See* reference staff
reference books, 4, 53
reference interactions
    behavior, 44, 48–49
    behavioral guidelines, 39–40
    communication, 40–41
    difficult patrons, 47–50
    emotional responses, 44
    metrics, 135
    reference interview, 41–46
    remote/virtual, 45–47, 77–78, 91–92, 135
reference interviews, 41–46
    common mistakes, 44
reference manuals, 26–27, 144–145
reference professionals. *See* reference staff
reference request forms, 149–151
reference staff
    defined, xiv
    interpersonal skills, 25–26
    search skills, 25
    self-care, 41, 49
    technology and technical skills, 24–25, 85, 141
    training, 27–29
    See also knowledge, archival; staffing models
reference transactions, 135
referrals, 43–44
registration, 56–58, 82
registration forms, 56–57, 82, 89, 109, 146–149
remote reference, 45–47, 77–78, 91–92, 135. *See also* chat reference; email inquiries; telephone inquiries
reproductions
    alteration of, 122
    attribution, 125–126
    copyright issues, 122–123
    delivery of, 118
    early forms of, 9
    fees, 121–122, 123
    format choice, 117
    permission to publish, 123–124
    preservation of materials, 121
    as preservation tool, 59
    request forms, 117, 122, 123, 158–160
    self-service, 118–120
    types of uses, 115–116
research, digital, 83–84
research areas. *See* reading rooms
research assistance tools, 76

research assistants, 43
researchers. *See* users
Resource Description and Access (RDA), 17
restrictions, access, 61, 82, 109–112
retrieval, 68
rights statements, 105, 106–107
RLG Partnership Working Group on Streamlining Photography and Scanning, 118
Roe, Kathleen, 20, 111
Ross, Catherine Sheldrick, 42
rotation model, 55
Rubin, Rhea Joyce, 48

S
samples
    Access/Excel file, 155
    camera use grid, 119–120
    citations, 125
    copyright status chart, 101–102
    data set, 157
    digital archive, 154
    FOIA request, 97
    job postings, 23
    mission statements, 14
    outreach activities, 129
    permission to publish form, 161–164
    reading room rules, 57
    reference manuals, 144–145
    reference request forms, 149–151
    reproduction request form, 158–160
    rights statements, 106–107
    takedown statements, 108
    training checklist, 28
    websites, 151–153
Samuels, Helen Willa, 44
Santamaria, Daniel A., 8, 17
Sarbanes-Oxley Act, 99–100
Schellenberg, Theodore R., 5
search engines, 71–72
"Search Room," 5
security, 60–62
security assessment, 62
service points, 52, 56
slides, 59
SnapChat, 131
social media, 80, 130–131
Society of American Archivists (SAA)
    accessibility best practices, 90–91
    born-digital records definition, 79
    Code of Ethics, 87–88
    Core Values Statement and Code of Ethics, 87–88
    collection/record group definition, 66
    formation of, 3
    on primary source literacy, 33
    on public services metrics, 135

Society of American Archivists (*continued*)
    reading room definitions, 52, 82
    reference interview definition, 41
    on reference skills, 22
    strategic plan, 15
    See also Dictionary of Archives Terminology
"soft skills," 26
stacks management, 61–62
staffing models, 54–56
standards, descriptive, 6, 8–9, 17, 69
statistics, 129, 131, 135–136
strategic plans, 13–15
surveys, 137, 138

T

tables, 53, 59
takedown statements, 105, 108
tampering, 61
technical skills, 24–25, 141
technology
    access and, 4
    historical overview, 8–10
    as part of appraisal, 15, 17
    in the reading room, 53
    reference and, 6, 140
    See also specific forms, e.g., content management systems; social media
Technology, Education, and Copyright Harmonization Act (TEACH Act), 104
telephone inquiries, 46–47
text mining, 83–84
theft, 61, 62, 112
time estimates, 43, 46
Torres, Deborah, 33
tours, 129
training, reference staff, 27–29
tutorials, 76
Twitter, 84, 130

U

University of California, Irvine, 82
University of Illinois at Chicago, 110
University of Oregon, 111
unprocessed collections, 112, 126
USA PATRIOT Act, 58, 89
usability testing, 77
use metrics, 137
use policies for cameras, 119–120. *See also* access restrictions; loans; reproductions
use types, 115–116
user-centered questions, 42–43
user data, 56, 57, 138
user demographics, 46, 57, 135
user expectations, 4, 6, 18, 45, 47–48, 78
user influence
    on acquisition, 17
    on digitization, 18–19
    on processing, 8, 17
user studies, 4, 136–138
users
    archival literacy, 32–34
    communicating with, 40–41, 45–46, 76
    copyright responsibilities, 107–108
    defined, xiv, 31
    difficult, 47–50
    eliciting cooperation from, 49, 59–60
    experience levels, 34
    historical overview of, 2–4
    influence of (*see* user influence)
    information-seeking behavior, 31–32
    involving in description, 131–132
    social media interaction, 131
    technical sophistication, 76
    types of, 3, 34–37

V

value, types of, 16
viewing aids, 49
virtual access
    accessibility issues, 91–92, 141
    born-digital records, 79
    digital collections, 77–78
    digitization, 78–79
    future of, 85, 140
    metadata, 81–82
    methods of, 80–81
    physical vs, 74
    research potential, 83–84
    websites, 75–77
virtual reading room, 82–83
virtual reference, 45–47, 77–78, 91–92, 135
visualization, 83

W

watermarks, 117, 118, 124
Wayback Machine, 81
websites
    as access point, 71, 80, 151–153
    accessibility, 91–92
    assessment, 76–77
    as digital archives, 84, 154
    components, 75
    recommendations for, 75–77
Weideman, Christine, 17
Word documents, 71
World Wide Web, 18
WorldCat, 70

Y

Yakel, Elizabeth, 33
Yale University, 7, 83